UNDERDOG POLITICS

MATTHEW N. GREEN

Underdog Politics

The Minority Party in the U.S. House of Representatives

Yale UNIVERSITY PRESS
NEW HAVEN AND LONDON

Published with assistance from the Louis Stern Memorial Fund.

Yale University Press books may be purchased in quantity for educational, business, or promotional use. For information, please e-mail sales.press@yale.edu (U.S. office) or sales@yaleup.co.uk (U.K. office).

Set in Janson type by Newgen North America
Printed in the United States of America

Library of Congress Cataloging-in-Publication Data

Green, Matthew N., 1970–
Underdog politics : the minority party in the U.S. House of Representatives / Matthew N. Green.
pages cm
Includes bibliographical references and index.
ISBN 978-0-300-18103-6 (paperback)
1. United States. Congress. House. 2. Political parties—United States. 3. Opposition (Political science)—United States. 4. Republican Party (U.S. : 1854–) 5. Democratic Party (U.S.) 6. United States—Politics and government—1945–1989. 7. United States—Politics and govenment—1989– I. Title.
JK1319.G74 2015
328.73′0769—dc23
2014017645

A catalogue record for this book is available from the British Library.

This paper meets the requirements of ANSI/NISO Z39.48-1992 (Permanence of Paper).

10 9 8 7 6 5 4 3 2 1

CONTENTS

PREFACE

It was a warm late morning in early August, but it was not the weather that made the day so peculiar. The Republican cloakroom, located just off the floor of the U.S. House of Representatives and normally off-limits to all but members of Congress and their staff, was being used as a thoroughfare for dozens of tourists. They were walking through a room normally used by G.O.P. lawmakers to get to the floor, make a phone call, eat a snack, chat with colleagues, or just rest in a comfortable chair. In fact, the presence of anyone in the cloakroom was unusual because the House was not even in session; the room should have been empty altogether.

But this was no ordinary summer day. Congress was indeed in recess, but many congressional Republicans had refused to go home to their districts. Instead, they were preparing to convene an extremely unusual "mock" session on the floor of the House. There would be no C-SPAN coverage and no microphones. The public would be welcome to come to the floor to watch. And with both the Democratic cloakroom and the chamber's other doors shut to outsiders, the G.O.P. cloakroom was the only entryway available to visitors. Groups of them were being guided through the room to the floor by congressional staff to join a growing audience of curious citizens.

By quarter past eleven, the cloakroom's low-lying chairs were littered with visitors' bags, cameras, cell phones, and other items that were prohibited in the House chamber. Over a hundred people were seated inside waiting to hear from the seventeen Republicans who would give speeches. The theme of the day—indeed, of the entire exercise—was that Democrats, the majority party in the House, had abdicated their legislative responsibilities: gasoline prices were $3.80 per gallon, just below an all-time high of $4.10 reached in mid-July, and yet the ruling party had recessed the House and its members had returned to their districts. It was the fifth day of the Republicans' "mock" floor session, and they would doggedly repeat the routine daily for another four weeks.

In politics, as in life, not everyone can be the winner. This book is about the losers. Specifically, it is about one set of losers in particular: those who belong to the party in the U.S. House that holds fewer congressional seats than the other party. Why do I focus on them? It stems in part, I suppose, from being raised by parents who often rooted for the underdog, whether it was people subject to discrimination, quixotic presidential candidates, or hapless sports teams. But I also chose this topic because I believe that the losers in a democracy are never hopeless. In fact, one of the themes of the book is that the minority party in the U.S. House *can* win: in elections, in policy decisions, in presidential politics, and in the way they are treated in Congress. Even when it does not, which is often, it still seeks out and exploits any opportunities it can to secure its goals and protect its interests, even occasionally innovating new ones like the August "mock" session.

The House minority party is a neglected stepchild, assumed to be a single-minded seeker of majority status without importance or influence. Perhaps this is why so few books have been written about it. But after collecting and analyzing a variety of data on the minority party, including archival material, floor votes, procedural motions, and speeches in the *Congressional Record*, and conducting forty interviews with current and former lawmakers and staff, I have concluded that the minority party is, in fact, not only important but also illustrative of key (and sometimes underappreciated) features of legislative politics. Its ability to influence political outcomes despite lacking many formal powers is a good sign, I think, for our democracy: the minority party does represent an important segment of the population. At the same time, however, the minority party's positive—as opposed to negative—contribution to policy-making has diminished in recent decades, and its primary means of influence have shifted from lawmaking to symbolic messaging. As I will argue in the conclusion, this trend is disturbing, the fault of both an irresponsible minority party and an arrogant majority party, Democrats and Republicans both.

There are many people I have to thank for helping bring this book to fruition. My seven-month-old daughter and I were fortunate enough to be present at the Republican "mock" session in August 2008, an experience that helped inspire this study. For that, I owe considerable gratitude to John Stipicevic, a leadership aide on Capitol Hill and former Catholic University student who invited my daughter and me to witness the unusual August protest. Colleen Shogan of the Congressional Research Service graciously invited me to present my early research on procedural motions by the minority party to her CRS colleagues. It was at a follow-up luncheon with some of those colleagues that one of them, Jim Saturno, suggested I turn what was then a rather narrow project into a broader study of the minority party in Congress. This book is the result.

Financial support came from several sources. The Institute for Policy Research and Catholic Studies (IPR) provided invaluable research funding, and I am particularly thankful to the Institute's director, Steven Schneck, for giving me a place to work when an earthquake forced the evacuation of the politics department at Catholic University. Additional financial assistance was made available by a generous research grant from the Dirksen Center.

I also am in debt to the many members of Congress and congressional staffers, both current and former, who willingly took time from their busy schedules to be interviewed (mostly anonymously) for this book. Their insights and observations were invaluable, enlightening, and often highly entertaining. Win Boerckel, Alison Dagnes, Linda Dooley, Rochelle Dornatt, John Feehery, Daniel Petri, Troy Phillips, former congressman Al Swift, James Wallner, Dan Wirls, and Don Wolfensberger were among those who provided help in securing interviews.

I was fortunate to have the help of several outstanding research assistants with gathering data for the book, including Josiah Baker, Robert Christian, Greg Collins, Daniel Davy, Darrell Rogers, Kristen

Sullivan, and Anne Roan Thomas. For assistance in identifying critical archival documents, I thank Molly Kodner and Dennis Northcott of the Missouri History Museum, Frank Mackaman of the Dirksen Congressional Center, and Judy Atkinson and Rod Ross of the National Archives. Special thanks to Douglas Harris and Ken Kato for guidance and advice in locating historical material. Thanks also to René Lindstädt, with whom I collected some of the book's data on discharge petitions as part of another research project.

As I developed the project many other individuals provided helpful suggestions. Besides Jim Saturno and Colleen Shogan, others from the Library of Congress who offered constructive suggestions at the early stage of this research include Andrew Austin, Richard Beth, Matt Glassman, Valerie Heitshusen, Bill Heniff, Megan Lynch, Walter Oleszek, and Elizabeth Rybicki. Don Wolfensberger graciously invited me to present my preliminary findings at a panel discussion of the minority party at the Woodrow Wilson Center, which was a valuable opportunity to garner constructive feedback. At the various IPR brown-bag lunches in which I discussed this project, I received useful ideas from many, including Dennis Coyle, Bill D'Antonio, Sandra Hanson, Maria Mazzenga, Jay McCann, Fr. Tony Pogorelc, Anthony Stasi, Sean Michael Winters, and Andrew Yeo. Dan Hopkins, Jonathan Ladd, Hans Noel, and Michele Swers were among those who offered both encouragement and suggestions when I presented a portion of my research at Georgetown University's Department of Government. Along the way I was also given valuable ideas and feedback from Richard Beth, Jeffrey Biggs, Win Boerckel, Chris Darnton, John DeCrosta (usually over beer and brats at Mozart Café), Diana Dwyre, Larry Evans, James Gimpel, Jeffrey Grynaviski, Laurel Harbridge, Edward Hasecke, David Karol, Greg Koger, Frances Lee, David Mayhew, Scott Meinke, Vince Moscardelli, Jason Mycoff, Andrew Platt, Jesse Richman, Laura Tam, Jeremy Tieger, and former congressman Robert Walker.

Bill Frucht at Yale University Press has been a wonderfully accommodating editor, and I am especially grateful to have had his guidance and encouragement from the beginning. Thanks also to the anonymous reviewers who took the time to share their wisdom and detailed, constructive advice on the manuscript.

I save the most important people for last. My family has been the keystone upon which everything else rests. My wife, Holly, patiently saw me through several long nights and early mornings of writing and revising, and Olivia and Joshua put up with their dad going on research trips or typing away on his laptop during playtime. My mother, Kate, and brother, Adam, continue to be greatly supportive of my work and career. Sadly, my father died before I was able to complete the book, but I tried my best to adopt his critical eye and sharp wisdom when writing the manuscript. This book is dedicated first and foremost to him.

one
THE POLITICS OF THE MINORITY PARTY

The minority is a perpetual frustration.
—Democratic congressman, 2003

But let me tell you that the delight of political life is altogether in opposition. Why, it is freedom against slavery, fire against clay, movement against stagnation!
—Mr. Joshua Monk, *Phineas Finn*

Frustration and freedom. Both are familiar to lawmakers unfortunate enough to be in the minority party. Though the two sentiments differ, they come from the same source: disempowerment. The minority party's lack of formal political power—an enduring feature of many legislative bodies, including the U.S. House of Representatives—understandably frustrates lawmakers from the minority who want to have an effect on national policy. But powerlessness also permits them to act with little worry for the consequences. Asked about serving in the minority, one House aide put it this way: "You can just sit back and say, whom do I want to mess with today?"[1]

In the contemporary House, minority party members do not respond to this disempowerment by meekly accepting their plight or, as the congressional aide implied, acting pell-mell. To the contrary, they take advantage of being *in* government without having *to* govern and look instead for ways to influence political outcomes on their own terms. Even though the party is outnumbered and the House's rules are stacked against it, the minority still tries to tilt the electoral playing field in its favor, make laws, protect its procedural rights, and steer presidential politics. And if the party is driven, creative, sizable, unified, and lucky enough, it can sometimes succeed.

Anecdotal evidence, at least, suggests that the minority party in the House of Representatives is not without influence, even if the chamber's rules grant it less legislative authority than the majority. Take for instance the closure or downsizing of over three hundred military bases around the country between 1989 and 2005, which displaced hundreds of communities and led to the creation of new schools, parks, homes, businesses, and other facilities on what was once federal property. This far-reaching and transformative policy came not from the president or leaders of the majority parties in Congress, but from Dick Armey (R-TX), then a member of the House minority party. Another example occurred in May 2000, when Mississippi Democrat Gene Taylor was refused the right to offer an amendment to a defense bill that would allow retired veterans to receive Medicare-subsidized care at military facilities. In protest, Taylor forced a number of votes on the floor to delay proceedings on the bill, votes that fellow Democrats overwhelmingly supported. The majority G.O.P. reversed course, Taylor's amendment passed, and it later became law. After losing control of the House in 2006, minority Republicans provided the needed votes to pass legislation that funded the ongoing war in Iraq; minority Democrats did the same on multiple occasions in the 113th Congress (2013–14) to enact major bills opposed by a majority of the majority party. Even the House's daily recital of the Pledge of Allegiance owes its existence to the minority party. The tradition was established in 1988 when minority Republicans tried to force a vote to institute it in the chamber, hoping to keep the Pledge's constitutionality alive as a presidential campaign issue. Though they failed to get the vote, Democrats adopted the Pledge anyway to defuse the controversy.[2]

These instances run counter to the conventional wisdom that the House minority party is irrelevant to policy-making. The party is considered especially immaterial when compared to its brethren in the U.S. Senate, where the filibuster reigns supreme and the chamber has become a "sixty-vote Senate" in which the minority party can seemingly stop anything if enough of its members join together on procedural votes. But suppose the conventional wisdom is correct and these examples are mere exceptions to the rule—that is, the House majority party is actually a "cartel" that monopolizes power, and the Senate minority is the only minority party in government with real influence. Why, then, does the minority in the House remain so active? Why do its leaders and members propose amendments to bills, hold press conferences week after week, offer delaying motions on the House floor, or hold sit-ins in the chamber? What explains these exceptions, if that is indeed what they are?[3]

The answers to these questions are not merely academic. If the minority party in the House of Representatives truly can shape politics and policy outcomes, it deserves at least as much attention as the minority in the Senate, for the laws Congress makes may well reflect the preferences and goals of both parties in the House of Representatives, not just one. Much of what the minority does, effectual or not, is also blamed for making Congress raucous, conflictual, and partisan.[4] If such blame is merited, any solution for that partisanship and conflict depends on a better understanding of minority party politics in the U.S. House.

Unfortunately, few scholars have bothered to explore the subject in depth.[5] One is Charles O. Jones, who in 1970 published *The Minority Party in Congress*. In his book Jones categorized the minority party of each Congress based on its degree of strategic flexibility, and he identified factors that dictate that flexibility, such as party strength, the power of the president, and the "temper of the times." Though ambitious, comprehensive, and insightful, Jones' book was a "big picture" study that did not try to explain an important aspect of congressional politics: why a minority party might employ a certain tactic in a given situation or for one issue over another. It was also written when Congress was a very different place for the minority, with no C-SPAN to air floor speeches, no twenty-four-hour news cycle to take advantage of, fewer recorded votes to exploit, and more open rules and procedures.[6]

Another noteworthy study of minority party politics, one that focused on the House and minority strategy in particular, was William Connelly and John Pitney's *Congress' Permanent Minority?* (1994). Adroitly incorporating a diversity of data, Connelly and Pitney explored the complex relationship between ideology, party leadership,

Table 1.1. Minority Parties and Party Leaders in the U.S. House since 1971

Year(s)/ Congress(es)	Minority party	Minority party leaders
1971–94 92nd–103rd	Republican	Gerald Ford (MI, 1971–73) John J. Rhodes (AZ, 1973–80) Robert Michel (IL, 1981–94)
1995–2006 104th–109th	Democrat	Richard Gephardt (MO, 1995–2002) Nancy Pelosi (CA, 2003–6)
2007–10 110th–111th	Republican	John Boehner (OH, 2007–10)
2011–112th–	Democrat	Nancy Pelosi (CA, 2011–)

and the minority status of House Republicans and evaluated the party's chances of becoming a majority. Their book appeared when Congress was more similar to what it is like today, with expanded media outlets covering congressional affairs, sharper partisanship in the chamber, and greater majority party power. But it too was overtaken by events: the year it appeared in print Republicans won a majority of House seats for the first time in four decades, and each party has since taken an additional turn in the minority (see Table 1.1). Unlike when Connelly and Pitney wrote their book, it is now possible to offer broader generalizations about minority party behavior shared by both Republicans and Democrats in a media-driven, highly partisan House.

That is the purpose of this book. Because I believe that the minority and what it does in the House is not well understood, the bulk of my analysis is dedicated to answering two questions: what kinds of things does the House minority party do, and why does it do them? In addition, I tentatively explore the answer to a third question: does the minority make any difference in political outcomes? I say "tentatively" because determining causal effects in politics can be maddeningly difficult, and it is well beyond the scope of this study to fully test all possible consequences of everything the minority party in the House has done since 1971, the starting point of my analysis. To simplify matters and at the same time establish a higher threshold for determining influence, I look at only the short-term, proximate consequences of select instances of minority party action. Then, in the book's final chapter, I speculate briefly about the political consequences of a legislative body, like the U.S. House, that gives disproportionate formal power to one party.

The House minority party and its members undertake a whole slew of collective and party-oriented actions that consume considerable time, energy, and attention. Generally speaking, these actions are motivated by one or more *collective party concerns*—goals or conditions of importance to the party—that derive from the nature of congressional parties and the lack of formal authority of the minority party in particular. Minority party politics is characterized by the use of various tactics and strategies to address these concerns; internal conflicts over which concerns, strategies, and tactics to follow; and efforts to overcome these conflicts and other hindrances to collective activity. When the minority does act collectively, it has a chance—not a great chance, but a chance nonetheless—to shape political outcomes.[7]

This way of thinking about the minority party and its "underdog politics" differs in subtle but important ways from other theories of political parties in the U.S. Congress. Most scholars identify no more than one or two party goals driving behavior; focus primarily, sometimes exclusively, on the majority party; and limit their observations to floor voting.[8] Attention to just the minority party, and with a more holistic approach as I take here, reveals a greater complexity in minority party politics than prior studies have uncovered. And while the majority and minority "are not mirror images of each other," some of this complexity may well apply to the majority party, too.[9]

My study begins in 1971 because it is a useful starting point for documenting how House minority party tactics have changed since Charles O. Jones' 1970 book, especially with the rise of a more partisan, media-centric Congress. Before discussing further these tactics and why they are utilized, however, it may be useful to put the subject in its larger historical and theoretical context. We take for granted, after all, that a legislature should have a minority party. But when and where did that idea first emerge? And what do political theory and historical practice suggest is the proper role of the minority?

The Development of the Minority Party: Its Rights and Responsibilities

Most democratic theorists agree that the minority in a free society should be valued and protected. However, under the principle of majority rule (*lex majoris partis*) as it developed gradually from ancient Greece to mid-1500s England, minorities were not entitled to political protection. Not until the rise of Western liberalism would concern with the rights of the minority in society become widely shared. James Madison, who agreed that "the fundamental principle of free government" was majority rule, also recognized the limits of that principle. It was "in some degree true," he admitted in *Federalist Paper* 10, that in government "measures are too often decided, not according to the rules of justice and the rights of the minor party, but by the superior force of an interested and overbearing majority." Five decades later, Alexis de Tocqueville warned that a minority is always at a serious disadvantage in a democracy because of the majority's social as well as political dominance. Writing in 1861, John Stuart Mill opined that a key problem for any government is to ensure that the minority in a democratic society is fairly represented.[10]

One way a minority group can protect itself is by organizing, seeking representation in government, and searching for ways to build a large enough coalition to become a majority—in short, becoming a political party.[11] In fact, opposition to the ruling government was an important impetus to the creation and development of the party system in the United States in the late 18th and early 19th centuries.[12] But the formation of an opposition poses two challenges to democratic governance. First, those in power may see it as a potential threat rather than a legitimate entity. The first organized groups opposed to the existing government in England or the young American Republic were often disparaged as disloyal "factions" that threatened the stability of the nation. Only gradually during the 1700s and early 1800s did Britain, and later the United States, come to acknowledge that an organized opposition was an acceptable, even desirable, part of political life, a development that roughly paralleled the growing acceptance of mass parties and the two-party system.[13]

The British thinker and legislator Edmund Burke was an important early defender of the political party (and, by implication, the opposition party) as an institution. In 1770 he described a party not as a threat, as many did at the time, but simply as a collection of individuals "united for promoting by their joint endeavors the national interest, upon some particular principle in which they are all agreed." Burke's acceptance, if not his endorsement, of parties soon spread to America. Despite warnings against parties and party opposition by early presidents, and even some efforts to eliminate political opposition altogether, a generation of politicians rose to power who saw mass parties, including an opposition party, as beneficial and believed the opposition should be treated following "certain canons of sportsmanlike decency." By the mid-19th century, political thinkers as well as politicians accepted parties and party conflict as an essential part of American democracy.[14]

The second challenge posed by the presence of an opposition party is how to balance its desire for representation in government against the majority's right to rule. An opposition may be welcomed or even encouraged to field candidates for public office, but what good is that if the party's members are totally excluded from decision-making because they are a minority? In England and the United States, as opposition parties became acceptable, so too did a belief that they should be granted representation, and even some limited influence, in the legislature. The U.S. Constitution grants a minority of legislators some powers, such as the ability to demand that the votes of their colleagues "on any question" be recorded. Lawmakers themselves have not always had charitable views toward the rights and powers of the minority: "The right of the minority is to draw its salaries, and its function is to make a quorum," as the House's acerbically witty 19th-century Speaker, Thomas Brackett Reed, notoriously remarked. But even the once-tough partisan John Dingell (D-MI), perhaps chastened by spending two stints in the minority, told a reporter that "the minority is important, I don't care whether it's Democrats or Republicans. In my view, every Member around here is supposed to be equal." Today, both the U.S. House and the British House of Commons endow a number of formal powers and rights to the minority party.[15]

An understanding that the opposition may not only exist but be entitled to legislative representation and some limited powers led to a new question: what is the minority's proper responsibility as a part of government? Lord Randolph Churchill, a member of the British Parliament from the 1800s (and the father of Winston Churchill), famously answered the question this way: "The duty of an Opposition is to oppose." Elaborated another British lawmaker in 1841, "it is to oppose everything and propose nothing." Others, however, have pointed to a more restrained, if not positive, role for the minority. At a minimum, for democratic governance to succeed it must agree "to be ruled by the majority until in orderly fashion the minority can make itself the majority," wrote one political scientist in the 1920s. When a nation's economic, social, and military security is at stake, it may also be obliged to help the majority govern. Some have further suggested that the minority must regularly offer proposals for voters to evaluate, not just attack the majority's agenda. In their noteworthy 1950 report "Toward a More Responsible Two Party System," a committee of political scientists argued that "the fundamental requirement" for parties to be accountable is an opposition that "acts as the critic of the party in power, developing, defining and presenting . . . policy alternatives." "A minority has various responsibilities," wrote former House Republican leader John Rhodes, "not the least of which is to put forward its own programs while analyzing and criticizing the programs of the majority."[16]

The classic model of how minority parties should conduct themselves is that of the "loyal opposition." It is the principle that the minority must remain faithful to the ideals and institutions of the country while respectfully disagreeing with, and perhaps suggesting alternatives to, the majority's legislative agenda. First coined in the 1820s British Parliament, it was rapidly accepted in other representative democracies, including the United States. Political scientist Clinton Rossiter went so far as to proclaim the loyal opposition as essential to a democratic state. Even hard-core oppositionists in the American Congress frame their tactics as serving national, not partisan, interests. Newt Gingrich, the famous Georgia firebrand of the House Republican Party from the 1970s through the 1990s, declared it to be the "civic duty" of the minority to be the critical watchdog of a corrupt ruling party.[17]

Needless to say, fulfilling the role of loyal opposition requires that the minority party maintain a careful balance between loyalty and opposition. This creates an ongoing tension between opposing the majority party's policies "just for the sake of opposing," wrote the scholar Nevil Johnson, "and 'constructive opposition' which, if pursued too zealously, may take the edge off the competition for public support." In the 1970s, '80s, and early '90s, younger House Republicans frequently complained that senior party members leaned too far in the latter direction, giving up opportunities to fight the majority in order to hold on to whatever influence they had in making policy. But those senior lawmakers in turn warned that excessive opposition for its own sake would hurt the party as well as the nation. As Senator Everett Dirksen (R-IL) put it, to "follow a course of solid opposition, of stalemate . . . is not in the interest of the country."[18]

Whether a minority party in Congress emphasizes loyalty, opposition, or both at any given time depends in no small part on what matters to the party—its central concerns. I explore these next. Afterward I outline the four basic types of tactics the minority in the House uses to address those concerns; discuss common obstacles to implementing tactics successfully; and review the role of innovators and entrepreneurs in developing and implementing those tactics.

The Collective Concerns of the Minority Party

Scholars often think of individuals in Congress as *goal-seeking*. If lawmakers within a political party share a set of goals, that party—as with any political party, in or out of Congress—is especially suited to "promote the achievement of [those] collective choices." It follows that the tactic of a minority party likely represents an effort to realize one or more such collective objectives—which, because they can encompass conditions for success as well as specific political goals, I describe more broadly as *concerns* (see Table 1.2).[19]

The preeminent concern of the minority party in the House is to alter its political status from minority to majority.[20] The House is a majoritarian institution, and from majority status all else flows: the right to chair committees, set the House's agenda, and craft the chamber's rules. It therefore makes sense that minority parties would

Table 1.2. The Collective Concerns of the Minority Party

Order	Concern	Primary tactics used to address
First order	Majority status (*goal*)	1. Electioneering 2. Messaging 3. Legislating 4. Obstructing
Second order	Policy (*goal*)	2. Messaging 3. Legislating 4. Obstructing
	Procedural rights and powers (*condition*)	2. Messaging 3. Legislating 4. Obstructing
Third order	Successful presidential party (*condition*)	2. Messaging 3. Legislating 4. Obstructing

care a great deal about winning a majority of the chamber's seats. The majority party cares about elections too, of course; the desire to win and keep governmental power is, for some, the very definition of a political party.[21] But because the majority party already possesses formal power, it has some flexibility in focusing on its other collective aims. Sometimes it even willingly subjugates its concern with elections in order to enact desired policy, as House Democrats did in the 111th Congress (2009–10) when they put their vulnerable members at risk by passing health care reform and energy legislation. By contrast, the minority party would like nothing more than to cease being a minority altogether.[22] Even during times when that goal seems remote, all members of the House minority recognize the inherent value in being in the majority, and the party's leaders always have this objective foremost in their minds, not least because they are often blamed (and even risk being deposed) if their party fails to win back power in a reasonable period of time.[23]

Parties do not exist solely to exercise influence, and even at their most ideologically diverse they attract members who share some policy objectives and beliefs. If we accept Burke's definition of parties as collectives organized around common principles to promote "the national interest," there follows a second, albeit less urgent, concern of the minority party: influencing policy outcomes.[24] Policy and electoral goals are certainly interrelated, for getting preferred legislation enacted might improve the minority party's reputation or allocate more government benefits to its supporters—outcomes that often translate into votes. However, as political scientist Richard Fenno and others have pointed out, policy influence also serves as a distinct objective in its own right. And even though the minority in the House is likely to discount its chances of influencing policy, since it is without formal power, its members are, after all, *legislators*: individuals whose very job is to make law and solve policy problems. This common concern is precisely why frustration is part and parcel of minority party life.[25]

If we think about congressional parties as goal-seeking, our consideration of what motivates the minority would probably end here, as it has with other scholarly studies. But not everything that a party does, or that preoccupies its members, has to do with reaching a goal or changing its political status. The minority also cares about maintaining, even enhancing, its political environment—the conditions under which it operates. Two features of that environment are of sufficient concern to the party to motivate collective activity.[26]

One of these concerns derives from the fundamental power asymmetry between the two parties in the House. This asymmetry extends not only to lawmaking, which the majority party dominates by dint of its superior numbers (its "policy majority"), but also to the very rules of the chamber itself (its "procedural majority"). Minority parties are accorded some privileges under the House's rules, but these are not cast in stone; the majority can change or ignore them as it sees fit. Accordingly, the minority is uniquely concerned that its members are guaranteed adequate procedural rights.[27]

Procedural protection, like policy influence, is of lesser importance than winning power, and it matters largely as a means of achieving other ends. Rights and privileges allow a party to advertise itself and take positions with the public so as to persuade voters in the next election. They are also tremendously important for influencing policy. As Congressman Dingell famously said, "I'll let you write the substance on a statute and you let me write the procedure, and I'll screw you every time." But procedural benefits are also of value to the minority party in and of themselves. They accord its members a degree of participation in the legislative process and allow them to voice the preferences of their constituents. They also enforce the general principle that a minority be accorded durable protection. "The only weapons by which the minority can defend themselves" against the majority, observed Thomas Jefferson, "are the forms and rules of proceeding[s]" of the House.[28]

The other collective concern of the minority, one that differentiates it from the opposition party in a parliamentary system, is the condition of the presidential party. The presidential party is the wing of the party that either seeks to control the White House or does control the White House and is thus led by the president.[29] To be sure, the presidency is relevant to both congressional parties, for it is the political (if not constitutional) center of American government. The president heads the executive branch and has formal and informal influence over the legislative process; his reputation rubs off on his congressional party; and as the leader of his party, he expects loyalty from his partisan brethren in Congress. Accordingly, the majority and minority parties will both expend considerable energy defending (or attacking) the incumbent president and doing what they can to help their party win the next presidential election. For the minority party, however, the presidency is essential. Lamented one House Republican in the early 1990s, "if you're a 'permanent minority,' or just a minority, and you don't have the White House, you don't have anything." A minority with a strong ally in the Oval Office retains a precious toehold of national power and influence, and a winning presidential candidate offers coattails that may pull his party out of the minority wilderness.[30]

Minority parties and their leaders are thus likely to dedicate a good amount of effort to helping their same-party president or presidential candidate and fighting the White House incumbent or candidate of their partisan opponents. When Richard Nixon faced the serious possibility of impeachment, Minority Leader Rhodes was deeply torn, fearing Nixon was guilty but understanding that as minority leader he was duty-bound to support a president of his party.[31] His successor, Bob Michel, responded to complaints that he was too willing to support compromises made by President Reagan with a Democratic Congress by declaring that "I was elected leader in a Republican administration to help a Republican administration." If Reagan were not president, he added, "we wouldn't be worth two hoots as a minority." Michel would later initiate a new campaign to use floor speeches as an organized weapon on behalf of President George H. W. Bush's reelection, and then against the Clinton White House (discussed in Chapter 3). A Democratic leader who served in the House minority in the 1990s described the development of a minority party's strategy thus: "The first question to be asked is, is the president of your party or not? And if the situation is as it was in the last six years of the Clinton presidency, then you conduct yourselves a little bit differently . . . Part of your role is to work in every way you can to help him . . . [You] raise as much Cain as you can, as much Hell as you can [for the president]." And if the White House is controlled by a Republican? Then "it's all-out warfare against the policies of the presidency." Republicans followed the same playbook after 2008, going after President Obama and avoiding cooperation with the White House as much as possible (see Figure 1.1).[32]

Figure 1.1 The House minority party versus the president. "Clenched Fist" by R. W. Matson, *Roll Call*, February 2, 2009. Reprinted with permission by CQ Roll Call, Inc. (www.cqrollcall.com).

Not that the presidential party will reciprocate favors given by a loyal House minority. Presidents do meet regularly with their party's leaders in Congress and often consult with them on legislative strategy.[33] But minority parties are just as often neglected or even mistreated at the other end of Pennsylvania Avenue. A same-party president has policy and electoral interests of his own that may differ from the congressional minority's, and his responsibility to govern requires negotiation with the majority party. Tensions can become exacerbated if the party of a first-term president loses control of Congress in a midterm election, because the chief executive is sorely tempted to read that loss as a message from voters to create distance from congressional allies. The same neglect sometimes comes from aspirants to the White House, too, who find Congress a tempting target on the campaign trail and make no rhetorical distinction between incumbent lawmakers from one party or the other.[34]

For these and other reasons, presidential politics is the weakest and most contingent of the minority party's four concerns. A minority tempted to sharply criticize a popular opposite-party president risks "look[ing] like . . . a nihilistic party of reactionary opposition."[35] The possibility of a policy victory sometimes trumps the political benefits of tarnishing the White House, as it did for minority Republicans who lent Clinton their votes and connections to help pass the North American Free Trade Agreement in 1993. Conversely, the constraints of having to support, or being affiliated with, a chief executive of the same party can be stifling to the minority. The 1992 election brought "liberation from the tentacles" of George H. W. Bush, explained Gingrich, and fellow Republican Tom DeLay (TX) agreed that "it was fabulous" that his party could now better paint a contrasting picture to voters.[36]

History, in fact, is full of examples of minority parties breaking, or coming close to breaking, with their presidential party on major bills. The Republican Study Committee, a highly influential organization of conservative-minded lawmakers in the House, was started by legislators disgruntled with President Nixon for being too moderate on policy. Nearly two decades later, Gingrich led a group of House conservatives into open revolt against President Bush's 1990 budget proposal for raising taxes. Then there are the scandal-ridden or deeply unpopular presidents or presidential candidates who threaten to drag the minority party's reputation down with them. The usual instinct of House party members in those situations is to flee. In the fall of 1998, when President Clinton's affair with a White House intern was revealed in graphic detail, Minority Whip David Bonior spent hours on the phone calming the panicked members of his caucus who might abandon Clinton, insisting that "we've got to stick together, because if we divide, we're *all* going down."[37]

Nonetheless, the House minority cannot free itself entirely from loyalty to the presidential party. Presidents are just too politically valuable and consequential to do otherwise. What hurts the presidential party usually hurts the party in Congress; its members may run from a tainted White House or presidential candidate like rats from a sinking ship, but many will still drown. Bonior's warning to fellow Democrats to stick with Clinton was, in this respect (and in retrospect), a wise one. It demonstrates how the American system of separated powers imposes an important limiting condition on the "freedom" of the minority party referred to by the character from Anthony Trollope's novel *Phineas Finn*.

These four collective concerns, the "four P's" that matter to the minority—power (by winning elections), policy, procedural rights, and presidential party success—are ordered by their degree of importance to the party, how much intra-party agreement there usually is to address them, and the extent to which they are instrumental toward addressing other concerns (see Table 1.2). But this ordering is not immutable and may shift with the political context. For instance, a minority party with no foreseeable means of winning control of the House, or one that has many ideologically moderate members, may often settle for bargaining with the majority on policy, as was the case in the early 1970s when Republicans were a more divided party and faced a majority that had strong incumbency advantages and some members willing to vote with the minority on occasion. In fact, all sorts of things may lead to some reordering of these concerns in the short or long term: the temperament and preferences of party members and leaders, the tactics of the majority party, the legislative agenda, the minority's size, which party controls the Senate and the White House, whether it is an election year, and so on.[38]

Conflict over which collective concern should take precedence over others is often "the crux of intraparty politics on Capitol Hill" for both parties, but can be especially heated within the minority. In addition, sometimes the minority party's leaders may follow personal goals that do not jibe with the concerns of their co-partisans. Minority Leader Richard Gephardt's (D-MO) presidential ambitions were a source of chagrin for many House Democrats, especially when some things he did, such as openly criticizing President Clinton in a December 1997 speech and taking several trips to early presidential primary states, seemed irrelevant, even hurtful, to the minority's collective concerns. Divisions often surface along the lines of seniority, with junior members chafing at what they perceive to be insufficient dedication from their older colleagues to certain collective concerns. The quintessential example from recent House history was the displeasure that younger Republicans, most notably Newt Gingrich, had with their elders in the 1970s and '80s for not working hard enough (in their opinion) to become a majority party. "My feeling from the beginning," reflected one former House Republican first elected in the early 1970s, "was there were too many Republicans who were content with being in the minority." As Gingrich later described it, these senior lawmakers saw themselves as the "subordinate wolf" that "spent a lot of time cultivating the dominant wolf" (that is, the Democratic majority) and in 1980 Gingrich declared that "the only *real* issue for Republicans in the U.S. Congress is, 'How do we win control?'"[39]

There are no obvious resolutions to these conflicts. Senior Republicans in the 1970s responded to their critics by insisting that not only were party leaders still fighting to win elections, but that it would have been foolish to abandon the minority's other concerns on a fruitless quest for power, given the Democrats' strong hold on so many House seats. "We had no real chance through most of that period [the 1960s and '70s] to hope to become a majority," recalled one former G.O.P. leadership aide, so "the goal was to find a way to get something valuable that we could take home, so to speak." Nonetheless, when conflict emerges, a general rule of thumb is that concerns of higher order—with majority status being the highest of all—will usually trump those that are lower.[40]

Emotion, Uncertainty, and Other Important Caveats

Collective concerns explain most of what the minority party does, but conceptualizing party politics this way relies on some implicit assumptions that do not always hold true in practice. One is that legislators make rational, rather than emotional, determinations of when and how to take action on behalf of their party. It is a reasonable assumption in many ways; and yet, if the philosopher David Hume was right that "reason is, and ought only to be the slave of the passions," his maxim applies no less to congressional party politics. "Emotion—over issues, over procedure—plays a larger part in parliamentary politics than people may realize," noted longtime Washington journalist Elizabeth Drew. The exclusion and disempowerment by, and dismissiveness of, the majority party can lead to frustration and anger among the minority's members, impede rational calculation, and propel (if not cause) them to move beyond mere rumination to actually do something.[41]

There have been numerous cases in which minority party leaders and rank-and-file members have acted out of emotion, not (simply) a utilitarian evaluation of costs and benefits. By the late 1970s, for example, a group of disgruntled younger House Republicans that included Gingrich, Carroll Campbell (SC), Bob Kasten (WI), Jack Kemp (NY), Trent Lott (MS), and Robert Walker (PA) had begun meeting regularly to discuss their party's lowly status. "We talked about our frustration with being in the minority and how oppressed we felt under the leadership of [Speaker] O'Neill," recalled one legislator in the group, which was known as the "Blow-Dry Guys" for their members' prominent coifs of hair. "We decided we weren't going to put up with it." In the late 1980s and early '90s, Republicans' exasperation at their treatment at the hands of the party in power contributed to their sporadic "war on the floor" against Democrats' bills and use of House rules.[42]

In addition to emotion, there are other reasons that action may take place that falls outside of, or that interweaves with, a careful consideration of the party's collective needs. "For it is Being that is dear to us," wrote Montaigne, "and Being lies in movement and action." Sometimes legislators act because it beats being idle—as minority members, excluded from most legislating, often are. If the majority party is being proactive it seems foolish not to respond with action in kind. From the perspective of minority party leaders, "there's a lot of stuff you have to do to keep people happy and show folks you're trying," explained one former Gephardt aide. Existing norms and practices matter, too: some tactics gradually accrete until they develop a sort of "autonomous motivational dynamic," done simply because they always have been done and there is an unquestioned faith that they work. They can become one of the "important social rituals" that make up so much of politics, as political scientists James March and Johan Olsen noted.[43]

Finally, even a minority party strategizing over how best to satisfy a collective concern faces uncertainty over which tactic will work best or what it might lead to. One Republican from the late-2000s explained his overall rationale for selecting particular tactics like so: "Some of my colleagues might ask, 'why would you do *that*?' But you never are sure which tactic's going to work, and ones that don't work, you don't remember . . . You never know where the sensitive point is going to be on the other side, so you keep pushing, and pushing, and pushing."[44]

Collective Tactics and Challenges to Collective Action

Whether to satisfy its collective concerns, out of emotional or other drives, or due to some combination thereof, the minority party in the House of Representatives employs a plethora of tactics and sometimes develops new ones, too. The next four chapters each discuss a broad category of tactics, listed in Table 1.3, defined by their primary effect (versus, say, their intent, which may not be the same thing). The first category of collective tactics is *electioneering*: fundraising, candidate recruitment, and other campaign-related activity. The second, *messaging*, includes press conferences, coordinated floor speeches, and other actions in the public sphere that have as their principal or sole effect the communication of messages or positions on particular issues. The third category of tactics is *obstruction and delay*, and the final is *legislating*: introducing bills, offering amendments, or using certain procedures to manipulate the content of, or perhaps defeat, legislation. These categories do not exhaust the list of possible tactics, tools, or techniques available to the minority party—including doing nothing, which sometimes can be the most politically profitable thing for the minority to do. But they incorporate the most common and important tactics used by the House minority party over the past four decades.[45]

For each of the four categories I discuss how particular tactics by the minority party have developed since the 1970s, then use case studies, aggregate data, or both to explain why the minority uses them. Intent is seldom obvious. For instance, a legislative act (say, an amendment) might be offered in order to alter a bill, make a political point, compel a vote that embarrasses or discredits the other party, or a mixture of these things. Floor statements, news stories, legislative text, and other clues are used to infer the motivation behind minority party activity whenever possible. When measuring the political effects of tactics—whether they actually "work"—I limit my attention to certain political outcomes for each category: for electioneering tactics, election results; for messaging tactics, shifts in public opinion; and for obstructive and legislative tactics, changes to bills, procedural rights, or the congressional agenda.

Two recurring features of minority party tactics are worth noting at the outset. First, the minority sometimes, and increasingly in recent years, uses different tactics within and even across categories

Table 1.3. Tactics Examined in This Book

Category	Specific tactic examined	Used by minority only or both parties?	Primary participants
1. Electioneering	Candidate recruitment	Both	Party org.
	Fund-raising	Both	Party org.
	Campaign-year agendas	Both	Party org.
2. Messaging	One-minute speeches	Both	Any member of Congress (MC)
	Leadership press conferences	Both	Party leaders
	Refusal to leave floor	Minority only	Any MC
	Floor walkouts	Minority only	Any MC
3. Obstructing	Quorum call	Minority only	Any MC
	Motion to reconsider	Minority only	Any MC
	Taking extra time to vote	Both	Any MC
	Motions to adjourn or rise	Minority only	Any MC
4. Legislating	Introducing bills and amendments	Both	Any MC
	Floor voting	Both	Any MC
	Discharge petition	Both	Any MC
	Motion to recommit	Minority only	Any MC

in tandem to address a common concern. Press conferences, for instance, may be held in proximity with the introduction of bills, amendments, discharge petitions, and delaying motions, all on an identical issue or grievance. I note examples of this integrative stratagem throughout the book, but for ease of analysis I do not attempt to capture them systematically.

Second, many tactics pose difficult trade-offs for the party. Pursuing legislative deals with the majority party may yield policy triumphs yet make the party look bad with its activists and loyalists in the electorate, for example, while obstructive tactics can block bills but annoy the majority party enough that it retaliates by curtailing minority party rights. To circumvent such trade-offs, the minority often delegates a talented party member to initiate or carry out a tactic without implicating leaders or the party caucus. A congressman with fund-raising acumen, say, may be tasked with finding new sources of campaign money from groups that party leaders would rather not associate with publicly. Aggressive communicators might make provocative statements that the party's leaders can disavow if they backfire. An influential committee member could be covertly charged with forging legislation in cooperation with the majority party. Floor watchdogs are appointed to observe chamber proceedings and use the rules to slow or stop the majority if they deem it best.[46]

Tricky trade-offs are hardly the biggest obstacle to collective action. True, lawmakers may have more incentives than disincentives to cooperate with their partisan colleagues.[47] But minority parties in the U.S. House face two major challenges to carrying out tactics collectively. Neither is unique to the minority, but they both tend to plague the minority party more deeply and durably. The first is to maintain, if not increase, *internal unity*. Voting unity is the most obvious manifestation of this challenge. The minority has little chance of winning a vote on the chamber floor or exercising leverage if it cannot cast its ballots as a unit. By contrast, if it is unified it can usually uphold any presidential veto (which needs a two-thirds vote to override) and, depending on the size and unity of the majority party, may kill bills altogether or at least force the majority to expend valuable energy and political capital crafting a fragile winning coalition within its own ranks. Voting unity also offers messaging benefits by signaling the minority's commitment to an issue, denying the majority an opportunity to claim bipartisan support for its initiatives, and creating a perception that the party is well organized.[48]

But the value of voting unity is easily overstated, especially because it is highly contingent on circumstances, and even the most ideologically unified parties will have some likely dissenters on any given vote. So minority leaders tend to pursue a strategy of selective voting unity. For example, Republican minority leaders readily let some of their members vote for Democratic bills in the early months of 2007 knowing the next election was nearly two years away, some of its members were in Democratic-leaning districts, and President Bush would veto many of the measures anyway. They were similarly sanguine about voting defections on several majority party bills in early 2009; explained one Republican, "You can't swing at every pitch." But not so for President Obama's high-profile economic stimulus legislation of 2009, nor his signature health care reform initiative in 2010. The latter was intensely disliked by conservative voters, and voting unity on health care was of such symbolic value to the party that Minority Leader John Boehner even asked its most endangered member, Joseph Cao of New Orleans, to vote no. Cao did. (He later lost reelection.)[49]

More fundamental for the minority party than voting unity is unity of purpose. If there is general agreement within the party over its common concerns and how best to address them, more members are likely to sacrifice time and effort to take part in collective actions. Unity of purpose leads to mass participation, which is essential to the success of many party tactics, like raising campaign money or walking out from the chamber in protest. It potentially encourages party activism, a highly useful resource. And it makes it easier for party leaders to whip lawmakers on key votes.[50]

Building and sustaining unity of purpose is not an easy task. The minority lacks levers of power that the majority party can pull to offer inducements in exchange for members' cooperation. Lawmakers who believe their reelection hinges on district casework or committee work may not be interested in doing things for the minority. Same-party presidents can also encourage factions to develop: Bill Clinton's middle-of-the-road positions on certain matters led to the creation of the New Democratic Coalition, a group of moderates who sometimes bypassed Democratic Party leaders to help the president win floor votes on trade and other issues. Because the most effective way forward is seldom clear, potential disagreement between party members over which strategy or tactic will work best is a looming roadblock on the path toward developing unity of purpose.[51]

Sometimes the majority party itself can unify the minority: as Speaker, Gingrich was "a galvanizer of Democratic opposition," as were G.O.P. Whip Tom DeLay, President George W. Bush, and Speaker Nancy Pelosi. But on the shoulders of minority party leaders usually falls the burden of finding ways to overcome hindrances to unity. Sometimes they use persuasion; other times, they find ways for members with different views of party strategy to work in a complementary fashion; other times, they compel agreement using promises to give or withdraw the few benefits they control, like campaign monies and committee assignments; and other times they follow a "politics of inclusion" strategy, involving the rank and file in party-wide decisions to inculcate loyalty. Many of the tactics that the minority employs to address its four core concerns can themselves build esprit de corps within the party. But perhaps the most intriguing unity-building leadership technique is to create what Minority Whip Steny Hoyer called "the psychology of consensus." Unity-building exercises are a common way to do this. The sociologist Émile Durkheim observed the power of this technique a century ago, writing that "within a crowd moved by a common passion, we become susceptible to feelings and actions of which we are incapable on our own . . . For this reason all parties—political, economic, or denominational—deliberately hold periodic meetings in which their members may renew their common faith by some collective demonstration." Examples of these "collective demonstrations" include the annual retreats held by both parties and Minority Leader Gephardt showing inspiring scenes from *Braveheart* and *Apollo 13* to unify Democrats before tough partisan votes. Over the long run, these and other moves can develop a lasting party culture in which defection is frowned upon.[52]

The second and related challenge to collective party action by the minority party besides maintaining internal unity is to build and sustain *party morale*. For either party, high morale, like strong unity of purpose, maximizes the odds of getting legislators to eagerly surrender their scarce time to help the party as a whole. But because the minority is disempowered, its members are especially susceptible to defeatism: "The sense of being in the minority is being left out," as one Republican congressman put it. One motive for Gephardt's movie screenings, according to former minority whip David Bonior, was to combat this defeatism: "You're not winning, okay? You're losing, day after day . . . So you've got to find things that keep people's spirits up, that keep their hopes up." As Gephardt himself explained, "It gets people motivated. It gets people fired up." And a minority party whose representatives are unhappy and demoralized can lose members to retirement, while those who stay develop a "permanent minority mindset" in which "you don't fight, you don't donate, you don't raise money, you don't do all the things necessary" to win power, said another Democratic leader. "If you act like you're in the minority, you're going to stay in the minority," warned Kevin McCarthy (R-CA) at a dinner with fellow Republicans following their losses in the 2008 elections.[53]

Disempowerment is demoralizing, but nothing stings worse than a rebuke by voters. "In defeat, morale withers," write Connelly and Pitney. Whereas the winning party can claim that its agenda represents the nation, the minority lacks that "moral ascendancy," and perpetually failing to become a majority can exacerbate a sense of rejection. Grisly election losses are especially injurious to the party's spirits. In the days, weeks, and even months that follow these kinds of defeats, particularly ones that reverse party control of the chamber, the minority becomes paralyzed, and submerged splits within the party are exposed. Its top leader frequently weathers internal grumblings, if not an outright challenge, by angry election survivors who blame the leader for their loss and hope a new leader will placate voters and party supporters.[54]

The Democrats' loss of the House in 2010—in which sixty-three Democratic-held seats went to the G.O.P., the single biggest one-party defeat in a House election in over six decades—was a huge blow to the party and may have depressed party members' desire for active confrontation in the following Congress. But minority status was still fresh in the minds of many incumbents, having become a majority only four years before. A better—perhaps the best—example of a demoralizing election loss from the past four decades is the Democratic defeat of 1994. Its devastating impact on the morale of the party, which had a seemingly invincible lock on power in the House, cannot be overstated. Quotes from a few of those who went through it underscore the point:

- We had always been in the majority, and thought we always would be . . . It was a huge shock that everyone had to deal with.
- Morale was low . . . it's very depressing when you go from the majority to the minority, especially if you don't know what it's like.
- After having lost the House after 40 years, it was very difficult for members to get themselves back on their feet again.

Democratic conservatives, their numbers greatly reduced, became embittered, even angry, that their liberal colleagues now "could really ignore us, to a large part," in the words of one former member. For senior Democrats who truly wanted to legislate, recalled a leadership staffer, "it was not a fun time." Some continued to try anyway, bringing to mind Ignazio Silone's account of being expelled from the Communist Party: "like someone who has had a tremendous blow on the head and keeps on his feet, walking, talking and gesticulating, but without fully realizing what has happened."[55]

The G.O.P. was also chastened, albeit to a lesser extent, after it was removed from power in the House in 2006 and lost the presidency in 2008. "Republicans basically did some pretty serious soul-searching about themselves," one G.O.P. leadership staffer recalled, "asking who we are as Republicans." But in the face of Democrats' bold partisan legislative proposals in the first months of 2009—particularly a new "card check" method to make it easier for labor unions to organize—the minority became rejuvenated, "unified and energized." It also quickly channeled its anger over the assertive use of chamber rules by the majority Democrats into strong unified support for using those rules for protest and delay. Recounted the same leadership aide, while Democrats took years to become a strong minority after 1994, "Somebody said to me, 'You guys figured it out in about twelve minutes.'"[56]

Besides waiting for the majority to charge up one's own rank and file, how do leaders improve party morale? Gephardt's movie screenings illustrate one way: use unity-building exercises that also boost morale. In addition, party leaders may play up grievances or acts of unfairness by the majority. Nancy Pelosi, for instance, "sought to galvanize the troops" in 2004 by proposing a legislative agenda that included greater protection of minority rights. Leaders will also spin any win, no matter how small, into a major triumph to strengthen morale: winning a presidential election, an off-year (or "special") congressional election, or a legislative or procedural battle. Just keeping active and fighting the good fight is itself a preventive, if not curative, medicine for low esteem. "You lose, but you feel good about it," recalled former congressman Robert Walker. G.O.P. leader Bob Michel even resorted to semantic changes to his job title to revive House Republicans in the face of continuing losses: in December 1980 he insisted that it be changed from "minority leader" to "Republican leader" because "I want to expel the word 'minority' from our vocabulary and bury it for all time."[57]

With respect to both unity and morale, thinking of parties as teams is especially apt. A sports team that is disunited, rife with internal disagreements over strategy and tactics, and demoralized is far less likely to win on the field, no matter how talented its individual members may be. Party leaders, like team captains and coaches, keep the party together and its morale high. At one of the lowest periods for the House G.O.P.—the slow unraveling of the Nixon White House in 1974—one former party member recalled that "after an hour or so of listening to John [Rhodes], we always came out reinvigorated and ready to continue the fight." "Think group. Think team," exhorted Gephardt to incoming Democratic freshmen after the 1998 elections.[58]

Much of minority party House politics in the 1970s through the early 1990s was about internal team-building. When Gingrich and other activist members worked to convince fellow Republicans that seizing power in the House was not only paramount but also possible, they were conducting a form of team-building. ("You've got to believe [you can win] before you can do something" to win back the House, as one former Republican member later put it.) Taking the advice of former president Richard Nixon to do something about the party's lack of "team-work, aggressiveness, or interest in ideas to make them an effective counterforce," Gingrich formed the Conservative Opportunity Society (COS) after the 1982 elections. The COS' occasional political and legislative successes, along with aggressive partisan moves by Democrats and the way Gingrich "brought an energy level to the place" (in the words of a former leadership aide), contributed to a growing consensus that Gingrich was right. John Rhodes, who stepped down as minority leader in 1981 following a stealth campaign by Gingrich to undermine his position in the conference, left the House altogether two years later—in part, he said, because he did not agree with the increasing number of Republicans who wanted everyone to "rally in Statuary Hall . . . and the leader would exhort them, and we would all march out on the floor and do battle with those 'bad Democrats.'" By 1993, every Republican leader except Robert Michel "believed in partisan confrontation," and that same year the G.O.P. Conference enacted rules to weaken the ties between members and their committees, putting party unity ahead of an individualistic pursuit of policy. Eventually Democratic leaders would follow the same team-building path in the minority, though as one party leadership aide remarked, "it's in our nature to compromise"—suggesting that there can be differences between the parties, irrespective of minority status, over the ability to forge oppositional team spirit.[59]

Change, Innovation, and Entrepreneurship

Constancy lies at the heart of my claim that the minority party in the House, at least since the 1970s, has held the same four collective concerns and has tried to address them with electioneering, messaging, obstructing, and legislating. This is plausible insofar as the root sources of these concerns—the House's majoritarian nature, the presidency as a central institution in American government, and the basic desire of lawmakers to make policy—have remained unaltered. Yet one cannot ignore the tremendous changes to congressional politics that have occurred over the past forty years. These changes include party control of Congress becoming more competitive; each party growing more internally unified and polarized along ideological grounds, with partisan differences emerging on issues like abortion and gun control; the Republican Party shifting to an emphasis on supply-side economics and social conservatives emerging as a growing force in the party; the Democratic Party's base in the American South dissolving; representational styles becoming less constituent-focused and more policy-oriented; new campaign finance rules being created, altered, or struck down; the minority's power in the Senate expanding relative to the minority's power in the House; and the number of outside interest groups and think tanks growing enormously. These developments did not, I would argue, add or take away from the collective concerns that are important to the minority, though many of them contributed to the development of new tactics to address those "four P's." They also paralleled an expanding degree of "team play" within both parties and a heightened emphasis of the electoral goal over other objectives and concerns.[60]

The introduction and acceptance of new tactics by the minority party since 1971 are discussed in each of the empirical chapters that follow, but two important patterns are worth noting at the outset: the *replication* of one party's successful tactic by the other, and the *innovation* of a new tactic or technique altogether. The former depends on creative lawmakers from the minority who often possess a seemingly preternatural gift of foreseeing the emergence of a new technology or voter attitude—raising their proverbial fingers against a light breeze and knowing not only which direction it blows, but if and when it will become a gale-force political hurricane. The latter depends on party members willing to use a novel tactic (or an old one in a new way), see it through, and accept the risk of failure.[61]

Both parties are potentially rich sources of innovating, entrepreneurial members, especially as the competition for power in Congress has become fiercer since the 1990s. But all other things equal, entrepreneurs are more likely to arise from within the minority party. Adversity breeds innovation.[62] There is a steady, at times insistent—even desperate—pressure from rank-and-file members, strong party supporters, activists, interest groups, and others to make the minority a majority. Even though minority parties face a particular danger of losing enterprising members to more alluring opportunities, every election brings with it the hope of new, energetic, and inventive lawmakers joining them in Congress.[63] The risks are also lower for minority legislators who want to try a fresh tactic, since the party is already without power; and, as the earlier quote by an activist Republican underscored, failure is usually forgotten. Innovators and entrepreneurs also have greater freedom of movement in the minority, for the party's leaders have less power to enforce social conformity. But more importantly, those leaders often seek out and actively encourage innovation and entrepreneurship. After the 1992 elections, Dick Armey proclaimed that "what we want to do is discover who our geniuses are and back them." In his party's next turn in the minority, Republican Policy Committee chair Thaddeus McCotter (MI) talked about the importance of "entrepreneurial insurgency" and would tell fellow G.O.P.ers, "Now, be constructive, don't be destructive—but if you have an idea, run with it." Wise party leaders, though, do keep an eye on such members, lest they and their supporters surface as rivals to their authority.[64]

The history of congressional minorities features many innovators and entrepreneurs who contributed in important ways to the party's electioneering, messaging, obstructing, and legislating. Some are well-known, colorful figures. Newt Gingrich looms perhaps the largest, both for his substantive contributions to House politics and his outsize personality. In his very first term in the House, Gingrich was already garnering attention in the national media and from conservative insiders for his aggressive style and relentless focus on defeating Democrats. (Party leaders nervous about Gingrich's ambitions sometimes tried—often in vain—to rein him in.)[65] But there have been many other important innovators, entrepreneurs, and "work horse" legislators and staff from the minority party, both Republicans and Democrats, since 1971. Gingrich himself was part of a larger team of bright, creative legislators that included Vin Weber, Jack Kemp, Robert Walker, David Stockman, and Guy Vander Jagt. Many became part of the COS, and in general it is not unusual for entrepreneurs and innovators to join together to share ideas and inspire each other. Some become trusted sources of advice to those who follow them in the House, such as former representative Robert Bauman of Maryland (briefly hired by Trent Lott in 1981 as a consultant on House procedure) and Gingrich. The history of the minority party—indeed, of Congress—would have been radically different without them.[66]

Defining Party and Measuring a Collective Act

Before exploring the various tactics employed by the minority to achieve its collective concerns, it is probably wise to explain briefly the sort of political party I examine here and how I determine what makes for a "collective party" tactic. Because American political parties are relatively decentralized and permeable, it is not always clear how to define them. Some consider a political party to be the set of candidates and officeholders that affiliate with it; others, its state and national organizations; others, the activists and interest groups that support its candidates and activities; and others, some combination thereof.[67] In this book my focus is primarily the party organization internal to the House, including its members, leaders, and leadership organizations. While this is an admittedly limited view of what constitutes a political party, it has the advantage of homing in on the primary subject of this study: the behavior of members of the House of Representatives who share minority party status. This does not mean that voters, interest groups, and other outsiders are unimportant for minority party politics. There are times, in fact, when their relationship with the congressional minority leads to important changes in the minority's platform, tactics, or strategy. But for purposes of understanding how lawmakers and their leaders in Congress perceive their partisan status, their collective objectives, and the ways to achieve those objectives, it is most useful to zero in on the minority party within the House.

However, this leaves unanswered an important methodological question: can one accurately measure the behavior and motivation of a large collective entity like a political party, even when limiting oneself to the party in Congress? Is it possible, in other words, to distinguish between individual activity undertaken on behalf of the minority party as a whole and activity undertaken on behalf of individualistic goals?[68] One way to answer this question affirmatively would be to consider a congressional party's leaders or its formal organizations, like the campaign committee, as representing the party in intent and deed. This is common in studies of congressional parties,[69] and I employ this method for collective activities like campaigning and media events that, when conducted by rank-and-file members, are more likely to be oriented toward individual, rather than group, needs. For these tactics (of which there are four in this book, as noted in Table 1.3), I focus on instances in which the party's official representatives in the House participated in, initiated, or organized a particular activity.

Since this method cannot be used for tactics undertaken by rank-and-file members but not officially sanctioned by party leaders, I use a second approach to determine if something represents the party's collective concerns: whether a tactic is supported by a majority of the minority party. This is most appropriate when the party's full membership can easily register its endorsement for a tactic (like a strategic floor vote, walking off the floor, or a motion subject to a recorded vote).

Finally, there are activities for which the minority party's members do not readily express their support (like individual floor speeches) or which are undertaken, initiated, driven, and done by a minority of the minority party. For these tactics I use a third measurement: whether they can be reasonably ascertained as being done on behalf of the congressional party, as implied by evidence like public statements or media accounts. I use this approach cautiously, however, since the motivation of an individual lawmaker's activity is often unclear or open to interpretation.

two
ELECTIONEERING

Holmes had encountered the challenger's paradox;
he couldn't win without spending lots of money, but people
wouldn't donate unless they thought he was going to win.
—Brooks Jackson, *Honest Graft*

Congressional races are won by inches.
—former DCCC aide

Above all else, the minority party in the House no longer wants to be a minority. That means it must win elections. And the most direct way to win elections is by electioneering: recruiting strong challengers, raising and spending money on campaigns, and developing election-year platforms. These three activities are the subject of this chapter.

Since the reason for electioneering is obvious, it is unnecessary to explain why the minority does it. Instead, I describe the development and use of these three basic campaign tactics since 1971, with particular focus on the role of party leaders, entrepreneurial members, and party campaign committees. The committees are an especially important resource for funding and information—especially for challengers, who are the key to a minority party winning power—and are obvious vehicles by which the party tries to help itself collectively. I also discuss whether these tactics are successful in achieving both their immediate goals (getting strong candidates to run, raising more money, improving the party "brand") and their ultimate objective of influencing election outcomes.[1]

In many ways, there is little difference between the electioneering activities of the majority and minority parties. Both recruit and train the best candidates they can, raise and spend lots of money, and employ advertising and other classic campaign techniques. The tactics of both parties are also tinged with uncertainty, even when campaign strategy is informed by experience or statistical analysis. What will the most salient issues be on Election Day? What kinds of candidates will attract swing voters? What sort of campaign ad will move the public? The answers to these questions are often unknown and can be given with little more than an educated guess.

Differences that do exist between the parties often have less to do with majority status than with the constituencies of the parties, which can determine where money, candidates, and votes come from. However, the electioneering politics of the minority do vary from that of the majority, whether Republican or Democrat, in four important ways. First, though both parties worry about protecting their incumbents while beating the other party's, the minority understandably focuses much more on the latter. Second, the minority operates with a greater scarcity of campaign resources. The "challenger's paradox" described by Brooks Jackson applies to the minority as a whole: to marshal enough outside support to compete, it must first overcome donors' skepticism that it can reverse its losing record.[2]

Third, the minority party's inherent disadvantages in electioneering, coupled with the highly competitive nature of campaigns in which victory is obtained "by inches," press the minority's members to innovate and replicate. The electoral environment has shifted tremendously since 1971 in part because of innovations by minority party members: Guy Vander Jagt's idea to have more businesses form fund-raising organizations, for example, or the Democrats' pioneering Red to Blue program in the early 2000s. The minority also has no qualms about copying the other party's winning recipes for victory. For instance, Democrats created an incumbent protection program called Frontline Democrats that was modeled after the G.O.P.'s Retain Our Majority Program, while the staff of the National Republican Campaign Committee intently read *The Thumpin'*, a book chronicling the successful electioneering tactics of campaign committee chair Rahm Emanuel (D-IL), to figure out how to win back control of the House in 2010. It should be noted, however, that the majority innovates and replicates campaign tactics too, especially when it greatly fears losing, as it has since the early 1980s.[3]

Fourth, the minority's tendency toward disunity and low morale puts it at an electoral disadvantage.[4] Hard work by party leaders and election committees is tremendously important, of course, but that can only go so far. Rank-and-file members who are dispirited, or who do not agree on the best way to win elections, are less likely to support the election strategies of their leaders or contribute desperately needed time and money to the cause. Consequently, minority leaders and campaign committee chairs often focus on improving party morale as a necessary precondition to getting their colleagues' vital electoral help.

The Development of Congressional Campaign Committee Activity since 1971

The ways that both parties campaign for Congress have changed enormously over the past four decades. In 1971, the percent of voters who were loyal partisans was declining, the partisanship of congressional districts was dropping, political action committees did not exist, and mass advertising for campaigns did not extend past television, radio, and print. By the end of 2010, none of these things were true. Looking just at how the electioneering activity of party-wide campaign organizations has changed gives a flavor of these massive developments and their impact on what the House minority, as well as the majority, does to win elections.[5]

There are two campaign committees in the House, one per party: the Democratic Congressional Campaign Committee (DCCC) and the National Republican Campaign Committee (NRCC). In 1971 the two committees were very different in the services they provided their respective parties. Under the leadership of Mike Kirwan (OH), who was "never an activist chairman," the DCCC provided "relatively limited" resources and focused mostly on protecting incumbents. Republicans, by contrast, were eager to end what at that point had been fifteen years of suffering as a minority party; their campaign committee offered a plethora of services—issue-specific research, candidate recruitment and training, media advice, and communication equipment—and it spent money to help both its vulnerable incumbents and viable G.O.P. challengers.[6]

New laws and court decisions in the 1970s altered the rules of the campaign game. Congressional campaign committees were allowed to raise and contribute far more money to candidates than the candidates could themselves. At the same time, the growth of television advertising and survey research pushed up the cost of the average campaign drastically. Together, these changes meant a much greater role for campaign committees as sources of money and other election resources.[7]

The major campaign innovator of the time was Guy Vander Jagt (MI), Republican chair of the NRCC from 1974 until 1992. In the 1970s, Vander Jagt established an independent staff for the committee, pushed corporations to create political action committees (PACs) and contribute to the party, created a massive list of small donors, and interpreted federal law in a way that allowed more spending on "coordinated expenses," or expenses related to individual campaigns. The NRCC became flush with cash, and with "so much money its biggest problem was figuring out how to spend it." It not only outraised the DCCC but was far more active in helping challengers. In the 1980 elections it even paid for a national television ad criticizing House Democrats, a rare occurrence at the time.[8]

Those elections delivered to Democrats their worst national defeat since 1952: the party lost the Senate and the White House, and many senior congressional incumbents were booted from office. It "created an atmosphere of fear that would drive Democrats for the next six years," wrote Jackson in his book *Honest Graft*, and the DCCC played catch-up with the NRCC under the energetic leadership of Tony Coelho (CA), who chaired the committee from 1981 through 1986. Coelho used both requests and veiled threats to get more donations from the now-substantial number of business

PACs in Washington. He mimicked the Republican National Committee, which gave special entrée to the Reagan White House for high-paying donors by creating a "Speaker's Club" that promised access, inside information, and favors for contributors. Coelho even built a television studio, just as the NRCC had done. "Whatever the Republicans had," Jackson writes, "Coelho wanted." He pioneered, too: the DCCC became the first to extensively collect and spend "soft money," unregulated funds given directly to the parties, to supplement the activities of individual campaigns. By the end of his tenure Coelho had "creat[ed] a permanent institution where before there had been little more than an annual fund-raising dinner."[9]

Two other significant developments in campaign committee activity followed this innovation-replication paradigm. First, to ensure the NRCC's money was prioritized for challengers, Vander Jagt set up a system to determine which incumbents would receive funding. Coelho did the same, albeit more informally. By 1990, the NRCC had stopped giving money automatically to incumbents and began spending funds more efficiently, to candidates in the most competitive races. Second, in 1991–92 the DCCC (led by Vic Fazio of California) began pressing for contributions from incumbents. When Bill Paxon (R-NY) became NRCC chair in 1992, among the many important changes he made to the committee's operations was the adoption of this tactic, and the proportion of House Republicans giving to the committee skyrocketed from almost zero to half. The amount of cash flowing to the campaign committees from incumbents grew further when then minority whip Newt Gingrich warned that these contributions would be part of leaders' determination of who received committee leadership positions. After Democrats were relegated to the minority in 1994, they followed suit.[10]

In the years that followed, operations by each campaign committee were added, expanded, and institutionalized, often at the instigation of the minority and then copied by the other party. After 2002, for instance, the minority DCCC began a mentoring program that paired incumbents with promising challengers, and the minority NRCC adopted the idea for the 2010 elections. By 2010 both the

NRCC and DCCC had come a long way from small outfits providing limited election resources mostly to incumbents; they were now "major support centers for House and Senate candidates."[11]

Before turning to the mechanics and immediate effects of specific electioneering tactics by these "major support centers" (and, in some cases, by other leaders and entrepreneurs in each party), it is worth briefly reviewing how the committees interact with party members and, in particular, try to encourage their cooperation and participation in collective campaign activities.

The Relationship between Party Members and Campaign Committees

The DCCC and NRCC are, first and foremost, creatures of their parties in the House. Both are headed by a member of Congress, with a "board of directors" consisting of other incumbents responsible for various committee operations. By delegating campaign decision-making to the committees, rank-and-file members can focus on other tasks and "keep the high ground" while the committee engages in aggressive partisan tactics. But that also means they subject themselves to the committee's decisions, and they don't always agree with those decisions. "You can't just tell an incumbent what to do," warned one former NRCC staffer, and unhappy lawmakers tend to have an "urge to purge" the committee of its staff and leadership. Nonetheless, campaign committee chairs have been known to pester incumbents who run lackluster campaigns, urge them to adopt better election tactics, or plead with them to cooperate less with members of the other party. After the 1994 elections, for example, the DCCC under Martin Frost (D-TX) worked on "getting members to think about turnout, about how you win a close race, and not just doing television." And challengers make things hard for themselves if they fail to follow the committee's instructions. In an extreme case from 1986, DCCC chair Tony Coelho threatened to withdraw all support from the congressional campaign of Kathleen Kennedy Townsend, daughter of former senator Robert Kennedy, if she did not "do what needed to be done to win," as one insider put it. "Do you know who I am?" she retorted, and Coelho followed through on his threat.[12]

As stakeholders in the campaign committees, incumbents may be largely spared that kind of hassling, but they nonetheless face near-constant pressure to contribute money to the committees. Their dues are substantial: in 2010, Democrats levied $125,000 from junior members and half a million dollars from the chairs of major legislative committees, and Republicans also asked for sizeable contributions on a sliding scale. The minority party and its leaders are arguably more assertive in this shakedown, both because the party needs money more badly and because minority party members have more time to dedicate to fund-raising. Ambitious members and those with "a sense of enlightened self-interest" may readily give, and team play is an important basis for encouraging such donations. In the words of one former NRCC aide, the contributions are like a "United Way campaign" where contributors are signaling, "yes, I'm part of this team." The rest of the party may need some prodding, however. That prodding has come in all shapes and sizes: showing members a film of an inspiring performance by an Olympic athlete, publicly outing those who don't give, conducting a "brutal exercise in peer pressure" on colleagues, threatening to deny desired committee slots to chary party members, barring non-givers from using campaign committee telephones to raise money, or issuing "a scolding letter" to recalcitrant lawmakers. Retiring legislators with big cash treasuries are targets, too. One aide to a departing Democrat who had a great deal of campaign money left over offered this story: "I remember, after my boss had announced he would retire, a short time later he gets a call from Pelosi . . . [Apparently] she asked him for $100,000 for the DCCC, pointing out that he had significantly more than that in his remaining campaign balance. My boss got furious. He said something like, 'Why don't you ask for the whole fucking thing?' 'No,' she said without missing a beat, 'just $100,000.'"[13]

It can take more than one election cycle for a minority's campaign tactics and strategy to bear fruit, to build the infrastructure and mechanics needed to win, and to convince local party officials that the national committee will support their homegrown challengers. In 1985, Republican leaders admitted that they did not expect to win a majority of House seats for at least another seven years and hoped only to stave off "massive losses" in 1986. Outgoing NRCC co-chair Ed Rollins warned in early 1991 that it would require "a six- or eight-year plan" for Republicans to win the House, requiring "a war of attrition" against a limited number of incumbent Democrats. In 2004, incoming DCCC chair Rahm Emanuel warned Minority Leader Nancy Pelosi to stop promising a takeover of the House in 2006: "We have to start realizing this is a two-cycle process," he told her. "You learn by doing," attested one former Democrat involved with the DCCC under Martin Frost, and "a lot of these things [that worked] we did in" Frost's second term as chair. Alas, lawmakers and donors are skeptical and think in the short term. According to one former DCCC staffer, "you always have to make the case that we will win the majority in the next election."[14]

Emanuel's warning to Pelosi is but one example of how much of a campaign committee's work, especially for the minority party, involves managing expectations. It also entails convincing other lawmakers that the committee's electoral strategies will pay off in the long run. Said one erstwhile DCCC aide, lawmakers are "not going to make an investment in an organization they don't believe in." A former (then minority) Democratic chief of staff recalled the DCCC periodically inviting chiefs of staff for presentations on the committee's progress, presentations that often ended with a plea for "anything you and your boss can do to help out." Though never made explicit, it was understood that the DCCC hoped staff might take leaves of absence to help with campaigning, or that even the lawmakers themselves might donate their time or money.[15]

Minority party leaders are also well aware that despondent legislators are unlikely to contribute resources to the campaign committee. Frost, who was the first DCCC chair after the Democrats' devastating losses in 1994, knew that "part of [his] job in the first eight or nine months was to be the cheerleader, because people were pretty depressed." Ten years later, DCCC chair Emanuel's responsibilities "involved not just enabling the Democrats to win but making them believe they could." As evidenced by the post-1980 House Democrats, the majority party can get dispirited, too. Following the G.O.P.'s unexpected seat losses in 1998, NRCC chair Tom Davis hosted a football-themed fund-raiser to inspire his colleagues and, using a "scared straight" approach, showed Republicans a movie depicting the Democrats as taking over the House.[16]

Finally, it should be noted that the committees' Congress-oriented nature can create tensions not only with incumbent members but with same-party presidential campaigns and the national party organization, which are often reluctant to share money with the committees and may not agree with their electoral strategy. In 1990 NRCC co-chair Ed Rollins advised Republican House candidates to openly run against George H. W. Bush after the president signed off on a budget that raised taxes. Rollins' move led Bush to cut off all help to the NRCC while Rollins remained co-chair, and he left the committee shortly after the elections that year. In the 2005–6 cycle, Emanuel engaged in a series of bitter fights with DNC chair Howard Dean over funding and whether to spend money only on promising races (Emanuel's view) or across the country (Dean's "fifty-state" strategy).[17]

Let us now look at three important electioneering tactics that both House parties, but especially the minority, undertake, and whether they make a difference in election results: recruitment, raising and spending money, and setting a campaign agenda.

Candidate Recruitment

The odds of a political party winning a seat without a candidate are, of course, zero. The odds improve if the party can recruit a candidate or, even better, a strong and viable one. Accordingly, both parties in the House actively seek out as many people they can to win newly vacant seats or seats held by the other party. Recruitment, however, "is always more important when you're in the minority," as one former Democratic Party leader remarked, because the minority can never win control of the chamber with just the reelection of its incumbents. And recruiting is one of "the two main things that a campaign committee can do."[18]

Unsurprisingly, then, innovations in candidate recruitment usually come from the minority party. The NRCC instituted a formal recruitment program in the late 1960s, and though the leaders of both party committees did draft candidates, the G.O.P.'s efforts were more extensive and institutionalized. Newt Gingrich demonstrated how recruitment could be a sphere for ambitious party members like himself to make their mark: GOPAC, his own fund-raising and recruitment organization, provided material to potential candidates—first independently, then in cooperation with the NRCC—and convinced a number of them to run. For some it even "transform[ed] their thinking about what it meant to be a Republican." By contrast, recalled one former Democratic Party leader, his party's candidate selection was "pretty much left to its own devices . . . Our ability to actually get someone to run, or keep someone from running, was usually laissez-faire." That all changed when the party became the minority in 1995, and the new committee chair, Martin Frost, concentrated intently on recruitment, as did his successors. Meanwhile, the NRCC sharpened its focus on incumbent retention, and when Republicans were sent into the minority in 2006, according to one campaign aide, "someone had to fill the vacuum" of challenger recruitment and training. Kevin McCarthy filled that vacuum with his Young Guns recruitment program, which was soon folded into the NRCC.[19]

Building a bullpen of worthy candidates is a multistep process. It begins not long (often within days) after an election, when the party committees start the "Monday morning quarterback period," looking at the previous results and the returns on spending in individual districts and gauging what they might mean for the election two years hence. One former NRCC aide described what the committee did shortly after the 2008 elections: "You look at all these maps of Democrats whose districts [Senator John] McCain won, and Democrats that won with 55% of the vote or less, and that becomes your target list."[20] The relatively low reelection rates of freshmen make them good targets, too. Even less-vulnerable majority party incumbents are still important to challenge, because an unforeseen scandal or national "wave" might suddenly put seemingly hopeless races in play.[21] Just over a month before the 2006 elections, for instance, Florida G.O.P. congressman Mark Foley resigned amid sudden explosive allegations of inappropriate sexual banter with a male congressional page. His Democratic opponent, who had been given little chance of success up till then, won the Republican-leaning seat.[22]

After the most promising districts are identified, the NRCC aide continued, "we'd start having members reach out to folks [and] call potential candidates to gauge interest." Lawmakers tasked with recruitment scour the countryside, visiting districts personally to "sound them out." What kinds of people in particular are they looking for? People with money, or the ability to raise it; prior electoral experience, especially in state legislatures; youth and energy; a reputation for electoral skill; and district "fit," meaning candidates "sharing the views, values and priorities" of the district's constituents.[23] Sometimes a certain background, or someone who "matches the mood" of voters, is predicted to play well in the next election. In 2005–6 Democrats looked for Iraq War veterans to bolster the party's national security bona fides; in 2010 Republicans wanted both "community leaders," betting they could plausibly ride the anti-incumbency wave of that year, and practicing doctors, assuming they would have more authority to speak out against President Obama's health care law. For the minority especially, these kinds of traits are far more important than ideological purity. Caring how a potential recruit might vote in the House is to put the proverbial cart before the horse: one must win a majority before one can worry about potential problems in governing. In fact, finding the right candidate can be so important, particularly to the minority, that a campaign committee will occasionally take sides in contested party primaries despite the very real risk of backing the wrong candidate. But even after taking all of these factors into account, there is always some uncertainty about who will get elected to Congress, and identifying the best candidates is "more art than science," as a former DCCC staffer put it.[24]

Party emissaries try all sorts of methods to convince people to run. But the House minority party has a real drawback in the recruitment game: it must persuade potential candidates with less to offer them and no guarantee that, even if they win, they will be joining a party with majority status. In 1999, Minority Leader Richard Gephardt promised to put former representative Jane Harman on powerful committees and restore her committee seniority if she ran again for Congress. Though Harman won, she had to tolerate serving another six years in the minority, and her situation was unusual: the incentives Gephardt offered her were unique to her previous service in the House. Not many will give up their careers and spend months campaigning for limited formal legislative power; and beating an incumbent, as would-be challengers know and research has shown, is a tough prospect. Accordingly, any sort of positive or encouraging news that hints the minority will retake control of the House—say, the unexpected victory of the party's candidate in a special election—becomes the pretext for a round of recruitment calls.[25] Help from other players with influence, particularly same-party presidents, is welcome as well.[26]

Campaign committees must also be prepared for an ever-changing electoral playing field. Seats "may not be in play now, but we've got to fill out the ticket," observed one former DCCC aide. Retirements within the other party create fresh opportunities, especially if the national mood or the district's party registration leans toward the minority. "Vulnerables"—incumbents that might be weak for other reasons, like personal scandal—are also identified over the course of time. In 2009, for example, Kevin McCarthy looked closely at "voting patterns [of incumbents] and how Democrats spent their travel allowances to spot incumbents who lost touch with voters."[27]

Though the minority party's primary focus is on challengers, if the political environment favors the other party, or too many of its incumbents choose to leave the House, the minority's goal of winning power becomes all the more challenging. And while the majority party also faces retirements among its ranks, the frustrations of minority life mean incumbent retirements "are always a risk when you're in the minority," remarked a onetime DCCC staffer. Gephardt aide Steve Elmendorf later recalled that after 1994 "our first goal was: how do we keep our members from leaving?" The other side of the recruitment coin for minority party leaders, then, is to "re-recruit" incumbents to run again (and, occasionally, to not switch to the other party). Again, leaders will turn to whatever goodies they can offer as incentives to keep incumbents. "What if we get your wife Kennedy Center tickets just so you see this [job] isn't all just castor oil?" as one former campaign aide put it. At one point, Gephardt gave a prime committee spot to a moderate Democrat, Bud Cramer of Alabama, who was being courted heavily by Republicans to switch parties.[28]

Anecdotal evidence implies that the parties and their campaign committees, particularly those with savvy and aggressive leaders, make the difference in who decides to run. John Boehner, eventual Speaker of the House, credited audio tapes from Gingrich's GOPAC with inspiring his first try for a House seat. Victorious Democratic candidates Mike Thompson (CA), Tammy Baldwin (WI), and Ronnie Shows (MS) were all carefully chosen by the DCCC under the leadership of Martin Frost, who was by one account "very hard-nosed about" getting only the best candidates. Frost even resisted a personal plea from Vice President Al Gore to back an alternative to Thompson, a young liberal who Frost believed was less likely to beat the incumbent Republican. In the 2005–6 cycle, Emanuel convinced former NFL quarterback Heath Shuler that a congressional campaign would not hamper his duties as a father of two young children. Emanuel asked other lawmakers, their spouses, and children to lobby the potential candidate, and for two solid weeks Emanuel himself called Shuler every time the DCCC chair was fulfilling a parental responsibility, like taking his own kids to or from school. In 2009, McCarthy successfully persuaded several ultimately victorious candidates in Alabama, Maryland, Tennessee, and Wisconsin to run for Congress.[29]

A more systematic determination of recruitment success is extremely tough to make. Recruitment efforts by both parties are confidential; the decision calculus of candidates is complex and difficult to discern; and there is always the possibility that a recruited candidate might have decided to run anyway. Some data do suggest that parties make the difference in who runs for Congress, but it is inferential at best. One can look, for instance, at the number of seats for which the minority failed to get anyone to run at all. Except in years when the minority won control of the House (1994, 2006, and 2010) plus the year 2000, the minority has had more trouble than the majority finding people to challenge incumbents from the other party, as can be seen in Figure 2.1. (The number of unchallenged minority party members is illustrated by the "M" marker, which is lower than the point for the majority party in all but those four years.) Or one can look at the number of quality candidates deciding to throw their hats in the ring against incumbents. Using one common metric of quality, previous electoral experience, political scientist Brendan Nyhan found a difference between the parties in the percent of competitive races fielding high-quality candidates, albeit more between Republicans and Democrats (with more Republicans than Democrats usually being of higher quality) than between the minority and majority.[30]

These data, however, are no more than suggestive that parties make the difference in who runs for office. A slew of factors beyond the control of the campaign committees, like the number of lopsided districts and the strength of state parties, affect whether seats go unchallenged. Most studies have found that factors outside the parties' hands affect the potential or actual decision to enter a race for Congress, including family and professional background, one's gender and ethnicity, a "general sense of efficacy as a candidate," and whether the district will be redrawn soon. "Macro" conditions that shape voter choice, like the economy and the popularity of the incumbent president, also matter. As NRCC chair in 1974, for instance, Bob Michel struggled to get Republicans to run in the wake of Nixon's scandal-plagued presidency. Strong candidates may decide to run because they recognize that an electoral wave is approaching, not

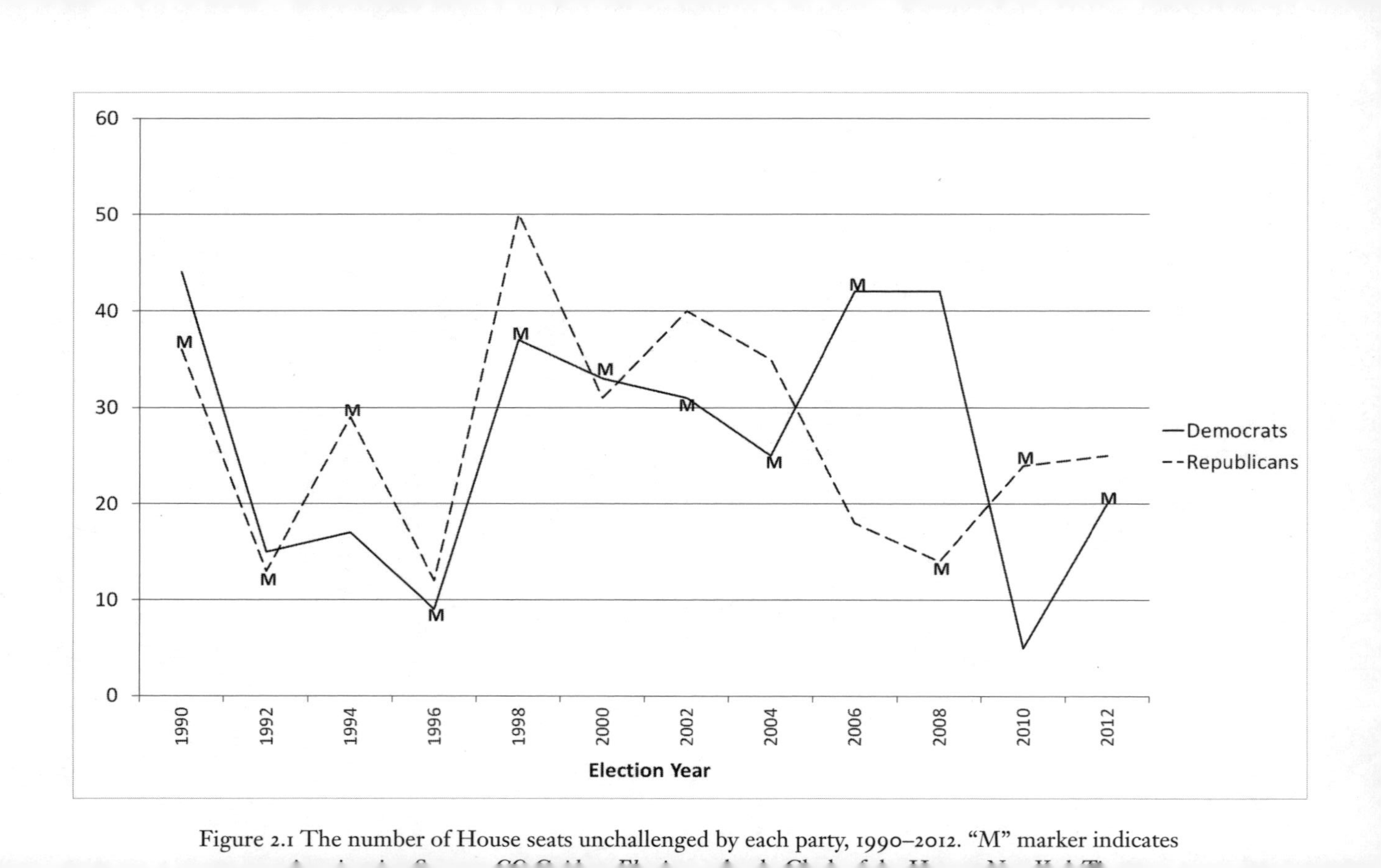

Figure 2.1 The number of House seats unchallenged by each party, 1990–2012. "M" marker indicates

because the party tells them so. For example, in 2008 House Republican leaders could not convince good candidates to try for office—even against vulnerable Democratic freshmen—in part because of an economic downturn and the public's dissatisfaction with the war in Iraq. By the end of 2009, however, Republicans were eagerly declaring themselves as candidates: some were driven by their own fierce opposition to the policies of congressional Democrats and President Obama, while others were encouraged by widespread "frustration about the economy, the deficit, and spending" among voters. The surprise victory of Republican Scott Brown in the race for a Massachusetts Senate seat encouraged still more Republicans to make a go at defeating incumbent Democrats.[31]

Nonetheless, the anecdotal data is compelling. Some research has also uncovered a positive relationship between a party reaching out to potential candidates and their serious consideration of running for the House, though not necessarily the actual decision to throw one's hat in the ring. It is probably safe to say that party recruitment does far less than the parties believe it does in getting the very best to run for office, but that it could make a difference in at least a handful of contests for Congress.[32]

Whether recruitment efforts alone are enough to propel the minority to the majority is another matter. The minority party does try to get the best people it can to run for office, and studies have revealed that more experienced candidates, unsurprisingly, do better in elections.[33] The party that had more unchallenged seats won a majority of House races in every election but one (the elections of 2000) and won a majority in seven of the ten elections from 1992 to 2010 in which it had more quality challengers in competitive seats (as measured by Nyhan). But the correlation between the number of (strong) candidates running for the House and the results of only a handful of elections tells us little. Weak candidates can get elected in big "wave" elections, strong ones can flounder against massive tides, and some incumbents are so vulnerable that even third-tier opponents might have defeated them. Prior experience is a liability, not an asset, if voters are in a strong anti-incumbency mood.[34] The number of good candidates running for office may be the result of a broad recognition that the election will go well for one party, rather than the candidates themselves influencing election results.[35] In short, it may be too difficult to say for sure whether the minority party's recruitment efforts are the sufficient cause of electoral outcomes.

Raising and Spending Money

In addition to getting the right candidate, it costs money—a lot of money—to wage a competitive congressional campaign. Money pays for staff, advertising, offices, and the many other necessities of a successful run for Congress. If "resources rule" an election campaign, money is among the most important of those resources. And if money is the mother's milk of politics, as former California State Speaker Jesse Unruh famously put it, then since at least the mid-1990s the minority party has been the hungry runt of the litter.[36]

Unsurprisingly, both parties make every effort to raise money for ever-more expensive elections. Party leaders and ambitious lawmakers are the most active players of the fund-raising game, as exemplified by the rise of "leadership PACs," fund-raising entities run by individual lawmakers to donate dollars to their peers. Also active are the party campaign committees. The exploitation of legal loopholes to raise more and more "soft money" in the 1980s and '90s, and the NRCC and DCCC's creation of "independent expenditure groups" in the 1990s to spend money without coordinating with campaigns, are but two examples of the creative ways the congressional campaign committees have tried to empty and replenish their coffers. The passage of the Bipartisan Campaign Reform Act (BCRA) in 2002, which prohibited "soft money" donations and limited the amounts that could be spent by the party committees, did little to stop the process. Instead, both committees pressed for more "hard money" donations, especially from members of Congress, and dramatically increased their direct contributions to campaigns.[37]

Figure 2.2 shows the total amount raised by the DCCC and NRCC since 1976 and how it compares to the average cost to win a House

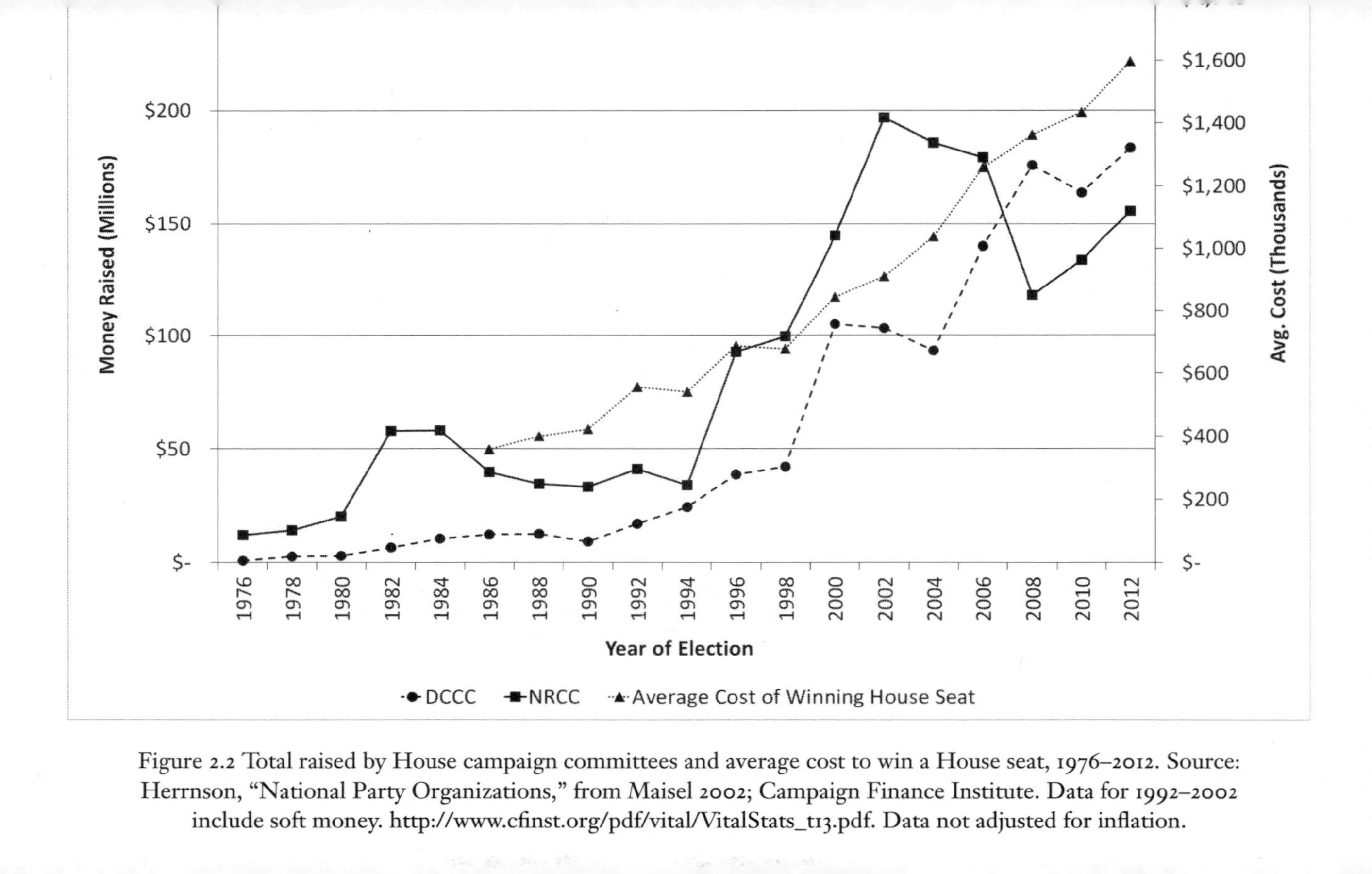

Figure 2.2 Total raised by House campaign committees and average cost to win a House seat, 1976–2012. Source: Herrnson, "National Party Organizations," from Maisel 2002; Campaign Finance Institute. Data for 1992–2002 include soft money. http://www.cfinst.org/pdf/vital/VitalStats_t13.pdf. Data not adjusted for inflation.

seat.[38] The NRCC long held a financial advantage over the DCCC, thanks in part to its well-developed database of individual contributors, but it was unable to convert that advantage into winning control of the House until 1994. After that year, the differences between the parties became more clearly a difference between majority and minority status. The Republicans, the new majority party, were raising and spending far more than the Democrats, though not for lack of trying by the latter. Democrats relied on "soft money" to compensate until it was outlawed by BCRA, widening the gap between the majority and minority even further. When control of Congress flipped in 2006, so too did the fund-raising edge—though interestingly, that edge remained in 2012 despite the Democrats' minority status.[39]

Both campaign committees look for money wherever they can find it. E-mails and phone calls are made routinely to big-name donors and ordinary voters, and building a database of reliable givers allows the party to receive steady funds over many cycles. The minority in particular will exploit any misstep by the majority party to solicit additional funds. Within three hours of Republican Majority Leader Tom DeLay's indictment in September 2005, for instance, the DCCC sent out an e-mail plea for cash, and did so again after Republican lobbyist Jack Abramoff pled guilty to federal crimes. Likewise, the G.O.P. solicited contributions following Scott Brown's unexpected Senate win in January 2010. Party leaders and chairs of both committees also push incessantly for money from PACs. Besides Vander Jagt and Coelho, others who have done so include Gingrich, who "browbeat" PACs to donate money to candidates in 1994; Tom DeLay, whose K-Street project to aggressively hit up PACs for dough earned him the media moniker "The Hammer;" and Greg Walden (R-OR), who in 2010 scolded PACs that donated insufficient amounts to his party.[40] The national party organizations (the Democratic National Committee [DNC] and the Republican National Committee [RNC]) can be a source of cash as well, though they tend to focus on presidential races, and when they do give money "it comes with lots of strings" attached. "The House election committees always end up being the red-headed stepchild in presidential election years," noted one former NRCC staffer. Same-party presidents, however, may be more willing to help raise money, particularly when they are not running for reelection. In 1999, facing the end of his final term in office, Bill Clinton helped convince California state lawmaker Mike Honda to challenge a Republican incumbent by offering to participate in a fund-raiser for him, and Barack Obama—who did relatively little to help House Democrats while running for reelection in 2012—promised to recruit candidates and raise campaign funds for the 2014 cycle. The committees also turn to other members of Congress for money, resulting in ever-rising dues that members are required to pay to their respective campaign committees. The urgent need for funds by the minority party has led it to deliberately select leaders of its campaign committee primarily for their fund-raising acumen. In the 2000s, Democrats picked Robert Matsui (CA) and, later, Patrick Kennedy (RI) in no small part because they were proven money-getters.[41]

The party committees spend virtually all of what they raise (and often more), and that spending has become an increasingly large proportion of the funds that flow into congressional elections. Its percentage of all money spent in congressional campaigns (House and Senate combined) grew from less than 10% in 1990 to nearly 30% by 2000, and in competitive races in 2006 the committees spent an additional 44% to 47% over and above what the candidates themselves spent.[42]

The parties can spend their money in several ways. They can give directly to candidates, but those amounts are sharply limited by federal law. A second and more attractive method is to spend their money on behalf of a candidate (the so-called coordinated expenditure) on such things as commercials, surveys, or solicitations, because the expenditure has higher legal limits and is more closely controlled by the parties. Or they can make independent expenditures (spending done without any coordination or advance warning to campaigns or the party committees), usually on negative advertising.[43]

There are no bottomless reservoirs of cash, however, so whom to spend money on and how to spend it are critical, and often tricky, strategic decisions. Competitive races and endangered incumbents are popular targets, for obvious reasons, and they become part of each party's target or "watch" list of races that usually number from twenty to one hundred or more.[44] However, "the minority party usually takes a more aggressive posture than does the majority party" in how it spends its money, focusing on seizing seats from the other side rather than on incumbent retention. Investing early in certain races might weaken the other party's candidates and force them to respond in kind, or help advertise those races to outside contributors. The minority, with fewer resources, sometimes succumbs to trying to "fake out" the opposition: one former NRCC staffer recalled that occasionally the minority Democrats would "go and 'lay in'—that is, reserve—all this [ad] time" to make a race appear important and as "a way of buying earned media" coverage if reporters fell for the gambit. One thing parties tend not to do is give based on the degree of a candidate's ideological loyalty; need matters more. Because the electoral terrain can change, sometimes quite quickly, committees must be prepared to shift their money across different campaigns over the course of an election cycle, and suddenly vulnerable incumbents and newly promising challengers can pull funds away from other races. The committees also try to keep cash on hand in the final weeks of campaign season should a new opportunity or unforeseen danger present itself.[45]

Neither party is above trying to make incumbents from the other party more vulnerable, eager to retire, or even consider switching parties. "Sometimes you want to hit 'em and see if they still remember how to run a race," explained a onetime NRCC staffer. "Can they still take a punch?" "You start firing press releases every single day" against vulnerable legislators, "just beating the snot out of them," said another staffer who once worked for the DCCC. Republicans, for example, targeted senior Democrat David Obey in the 2009–10 cycle, running negative ads in his district to put him on the defensive. Obey ultimately retired. Recognizing this potential threat, each party also spends money early on behalf of its weak incumbents "to make them look as invulnerable as possible . . . so that it's more difficult to recruit against them."[46]

In recent years the minority has signaled out certain candidates running for seats held by the other party for financial (and other) assistance. In 2004 the DCCC created the Red to Blue program to draw the attention of donors distracted by the presidential election and Senate campaigns, and in 2007 Congressman McCarthy followed suit with the Young Guns program. Both were designed to identify particular candidates worthy of contributions, give those candidates priority in receiving assistance from the campaign committee, and encourage other candidates to improve their campaigns in hopes of being added later. They also serve as a useful test of how effectively the minority party can raise money for the races it cares most about.[47]

Evidence suggests these programs have been quite effective. Figures 2.3, 2.4, and 2.5 show the median amount of money raised before and after certain candidates were added to the lists: Democrats to the two 2004 Red to Blue groups (combined), Democrats first added to the Red to Blue list in 2006, and the second round of Republicans added to Young Guns in 2010. To be sure, most of these candidates were already proven money raisers, and they might have continued to do well without the campaign committees' help. But compared with the median fund-raising of "matched pairs" (same-party candidates not selected to those groups but from similar districts who demonstrated some degree of fund-raising prowess), one sees that candidates in these programs were able to maintain a healthy advantage in fund-raising over those who were not. This strongly implies that these programs—and, by extension, campaign committee fund-raising efforts in general—work well.[48]

The favored candidates often win, too. In 2004 all but five of the Democrats' twenty-three Red to Blue candidates were victorious in their elections, constituting nearly a third of the party's new members elected that year; four of those five snatched seats from Republican incumbents. The 2006 Red to Blue Democrats also did well:

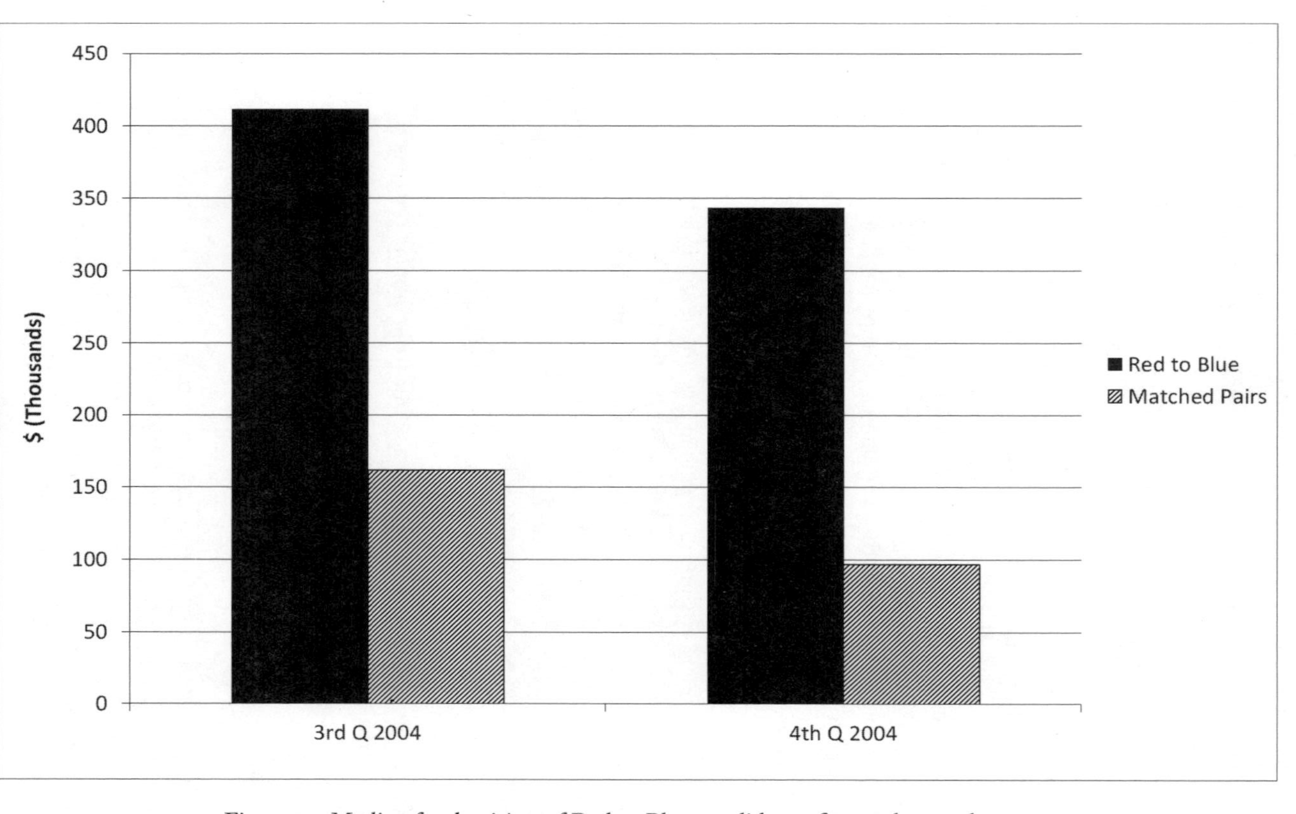

Figure 2.3 Median fund-raising of Red to Blue candidates, first and second groups

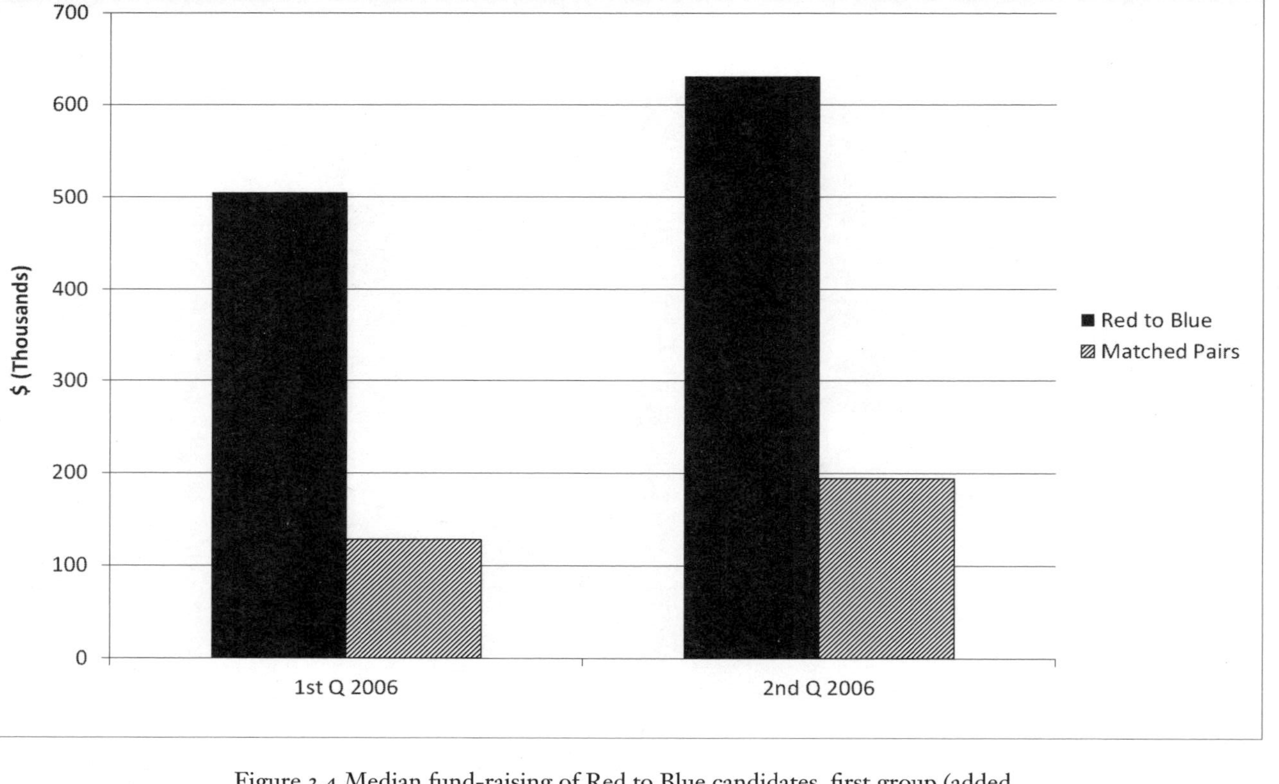

Figure 2.4 Median fund-raising of Red to Blue candidates, first group (added April 2006). Source: Federal Election Commission.

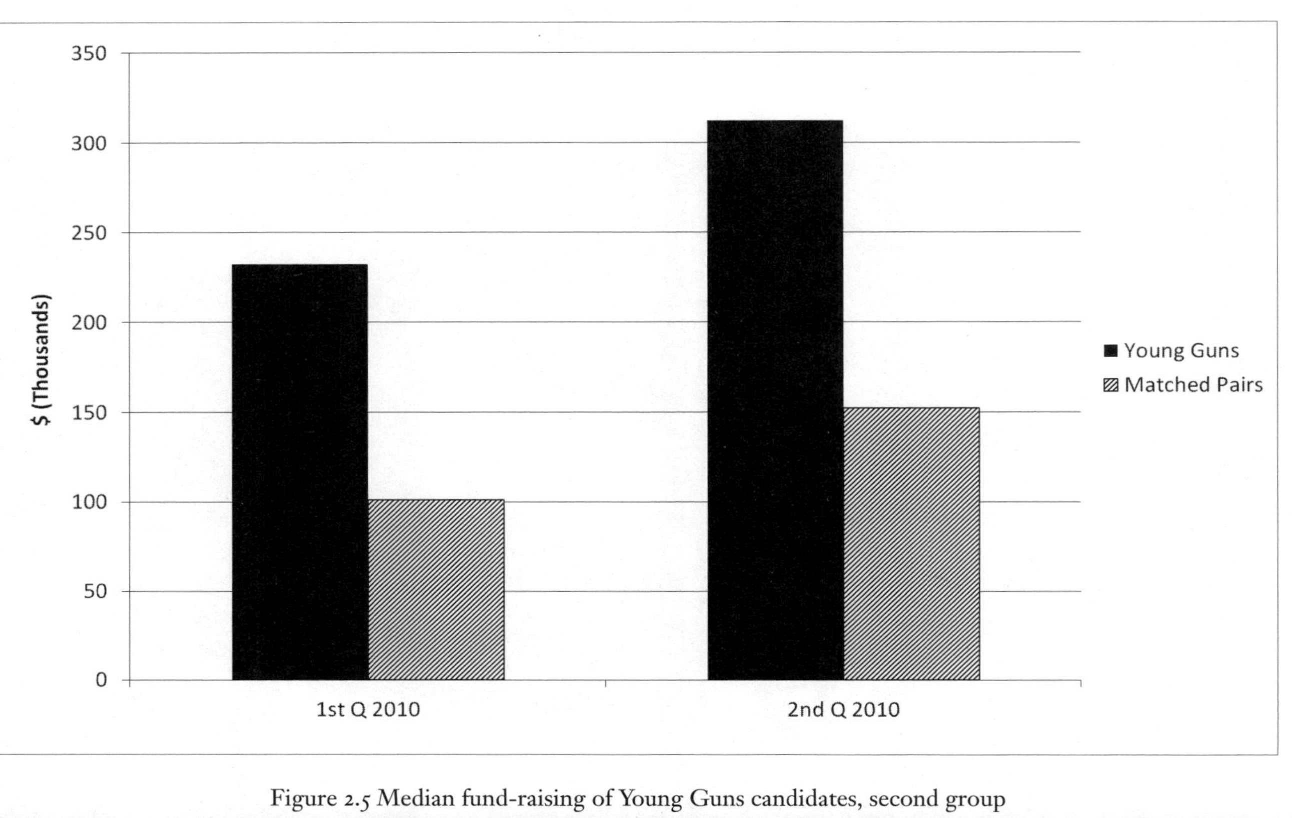

Figure 2.5 Median fund-raising of Young Guns candidates, second group

eighteen of the forty-four running in Republican-held seats won, as did another five who ran for vacated Democratic seats. One must be cautious, however, in directly connecting a sizable campaign war chest with electoral victory. We cannot know if those winning Red to Blue candidates would have been victorious without joining the program.[49] Though it is a safe bet that a reasonable minimum must be spent for a candidate to have a decent shot at winning office, political scientists have yet to reach a consensus on exactly how, and to what degree, spending affects elections. Some have found that it makes only a marginal difference in elections; others, that it helps challengers more than incumbents; others, that it does matter in changing voter attitudes or encouraging supporters to turn out to vote, depending on how it is spent.[50]

Setting the Campaign Agenda

Agenda-making is the third important element of the minority's campaign arsenal. Voters tend to base their judgments on what incumbents have done, not what challengers promise to do—or, as former House doorkeeper Fishbait Miller succinctly put it, "People do not vote *for* someone. They vote *against* someone." Nonetheless, the minority party cannot assume that just criticizing its opponents will translate into election-night success. It therefore develops and advertises a positive agenda, an election-year pledge of what the party would do with power.[51]

Both parties put forward campaign agendas. An agenda can promote a positive brand name for the party, create an impression of competence and foresight, distinguish it from the other party, and give its candidates an additional resource from which to draw for speeches and advertising.[52] The majority offers them less often, however, because it can usually run on its legislative record, while the House minority has little or no positive record on which it can be judged. Recent minorities may also feel the need to distinguish themselves from their party's recent past. "We had to make some promises because we had made some mistakes" when last in the majority, explained one House Republican staffer for why the G.O.P. developed an agenda in 2010. Also, as the minority party has increasingly used delay, obstruction, and unified voting opposition against majority party measures, it can feel pressure well before election season to craft a positive message lest it be seen as the "party of no." Though campaign agendas risk subjecting the minority to criticism from the majority, their upsides are seen as outweighing their downsides.[53]

The Contract with America, proposed by House Republicans in 1994 just a month before they won control of the House, is the most famous example of a minority party election-year agenda. It was not the first of its kind, however. Minority Leader Joe Martin promised action on a number of conservative policy goals to voters in exchange for a Republican majority in the 1946 election. In the mid-1960s, several Republicans developed a Constructive Republican Alternative Program, and in the fall of 1968 then minority leader Gerald Ford suggested twenty items the party would pursue if it won control of the chamber. In 1975, the House G.O.P. proposed a legislative agenda that was criticized for being developed separately from President Ford's own campaign. Having failed to see presidential victories translate to congressional ones, however, John Rhodes explained that "the days of presidential coattails are gone, gone forever," so "if House Republicans ever expect to become the majority in Congress, it's up to us to tell our own story." Five years later, Newt Gingrich and other G.O.P. representatives reconnected with their presidential party by presenting an agenda jointly with White House candidate Ronald Reagan. As the efforts to develop and advertise agendas continued in the 1980s, both parties began circulating their agendas to congressional challengers along with briefing materials on nationally oriented issues.[54]

The 1994 Contract may not have been a novel idea, but it can be credited with introducing several new wrinkles to the content and development of election-year agendas. As a "contract," it intimated a high level of candidate commitment; one G.O.P. advertisement advised readers that "if we break this contract, throw us out.

We mean it."[55] It also pledged a specific timeline for action (votes within the first one hundred days of the next Congress) which Nancy Pelosi echoed in 2006 by proposing consideration of the Democratic agenda in the party's first one hundred *hours* of rule. In addition, the Contract's content and presentation were the first shaped in part by a poll of incumbents and party candidates as well as voters. It is now de rigueur for the minority to do the same. In 1997, for instance, Gephardt's office commissioned polls and focus groups and met with top consultants like Celinda Lake and Stan Greenberg to identify promising proposals for the party's 1998 agenda.[56]

The Contract with America was also pathbreaking in its presentation. It was officially unveiled at a carefully orchestrated media event, with over 170 G.O.P. challengers and nearly every single incumbent House Republican standing at the steps of the Capitol, and its provisions were printed in widely read magazines like *TV Guide* and *Reader's Digest*. Minority parties now routinely use aggressive marketing and communication tactics to advertise their agendas to broad audiences. They are officially unveiled at televised press conferences, promoted extensively in print and electronic media, and distributed along with talking points to candidates.[57] Minority party members also give floor speeches touting the agendas and introduce bills implementing agenda items. Of course, none of this can guarantee that people will know or care about minority party campaign agendas, especially given that the minority must compete against the majority party's bigger soapbox and, sometimes, the White House or a presidential campaign. A vivid example occurred during a 2002 rally by Democrats at the Capitol to tout their election agenda: the audience was distracted when President Bush's motorcade happened to drive by, and speakers strained to be heard above the sound of hovering police helicopters.[58]

The format, presentation, and marketing of these agendas not only follow tactics that have come before, but also give individual members of the minority an opportunity to innovate and find an outlet for their creativity. Newt Gingrich, who was a major organizer of the widely covered 1980 and 1994 party agendas, is a quintessential example, though for both agendas he was one of many Republicans who helped put the documents together, including Jack Kemp (in 1980) and Dick Armey (in 1994).[59] Another ambitious party entrepreneur, Kevin McCarthy, headed the development of the 2010 Pledge to America agenda, drawing on ideas proposed by other Republicans like Tom Price (GA) and Jeb Hensarling (TX).[60]

One important variable in the creation and publicity of campaign agendas is party unity. An agenda without the support of a significant number of lawmakers will seem like an empty promise and fail to project an image of consensus. It may be no coincidence that the Contract with America garnered as much attention and heft as it did after it had been signed by almost the entire Republican Conference as well as more than 150 of the party's congressional candidates. Unfortunately, while agendas might themselves help create a greater sense of unity and team purpose within the party, more often minority parties struggle to find agenda items that their members uniformly support. The result is often a "fluff" document long on rhetoric and short on specifics, or excessive and sometimes embarrassing delays in putting an agenda together.[61] Since disagreement is probably inevitable, the challenge for the minority party is to resolve it successfully, as was done for both the 1994 Contract and the 2006 Six for '06 agenda, and if not then to find ways to downplay it to the press.[62]

Table 2.1 lists the election-year agendas offered by the House minority party every election year from 1992 through 2010. (In a break from tradition, House Democrats did not develop a specific agenda in 2012, though they did adopt a general theme—Reigniting the American Dream—which emphasized job creation, small-business development, and aid to the middle class.) Though the agendas reflect the policy goals of the vast majority of party members, and they are developed by party leaders and entrepreneurs rather than campaign committees, they should not be considered policy documents but rather campaign manifestos designed to win elections.[63] Their brevity—no more than ten, and usually between four and six, items

Table 2.1. Election Year Agendas by House Minority Party, 1992–2010

ear	Minority party	Title of agenda	Number of items, topics, or themes	Some major proposals
992	R	A Manifesto For Change	10[a]	Tougher criminal laws, tax cuts, health care reform, educational choice, welfare reform, congressional disclosure, term limits, balanced-budget amendment, line-item veto, school prayer
994	R	Contract with America	10[b]	Balanced-budget amendment, line-item veto, tougher crime laws, welfare reform, child support, child tax credit, no U.N. command of U.S. troops, Social Security earnings-limit increase, small-business incentives, tort reform, term limits
996	D	Families First	3 (21 proposals)[c]	Health care for children, college-tuition tax credit, balanced budget without cutting Medicare, pension portability

(continued)

Table 2.1. (*continued*)

Year	Minority party	Title of agenda	Number of items, topics, or themes	Some major proposal
1998	D	New Solutions for a New Century	5	Saving of Social Security surplus, hiring of teachers, passage of patients' bill of rights, expansion of Medicar to older workers, minimum wage increase
2000	D	Families First 2000	4	Saving of Social Security surplus, making Medicare solvent, improvement of public schools, passage of patients' bill of rights
2002	D	Securing America's Future for All Our Families	5	Protection of Social Security, Medicare prescription drug coverage, school modernization, pension protection, environmental health
2004	D	New Partnership for America's Future	6	More job creation, support for strong military, child health care, improvement of early child education, strong law enforcement, greater fiscal discipline

Year	Minority party	Title of agenda	Number of items, topics, or themes	Some major proposals
2006	D	A New Direction for America	6	Alteration of Bush's foreign policy, minimum wage increase, college-tuition tax credit, more energy efficiency and domestic energy production, Medicare reform, no Social Security privatization
2008	R	The Change America Deserves		Health care reform, repeal of tax increases and passage of new tax cuts, more domestic energy production, passage of anti-drug crime bill, strengthening of borders
2010	R	A Pledge to America	5	Ending of tax increases, halting of spending, repeal of Obama health care, printing of bills three days before a vote, "clean" military bills to ensure "checks and balances"

a. The 1992 "Manifesto" included thirteen chapters on various subjects, but Gingrich's chapter included ten specific proposals that would be subject to votes.
b. The 1994 Contract promised votes on a series of congressional rules changes as well as the ten policy items.
c. The 1996 agenda had twenty-one items organized around three "principles."
d. Originally titled "The Change You Deserve" but renamed after it was discovered the same slogan was used by an anti-depressant medication.

or themes—and the general popularity of their proposals suggest that catching voter attention and ensuring that items stick in people's minds are critical considerations.[64] In 1994, for example, Gingrich wanted the Contract to have proposals supported by "at least 60 or 70 percent" of citizens, and in 2000 the Democratic agenda emphasized issues like health care, education, and Social Security that voters believed were better handled by Democrats. Even the electoral impact of an agenda's name is taken seriously. In 1996, Democrats considered many possible titles for their platform—Fighting for Our Kids, Rebuilding America, For Families, For a Change—before coming up with Families First.[65]

Campaign agendas are not really written to help the minority address its procedural or presidential party concerns either. To be sure, presidential elections are occasionally taken into account—in 1980 and 2000, for instance, the House minority coordinated its agenda with its party's presidential candidate—but the minority's primary target is congressional elections. In fact, when Gingrich attempted to develop and unveil an agenda in 1992 jointly with the Bush White House, the president demurred, leading House Republicans to offer an agenda of their own. On the very few occasions that the agendas include items related to minority rights, they tend to be buried. In the Democrats' 2006 platform, for instance, there was no reference to the subject among its top six proposals; its twenty-five-page report did mention pro-minority party reforms, but at the very end, and they were written as changes that "should" rather than "will" happen if Democrats won power.[66]

Do campaign agendas influence election outcomes? Examples from recent history suggest they do. House Republicans made the creation of a "positive governing agenda" one of its three central strategies to win control of the House in 1994, which they did—as did Democrats after advertising their Six for '06 agenda, and Republicans following their New Direction for America platform in 2010. Some scholars have argued that, at a minimum, the G.O.P.'s Contract with America established a successful brand for the party and had a major impact on news coverage and rhetoric in election campaigns. As Walter Lippmann noted, "once a party can induce the country to see its issue as supreme the greater part of its task is done."[67]

And yet: in every other election year between 1972 and 2010 in which the minority produced an election-year agenda, that agenda either failed to yield many seat gains or was followed by a loss of seats for the minority party. Even the 1994, 2006, and 2010 election results may have owed little to minority campaign agendas. For one thing, as noted above, voters tend to be retrospective, not prospective.[68] "The victory in a campaign," Lippmann also wrote, "is far more likely to go to the most plausible diagnosis than to the most convincing method of cure." One study found that campaign messages that influence voters' perceptions work best when individually tailored to feature a candidate's record.[69] Agendas are also usually ignored by the news media or overshadowed by other events, the 1994 Contract and 2010 Pledge being notable exceptions.[70] Even well-publicized agendas tend to make only a minor impression on the public. Surveys revealed that little more than a third of voters had even heard of the Contract with America and indicated a similar lack of familiarity or interest in the Democrats' agenda after the 2006 election and the Republicans' 2010 agenda after it was unveiled. When asked about the electoral impact of the minority Democrats' platform in the 1990s, former Gephardt aide Elmendorf replied, "Did it make a difference? No . . . Members think that more people are listening to them than actually are."[71]

To be sure, issues raised in a campaign can lead voters to cross party lines, and we cannot rule out the possibility that agendas affect some races, at least at the margins. Wrote one staffer in a memo to Gephardt regarding the party's 1998 agenda: "This agenda is not going to win the election for us . . . But it is a critically important arrow to have in our quiver when we make our case for putting Democrats back in the Majority." Nonetheless, available evidence strongly suggests that agendas are, at best, window dressing on the campaign house.[72]

Conclusion

These three electioneering tactics—recruiting strong candidates, raising and spending sufficient funds, and crafting clever and popular election agendas—are the tip of the iceberg of what both parties and their campaign committees do to win elections. Both committees develop and air campaign advertisements and make robo-calls on behalf of individual candidates, the party, or even on bills prior to floor votes.[73] They offer training seminars, mentors, and informal advice on campaign tactics; lend their own staff when needed; and encourage the use of certain themes or messages. (Perhaps the most famous example of the latter, albeit not by a campaign committee, was Gingrich's 1990 memo to G.O.P. candidates extolling language as "a key mechanism of control" and encouraging the use of both "optimistic" and "contrasting" words—the latter including terms like *bosses*, *corrupt*, *liberal*, and *sick* to describe Democrats and their party.)[74] Committees also fund efforts to turn out voters, provide data on voter demographics, and conduct opposition research.[75] But the activities examined here not only exemplify the importance of campaign committees, party leaders, and innovators in the minority's constant quest to win power; they also illustrate how those activities may, with varying degrees of success, help the party achieve its immediate goals of getting good candidates into the field, funding them sufficiently, and having a national platform on which those candidates can run.

Less certain is whether the electioneering of the minority actually yields results at the ballot box. Anyone who has been in the trenches of a campaign probably has at least one story of a candidate, a campaign decision, or an event that seemed to make the difference in who won the election. But persuasive and conclusive empirical data to support such stories are fleeting.[76] Other elements out of the hands of the minority seem to matter more: the party and popularity of the president, the natural advantage of incumbents, if it is a midterm or general election, the economy, district boundaries, and so on.[77] These elements can coincide in the right way to create a large "wave" election that helps the minority. The massive 2010 G.O.P. "wave," for instance, was largely the consequence of distaste toward President Obama by voters, unpopular votes taken by House Democrats, and the fact that the president's party usually does poorly during midterm elections—though Republicans did help their candidates through strong fund-raising efforts. Even members of Congress who claim they can sense when a wave is coming rarely take full credit for creating, expanding, or curbing it. Trent Lott recalled that by 1978 "we [Republicans] were beginning to smell blood," yet he and other party members recognized that demographics and district boundaries remained insurmountable barriers to a G.O.P. majority until the South would turn durably Republican, as it finally did in the early 1990s. Rahm Emanuel, widely praised as the architect of his party's 2006 victories, himself admitted that the elections would be shaped by things out of both his hands and those of the NRCC chair. "Neither one of us has a bucket to piss in or a window to throw it out of," as he eloquently put it. "Events create waves, history creates waves," remarked one former Republican campaign aide, adding pessimistically, "at the end of the day, members are corks in the ocean."[78]

Still, members of the minority party and the party's campaign committees are not irrational for investing so much time in electioneering. Unless both parties agree to stop, it makes little sense for one party to unilaterally halt or curtail its recruitment or fund-raising. Many of the things the parties do may be necessary, if not sufficient, to exploit favorable election conditions. Emanuel, wrote one journalist, "position[ed] the Democrats so that if a political tidal wave did emerge, the party would reap the benefit." When competition for control of Congress is tight, as it has been for the past several election cycles, it makes sense to do all one can to win elections. One never knows what difference that extra dollar, new candidate, or agenda might make. Other activities are similarly important: the "relentless" Martin Frost, for example, "created the modern DCCC" by improving its fund-raising and voter mobilization operations and, by spending its limited resources intelligently, "did more with less than any campaign committee in modern history." And legislators from the minority need to be assured that *something* is being done to change their status. Explained Steve Elmendorf, Democrats wanted to develop election-year agendas because "a lot of them are *positive*—they want to be *for* something." Electioneering, in short, is too important to give up, no matter how much or how little difference it makes in winning majority control of Congress.[79]

three
MESSAGING

The only thing you have in the minority is your voice,
and your strongest weapon is your message.
—House (minority) Democratic aide

They [House Republicans] ought to get the idea out of their minds
that they are legislators. But what they can be is communicators.
—Minority Leader John Boehner (R-OH)

Members of Congress are masters at messaging. With hundreds of thousands of constituents, representatives cannot realistically hope to win reelection solely through retail politics—knocking on doors, doing favors, holding coffee klatches, and so forth. Instead, spinning a story, providing a pithy quote, and touting one's accomplishments through mass media are far more efficient ways to make a good impression on many voters at once.[1]

This holds true for the day-to-day activities of lawmakers as well as what they do on the campaign trail. The three basic election-oriented behaviors of incumbent legislators—position-taking, credit-claiming, and advertising—all involve, to varying degrees, crafting and communicating a positive public image. As a result, much of the daily public spectacle surrounding Congress consists of non-legislative messaging: press conferences, floor speeches, faux committee hearings, and staged media events. Occasionally these activities become part of larger dramas or "pseudo-events," with reporters and news analysts eagerly discussing clashes between lawmakers or the two political parties.[2]

Messaging, then, is a central activity for individual members of the House of Representatives. Likewise, both congressional parties have incentives to develop and present messages collectively.[3] A message that is associated with an entire party, versus just one lawmaker, carries more weight and potential punch. Party activists expect their fellow partisans in Congress to be visible and can get ornery if they are not. And, ever aware of the potential for a "wave" election that benefits one party over the other, leaders see messaging as a powerful means of carrying the party's election candidates along that wave, if not creating it.[4]

Both parties conduct extensive messaging operations, and neither could stop developing media strategies even if it wanted to; otherwise, explained one legislative aide, "you are unilaterally disarming yourself against people who don't share your interests who have those strategies."[5] But in the House majority party, as former Democratic whip David Bonior put it, "you really don't have as much time to spend on messaging. In the minority, you can spend *all* your time on messaging." "It's easier to stay on message if you're in the minority," observed a Republican aide. "If you're in the majority, you've got to deal with all the fires that you're putting out." Recalled a former G.O.P. staffer, "You don't have that much [in the minority], so what you do have is to pound home your message."[6]

The most obvious reason that the House minority party engages in public communication is to achieve its collective goal of winning elections. A powerful message may rally the party's electoral base or convince undecided voters to support its candidates in the next election cycle. If a message can improve the minority party's own reputation or denigrate the other party's image, it may influence the minority's standing in the polls. Because "citizens receive and process political information regularly, not merely in the campaign season," observed the political scientist Douglas Arnold, it is considered vital that parties wanting to win elections have a communications strategy and continually implement it.[7]

Yet electoral victory is not the only purpose of messaging. A strong message could help the minority party shape policy by shifting public opinion on a forthcoming bill or placing pressure for action on other policy-makers in Washington. Messaging may also address the minority's concern with its procedural rights by drawing attention to abuses and creating an outcry that forces the majority party to relent. (Although, as Republican Minority Leader Bob Michel lamented, the press and voters usually respond to such complaints as "'MEGO'—my eyes glaze over.") In addition, the minority party can try to influence the reputation and popularity of their party's president or presidential candidate with messaging.[8]

Then there are reasons for party-wide messaging that cannot be explained by the strategic pursuit of collective concerns. By organizing and coordinating messaging activity, the minority party can build internal unity and a greater sense of shared purpose, which in turn may help with future collective endeavors designed to address core concerns. A surprisingly strong speech, or messaging from unexpected quarters within the party, can strengthen morale. Minority Republicans in the 2000s saw that even senior members of their party, like Hal Rogers of Kentucky, were willing to wait on the floor a long time just to speak against Democratic legislation. "That was the kind of thing that was a shot in the arm" to other members, recounted one Republican leadership aide. "I think we inspired each other," explained a G.O.P. lawmaker for why she and others conducted messaging activity on the floor. Messaging serves as an outlet for frustration as well. When Republicans quickly passed one conservative bill after another following their 1994 takeover of the House, "there needed to be a response to what was happening," recalled one House Democrat. "We couldn't just sit on the sidelines and watch." Finally, messaging is a rare avenue for creativity and fulfillment that keeps minority party members busy. John Feehery, an aide to Bob Michel who worked on the development and use of coordinated, provocative sound bites by House Republicans in the early 1990s, noted that "it was a lot of fun to do this . . . We had nothing to lose because we were in the minority;" and what was more, "you gave folks something to do."[9]

Since almost any act in the public sphere can serve a messaging purpose,[10] I limit my discussion of minority party messaging to the most obvious kinds, excluding tactics that have messaging as a secondary intent or effect (like obstructing floor proceedings, discussed in Chapter 4, or legislating, discussed in Chapter 5). Table 3.1 lists

Table 3.1. Major Types of Messaging Activity by the Minority Party

Activity or Tactic	Principal effect(s)			
	Conveying a message	Enacting, altering, or killing legislation	Delaying proceedings	Forcing opponents to take a position
Press conference, planned media event	X			
Press release	X			
Interview program	X			
Social media, Internet communication	X			
Faux hearing	X			
Refusing to leave chamber	X			
Symbolic amendment	X	X	X[a]	X[b]
Discharge petition	X	X	X[b]	X[b]
Motion to recommit	X	X		X[b]
Floor speech	X		X[a]	
Walking out of chamber	X		X[c]	
Raising a question of privilege	X		X[a]	X[b]

Note: Shaded rows indicate tactics examined in this chapter.
a. Contingent on the number offered or delivered.
b. Contingent on whether a recorded vote is, or must be, held.
c. Contingent on number of majority party members available to make a quorum.

the most common kinds of messaging activity by the minority party (and, in many cases, the majority party). Particular attention is given to one-minute floor speeches, press conferences, walkouts during House proceedings, and refusals to leave the floor when the chamber is in recess. Though these four tactics differ in frequency and level of participation, they all exemplify how the minority uses messaging to address its collective concerns.

I also explore the effects of party messaging. Unfortunately, those effects are nearly impossible to trace accurately, especially since they may be diffuse and take a long time to emerge. In determining the efficacy of a message, according to one minority leadership aide, "the ultimate measure is the next election," but making a causal connection between a message and an election outcome is too complex a task to undertake here. Instead, I look at how minority messaging may shape public opinion, especially toward Congress, which studies show is positively, if weakly, related to congressional election outcomes, with the majority party being punished by voters when Congress is disliked.[11]

One caveat to my analysis of messaging should be mentioned at the outset. A great deal of the minority's (and majority's) communications strategy involves multiple messaging tactics—floor speeches, press conferences, district town-hall meetings, and so on—to convey the same message. Messaging may also be done in conjunction with the Senate or the White House,[12] or used simultaneously with electioneering, delaying, or legislating efforts that highlight the same theme.[13] The reader should be aware that much of the messaging examined in this chapter occurs in conjunction with these other activities, though space precludes discussing this in detail.

The Development of Party Messaging since 1971

Innovative lawmakers have long found ways to exploit existing avenues of communication, or create new ones, to grab the attention of the American public. Even so, in the late 1960s and early '70s Congress, and particularly the House, was not given much notice by the press. The vast majority of newspapers had few if any reporters dedicated to covering just the legislative branch. One congressman lamented that "if the House were to become any more ignored than it was already, it would become as obsolete as the House of Lords," and an observer noted that "Congress may well be one of the worst covered stories in Washington." What reporters did pay attention to was the White House—often to the chagrin of minority Republicans, especially when presidents like Lyndon Johnson used the bully pulpit to steer or circumvent Congress.[14] Though the two parties did some press-related activities—leaders holding news conferences, congressional groups like the Republican Policy Committee issuing policy briefs and press releases—by far the greatest use of the media in Congress was by individual lawmakers trying to reach their own voters through the local press.[15]

The kind of regularized, coordinated, carefully crafted, and nationalized messaging by congressional parties that we see today owes a great deal to one man: Newt Gingrich. Not long after he entered the House in 1978, Gingrich joined forces with other young conservatives to seek out new tactics in communication, or find new ways to use old messaging devices, on behalf of his party. Speeches on the House floor were an example of the latter. Republicans had tried collective partisan messaging via floor speeches as far back as 1960, but in 1979 a new cable channel, C-SPAN, began airing live coverage of House floor proceedings. A collection of restless Republicans that included Gingrich, Jack Kemp (NY), and Trent Lott (MS) saw the new network as a useful way to reassert themselves and their party. They also realized that what was said, and how it was said, was as important as who was listening. Kemp complained that "part of our problem is language. You know, 'cut this,' 'cut that' . . . It was all 'root-canal' politics," and Lott recalled that Gingrich's "first step was to make us aware that the words we chose to use in the public square had an impact on our status as a national party."[16]

They and other mostly junior House Republicans began using one-minute floor speeches and longer "special order" speeches at the end of each day to make sharp partisan arguments. Members of the Conservative Opportunity Society (COS), the group formed by Gingrich in 1983, used floor rhetoric to extol conservative viewpoints and criticize majority Democrats. G.O.P. leaders also helped organize and recruit members to participate in special order speeches, and Democrats, both in response to these efforts and to compete with the press-savvy Reagan White House, conducted more messaging on the floor and in the press. However, the COS scored a major public relations coup when, upset by one of their more provocative special order speeches, Speaker Tip O'Neill excoriated Gingrich on the floor and was admonished for breaking the chamber's rules of decorum. The brouhaha got national press, including a story on all three major network evening news shows, making Gingrich a national figure and validating the COS's messaging tactics.[17]

When Gingrich became the G.O.P. whip in 1989, he created a new whip officer whose job was to encourage party participation in communication-oriented activities. The Democrats' new majority leader, Dick Gephardt, responded by forming the Democratic Message Board (DMB), an organization of party members charged with developing a "message of the day." Gephardt was well suited to the task, having contributed to his party's early efforts to develop unified responses to President Reagan's messaging machine. Both Gingrich and Gephardt were also emblematic of the era's newer, younger party leaders who were far more willing and eager to use mass media for spinning stories than the leaders who had come before them.[18]

After the 1992 elections, Republicans were completely removed from power at the national level, and the House G.O.P. responded with new communication initiatives. They included a "Theme Team," which acted much like the Democrats' DMB, and a "rapid response team," modeled after a campaign tactic used by Bill Clinton, to quickly rebut proposals or speeches by the other party. The minority also created a task force to develop messages that would shine a spotlight on restrictive floor rules. House Democrats stepped up their messaging game when they lost power in 1994. A new position of "message chair" was created to coordinate media communication, and the Democratic Policy Committee (DPC) issued regular messages of the day to members, announced press opportunities, and distributed talking points with titles like "reality check" and "outrage of the week.[19] When George W. Bush was elected president in 2000, Democrats formed rapid response teams of their own to rebut the White House. As for floor speeches, they took "a page out of Gingrich's book," recalled one Democratic member of Congress. "Gingrich utilized that time for one-minutes and special orders to confront Democrats, to tell a story about Democrats. It was, if you will, a weapon to go after the majority. So we began to use those opportunities to fight back."[20]

By the early 2000s, both parties had mastered many different kinds of messaging techniques. One-minute speeches were dominated by party-directed themes of the day or the week, and it was no longer unusual to see groups of members monopolizing special order speeches—groups like the 30-Something Working Group (Democrats) and the Official Truth Squad (Republicans). The two parties had also perfected the art of staging public media events outside the halls of Congress, appearing in front of gas stations when fuel prices were high or holding pretend committee hearings at which handpicked witnesses would "testify" on issues favorable to the party. To keep all members "on message," leaders distributed periodic bulletins and packets to lawmakers with weekly messages and included instructions for how to conduct events in their districts. Party communication was now far more centralized and leadership-driven than it had been three decades before.[21]

The Art, Science, and Politics of Effective Party Messaging

Lawmakers from the minority party can give speeches, hold press conferences, and do interviews until they are blue in the face, yet never be heard by the public at large. A typical speech in the House is unlikely to raise eyebrows, and getting reporters to write about the minority party is difficult. The minority must compete with the president and the House majority party, considered the real "players" in government—not to mention the U.S. Senate, Washington think tanks, government agencies, and interest groups—for an audience, amid a daily panoply of news events in the capital, the nation, and the world. "It's really hard for the minority party to get any kind of press, unless it's really outrageous," commented one Republican who saw life in both the minority and the majority. "And even then, the press is usually looking for something negative."[22]

An effective message by the minority party in Congress is one that finds ways to overcome these obstacles and get the public's (or at least reporters' or bloggers') attention. Alas, the minority party does not have the power to craft the House's legislative agenda or convene committee hearings, which could be used to shape news coverage or bring attention to helpful issues. On the other hand, because it is free from the expectation of governance, the minority can more easily pick and choose which issues it cares to discuss. In any event, because "newsworthiness is inherently an elusive quality," as the scholar Timothy Cook aptly put it, both the minority and the majority use consultants, public opinion polls, and constituent feedback to identify themes and sound bites that might gain traction. Every congressman is "constantly bargaining" with reporters (and vice versa) over what is covered and how, trying to win what Cook described as "a struggle to lead a dance."[23] Innovators and entrepreneurs in the minority party often introduce, develop, or institutionalize new tactics of communication, as well as novel themes, lines of attack, or rhetorical phrases. For example, minority Republicans became early users of Twitter in the 2000s, sending twice the percentage of tweets in two weekly periods in 2009 as House Democrats; Democrats in turn tried to make greater use of social media after losing the House in 2010.[24]

Though one Republican staffer opined that "basically, if you're in the minority, you can go out there and yell and scream about whatever you want," some rhetoric can go too far, hurting the reputation of the party or its leaders. Accordingly, messaging is often delegated to entrepreneurs or willing activists who can absorb any negative fallout and not implicate party leadership. For instance, Minority Whip Gingrich supported the harsh anti-corruption rhetoric of a group of Republicans called the Gang of Seven (a group that included future speaker John Boehner) but "let them do a lot of the dirty work" while he negotiated with majority Democrats on other matters. In 2003 Nancy Pelosi recruited Tim Ryan (OH) and Kendrick Meek (FL), self-described Young Turks, to form the 30-Something Working Group, a collection of younger Democrats eager and willing to "fight fire with fire" and use bold and creative messaging tactics unafraid of any negative repercussions.[25]

Some subjects in particular are believed to get people's attention. For instance, noted one Republican staffer, "from the minority you really have to latch on to what gets people angry. It comes down to what people are fired up about." This is one reason why ethical lapses by the majority, which can certainly anger and disgust voters, make for a popular topic. The Gang of Seven discussed ethics problems relentlessly in the early 1990s, and some House Democratic leaders later pointed to the G.O.P.'s pursuit of banking and post office scandals as a major reason their party lost the 1994 elections. Democratic messaging touched upon G.O.P. ethics quite a bit thereafter. "Quite frankly, we didn't leave a stone unturned," recalled one particularly vocal House Democrat from that period.[26]

Regardless of its specific topic, a message must be structured and framed in ways that maximize its effectiveness. An ideal message is "simple, clean, and emotional," according to one Democratic leadership aide. "Tested, solid, short, cogent, to the point, and show[s] a substantive difference" between the parties, in the words of a Republican aide. Reporters always look for a "news peg" on which to hang a story and prefer the "exciting, novel, or controversial" over the "complex and mundane." Strong, colorful, even inflammatory language gets notice. Criticism may be tempered by attention-getting humor. In the early 1990s, for example, members of the G.O.P. Theme Team often delivered oddball and witty one-minute speeches that included poems, top-ten lists, and references to Beatles songs and contemporary pop culture because "our goal was to make it interesting to reporters," according to Feehery. Of course, the specific message that will yield the best results in a given situation is never known with certainty. This is especially true because a message may bear fruit weeks or even months after it is delivered, depending on whether the press picks it up and how the other party reacts, if at all. Not even a sophisticated survey or focus group can perfectly predict what minority party message will move the public.[27]

A speech or statement delivered once by a lone congressman is not likely to be heard. Accordingly, both the majority and minority use repetition, recruit outside groups to echo their messages, and coordinate messaging with other kinds of activity such as obstruction and campaign advertising.[28] "You always want to have a coordinated message," advised one Republican leadership staffer, and "that's true . . . whether you're in the majority or the minority." A unified front—"a Radio City kick line where all the dancers are in sync," explained a G.O.P. leader—is also useful for connecting a message to the party label and preventing news stories of party disunity and defection. "Unity is a message in itself," Nancy Pelosi once declared. Leaders of both parties use many devices to maximize this unity, including weekly themes or arguments and "tool kits" to guide legislators in setting up local media events to echo party messages. In the summer of 2010, minority Republicans were asked to tell their constituents that over 2 million jobs had been lost since January 2009, while majority Democrats received a "Job Fair in a Box" kit that emphasized the party's efforts to improve the economy. In the 111th Congress (2009–10), Republican leaders even whipped their members to host district events on party-chosen themes.[29]

However, it can be hard to get everyone to agree to participate or repeat the party's rhetoric, especially lawmakers from less partisan districts. Recalled one former aide to a moderate Republican, "ninety percent of [the leadership message packet] would not resonate [with our voters] and would really make us look out of touch." Some messages play so poorly in marginal or swing districts that their representatives may plead with the party to cease using them.[30] Members in the minority, especially those new to their status, may be unaccustomed to (or too demoralized to try) novel communication tactics or strategies. "After having lost the House after forty years, it was very difficult for members to get themselves back on their feet again," remembered one Democrat who was in the minority after the 1994 election and responsible for developing party messages. Recalled Gephardt staffer Steve Elmendorf about the post-1994 period: "You have to convince your members that no, you have to go to the floor and give speeches and talk about how bad the other side is." Then there are the maverick-type lawmakers who may seek the limelight by openly opposing their party's official theme. And a party leader with his or her own agenda may develop messages that might not necessarily help the congressional party.[31]

Besides content, delivery, and unity, the effectiveness and reach of a message, especially for the minority party, is contingent upon who occupies the White House. Having a same-party president makes it much harder for the minority to be heard. Presidents routinely dominate news coverage of American politics, as reporters view the president as the party's spokesperson and see no need to interview his party's leaders in Congress as well.[32] Voters often falsely assume that the president's party controls Congress, placing a further burden on a minority trying to advertise its powerlessness. At the same time, if the president decides to criticize a Congress controlled by the opposite party, the danger is that he will hurt the reputation of everyone on the Hill, including his partisan allies.[33] And if the chief executive reaches an agreement on legislation with the majority party, he creates an impression of bipartisanship that makes it harder for the minority to draw distinctions with the party in power. In short, since competing with the presidential bully pulpit is so challenging, a minority party with a friendly White House has to make a difficult choice. It can openly defy its president, since "you really get the news by attacking" him, as John Feehery observed, but then risk conveying an impression of infighting that hurts the party brand. Or, as Elmendorf put it, it can "tie [itself] to the president and hope that a rising tide lifts all boats." In late 1997, Democrats chose the latter: its leaders in both the House and Senate planned a "non-partisan" media event with President Clinton after his State of the Union address and hoped to send party members "home for press events which reinforce the President's message."[34] In 2011, they steered from one strategy to the other: House Democrats excoriated President Obama's final deal with congressional Republicans to raise the debt ceiling, with one congressman (Emanuel Cleaver of Missouri) calling it a "Satan sandwich," but Minority Leader Pelosi then tried to change the subject and told reporters, "enough talks about the debt, we have to talk about jobs."

Things are easier when the presidential party is out of power, but the minority party is still not always entirely free to criticize the White House. In particular, the minority must be cautious if an opposite party president or presidential candidate is popular. In 1999, for instance, many House Democrats were hesitant to criticize the seemingly popular G.O.P. nominee George W. Bush in their own speeches (though most were later convinced to do so by the Gore campaign). And in early 2009, Republicans tried to follow a carefully nuanced message of praising Obama for his bipartisan rhetoric while criticizing the House majority for being too partisan. Nonetheless, being in the "deep minority" gives the minority party many more opportunities to communicate powerful partisan messages. Noted one House Democrat who was active on the chamber floor: "When you can address the majority in the House as carrying out the policies of the president, you've probably got a stronger wedge."[35]

It is also important to note that party communication may not always be calculated to reach a national audience. Patrick Sellers identifies three possible audiences for a message—the public, other elected politicians, and the media—and a Democratic leadership aide agreed that "some messages are meant for inside the Beltway and some for outside the Beltway." One Republican lawmaker who spoke often on the floor admitted that floor speeches may not be seen by many people, but "at least I could say to my base, 'Yes, I made a speech about this.'" Different audiences may be reached with different platforms, and some communication may not need to attract reporters or bloggers to be heard by targeted listeners. Messages related to House procedure, for example, may be conveyed to the press but really directed toward other lawmakers.[36]

The One-Minute Floor Speech

Perhaps the easiest place for the minority party to deliver a message, regardless of its content or audience, is the floor of the House of Representatives. Talk consumes more of Congress' time than anything else. Recorded votes in the House last no more than fifteen minutes, but debate on bills can take hours or days to complete. Plus, the daily schedule grants lawmakers many chances to speak out on the floor, be it in a one-minute speech (the "one-minute"), in a five-minute speech, or in hour-long, multi-member dialogues during special orders at the end of the day.

Minority (and majority) party members take advantage of all of these opportunities to be heard on matters important to their party. But one-minute speeches are preferable for studying floor-based communication, at least in the aggregate, because many lawmakers use them and both parties try to coordinate their content.[37] "One-minutes are a way to have everyone speaking about the same issue, the same thing," explained a Democratic member who organized them while in the minority. "We were encouraged to do one-minutes," remembered one Republican who served in the minority.[38]

House members have long had the right to ask unanimous consent to address the floor "out of order" (i.e. on a matter distinct from the bill being considered at that moment), but requests to do so became so common by the 1930s that the leaders of both parties agreed to limit such speeches to no longer than one minute in length.[39] Starting in the late 1970s, and especially after C-SPAN's arrival in 1979, minority Republicans began delivering floor statements that were not only more partisan in content but shriller in tone. Many of these Republicans, though not all, were junior members.[40] They also began repeating the same message in multiple one-minute speeches. In 1980, for instance, John Rhodes and some of his colleagues gave speeches that criticized the last quarter century of Democratic rule in Congress.[41] Democrats complained about the minority's new partisan tone: Parren Mitchell (MD), for example, decried the speeches as "puerile, partisan" and emblematic of "the children's hour."[42] But when the tone of the speeches did not change, and an effort to reschedule them to the end of the day was vociferously opposed by Republicans, Democrats joined in. Peter Peyser (D-NY), who had previously lamented "wild phrases on the floor," returned after a week and lampooned Ronald Reagan for an "on-again, off-again China policy" and for doubting Darwin's theory of evolution.[43]

By the 1980s Democrats had accepted one-minutes as a new tool for partisan messaging. In August 1984, Speaker O'Neill effectively institutionalized their partisan nature by alternating between one party and the other in recognizing members to give them. In the 100th Congress (1987–88) Deputy Majority Whip Steny Hoyer organized one-minute speeches around common themes on dozens of separate occasions, and in 1989 the party established the DMB to develop messages, recruit other Democrats to repeat them in their one-minutes, and hand out speech transcripts to the press gallery. By the end of the decade, the presiding officer of the House was giving priority of recognition for one-minute speeches to members who were on lists drafted by party leaders.[44]

Republicans formed the Theme Team in 1993 to develop humorous partisan remarks that might better capture the media's interest. Concerns about presidential politics were as important as House elections to the group's creation and development. Recounted John Feehery, the leadership aide who worked on behalf of the Team (which was chaired by Rep. Lamar Smith of Texas): "[In 1992] we had made a decision to use one-minutes to help Bush out. And so I started writing a bunch of one-minutes for a bunch of different members . . . [Then in 1993] Michel is trying to find a way to come up with a communications plan to counter Bill Clinton and his microphone . . . Our goal was to make things as hard for Bill Clinton as possible." Feehery also noted the Theme Team's salubrious effect on party unity and morale: "It was a unifying experience for the conference. After the 1992 elections everyone was really down, and it gave our guys something to do that was positive, that was fun."[45]

Both the DMB and the Theme Team still exist today, and frequent, synchronized, and partisan one-minute speeches are the norm. On July 21, 2009, for example, Republicans consumed three hours of floor time with speeches repeating the same four-word question ("where are the jobs?"). On the morning of February 21, 2010, the House was regaled with a whopping eighty-nine one-minute speeches—forty-three from Democrats (twenty-two of them touting Obama's stimulus or health care reform bill), and forty-six from Republicans (nineteen criticizing either or both bills).[46]

A typical legislative day in the House begins with a series of one-minute speeches, a period known as "morning business."[47] Occasional one-minutes are delivered during the day, and another cluster of one-minute speeches are usually given, along with longer "special order" speeches, after legislative business is completed. Though one-minute speeches have been a fixture of the House for decades, their frequency has varied from one Congress to the next. Figure 3.1 shows the average number of one-minute floor speeches delivered daily every five years since 1970 and annually since 1989.[48] Observe the increase in the average from the late 1970s through the early 1990s, roughly matching the rise in the percentage of households with the ability to watch floor proceedings at home. There are also notable upward jumps in 1993, 2005, and 2009—years that, interestingly, followed congressional and presidential elections in which the House majority party was banished to the minority.[49]

Scholars have traditionally regarded one-minute speeches as a function of individual goals, particularly the goal of reelection. This was certainly the case with one-minutes through the early 1970s, when a good number of them were about local matters, whether it be the death of a prominent constituent or an award won by a high school student from the district. Even now, parties cannot exercise total control over what their members will say. "You might be [prepared to speak] on the [party's] theme of the week," observed one House Republican, but "the person ahead of you says something outrageous, and you just want to say, 'to Hell with the theme of the week.'"[50]

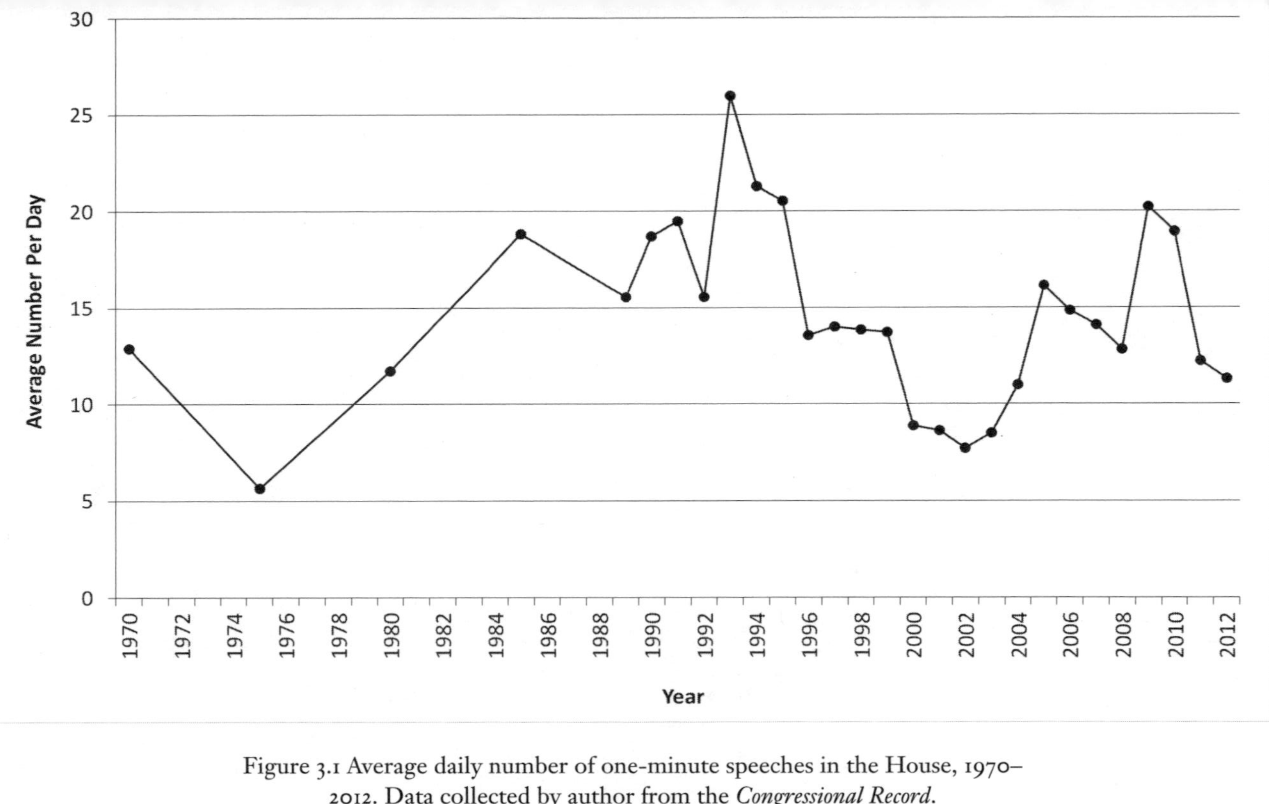

Figure 3.1 Average daily number of one-minute speeches in the House, 1970–2012. Data collected by author from the *Congressional Record*.

However, as already noted, one-minute speeches have evolved into important tools for each party to achieve collective purposes. They are often organized around common messages, and party leaders recruit fellow partisans to deliver them.[51] Even before the DMB and the Theme Team, groups of lawmakers (notably the COS) developed coordinated themes for one-minutes. The representational strategies of legislators since 1970 have also shifted from being "person-intensive," emphasizing personal relations with constituents, to "policy-intensive," in which one's position on issues matters most. So even lawmakers who deliver one-minutes to get themselves elected may believe that speeches echoing the party line are the best way to achieve that goal.[52]

Because the two parties cannot force lawmakers to speak on preapproved topics, there is no easy way of determining each speech-giver's motive for delivering a one-minute speech. For obvious reasons, members of Congress do not readily give honest explanations for why they say what they say. Inside information on the coordination of speeches would be ideal for figuring out the salience of party-wide concerns, but that is hard to come by. A less precise but more viable approach, which I use here, is to infer motive based on the content of statements themselves. We can, for instance, safely assume that speeches driven by collective party concerns will not refer to purely local matters, advertise a speech-giver's own bill, or announce routine administrative topics like an upcoming committee hearing. Conversely, speeches that make references to the president, minority party rights, or one or both political parties are more likely to reflect the orator's concern with collective partisan interests.[53]

Let us look first at recent speeches that were obviously individualistic. The fourth pair of columns in Figure 3.2 shows the percentage of 557 randomly sampled one-minute speeches from each party in 2010 that referred to a district or state matter,[54] and the fifth pair of columns indicates the percentage that advertised a lawmaker's own bill or resolution. Together they indicate that about 25% of floor speeches were oriented solely toward one's district or burnishing one's legislative record. Now consider the first pair of columns, which

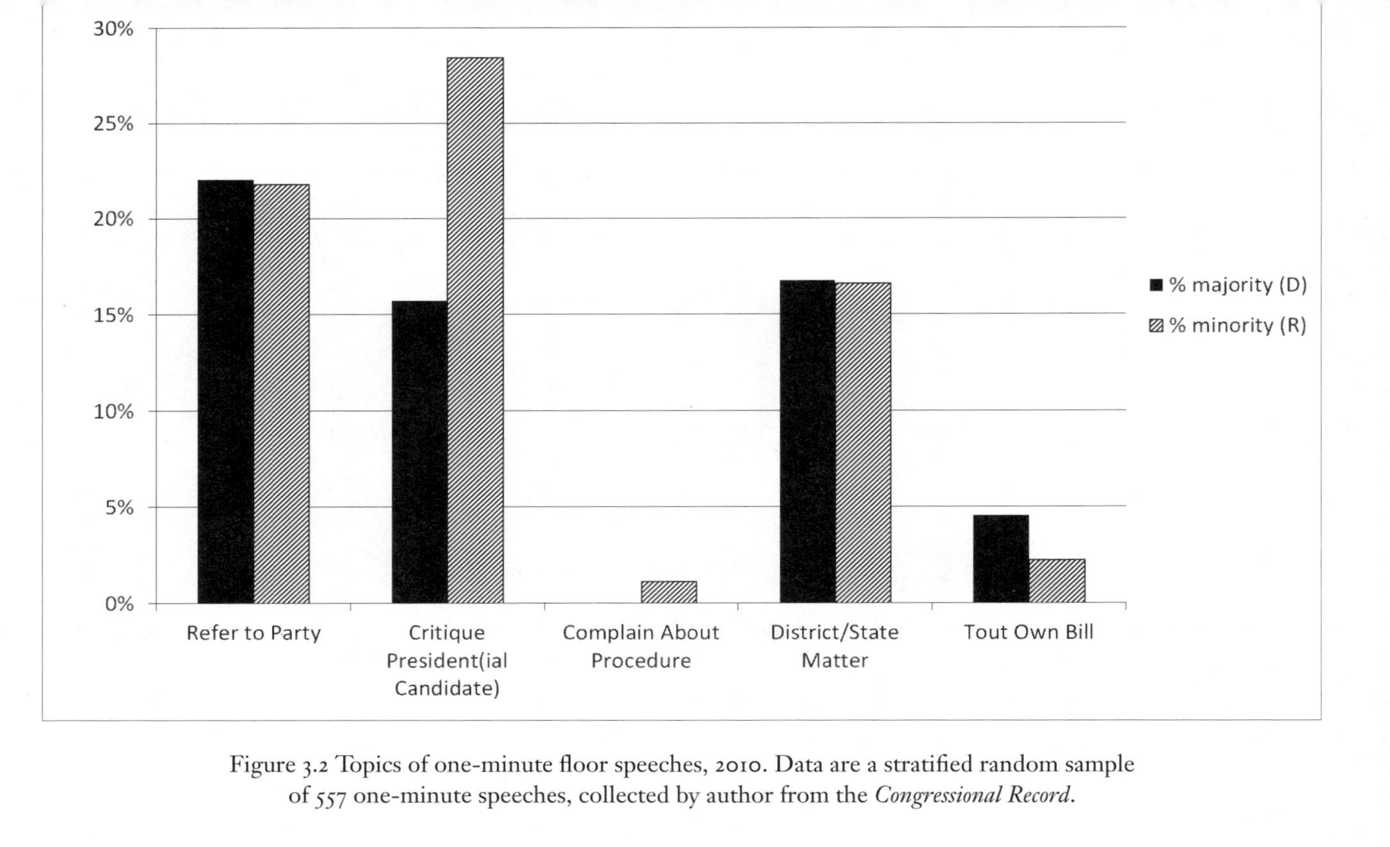

Figure 3.2 Topics of one-minute floor speeches, 2010. Data are a stratified random sample of 557 one-minute speeches, collected by author from the *Congressional Record*.

show the percentage of these sixty-second sound bites that referred to parties or used partisan labels like "liberal" or "conservative."[55] These are most likely delivered to help win the next election by praising one's own party and trashing the other in the hope of swaying public opinion, though they could (also) be used to advance each party's policy objectives by convincing other lawmakers, either directly or via their constituents, to side with them on legislation.[56] The data reveal that over 20% of each party's one-minute speeches that year were explicitly party-oriented. This may seem low given how extensively the parties craft and organize one-minutes, but the true level is likely higher since many coordinated speeches are devoid of party references but still framed to benefit the electoral or policy goals of one party over the other.

The minority party's two other collective concerns, procedural rights and the presidency, also appear to have driven the use of one-minutes in 2010. The former was an infrequent subject, making up a mere 1.1% of the minority's floor speeches sampled from that year (and, unsurprisingly, none of the majority's).[57] But the presidency was a far more popular topic. As shown in the figure, over a quarter (27%) of the minority party's speeches praised or criticized the president or a presidential candidate in 2010, far above the proportion of the majority's speeches on the same subject. Even if these statements were being given with an eye toward influencing the upcoming congressional elections or convincing the president to take a certain policy position, their most obvious and immediate target was the reputation of the chief executive or a candidate for president.

Particularly striking is the stark and statistically significant disparity between the two parties in critiquing the presidency.[58] Does that disparity stem from a fundamental difference between the majority and minority parties in their concern about the presidential party, or is it due to the politics of that particular year—an incumbent president struggling in the polls, tied to an unpopular health care reform initiative, and facing a stringent and united opposition? Figure 3.3, which shows the percentage of one-minute speeches sampled every five years from 1970 to 2010 that critiqued the president or a

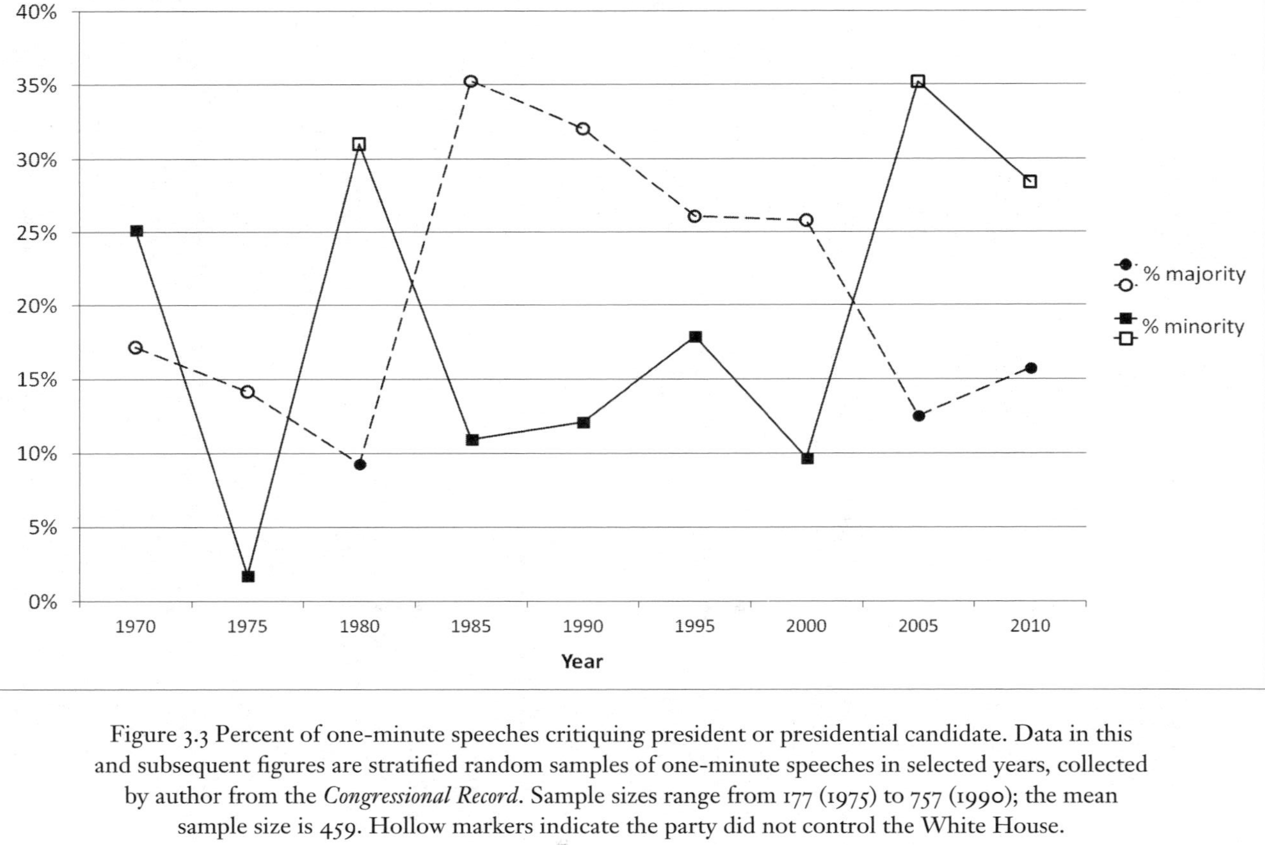

Figure 3.3 Percent of one-minute speeches critiquing president or presidential candidate. Data in this and subsequent figures are stratified random samples of one-minute speeches in selected years, collected by author from the *Congressional Record*. Sample sizes range from 177 (1975) to 757 (1990); the mean sample size is 459. Hollow markers indicate the party did not control the White House.

presidential candidate, reveals an enduring political logic at work. It is the party that does not occupy the White House, regardless of majority or minority status, that gives more speeches about the presidency. (The sole exception to this pattern was in 1970, when minority Republicans gave more White House–oriented speeches despite Nixon being president.) The minority party, then, sees presidential politics as a worthy talking point provided the chief executive is a partisan opponent, but finds it unnecessary to discuss the White House—or perhaps impossible to be heard on the subject—when its partisan ally occupies it.[59]

A more consistent difference based on majority versus minority status emerges with speeches that are explicitly partisan. As can be seen in Figure 3.4, in all but two years (1995 and 2010) the minority party delivered a larger percentage of its one-minute speeches with a partisan perspective than did the majority party. Perhaps this partisan rhetoric was used to persuade the majority to change its policy positions—directly, or indirectly by shifting public opinion—but it is a safer bet that these references to party were made principally to win the next election by influencing each party's public reputation. Finally, Figure 3.5 tracks the percent of sampled speeches that praised or criticized House procedure. It is hardly surprising that the minority party almost always critiqued the chamber's rules (usually negatively) more often than the majority party, nor that it was a seldom-seen subject given its low salience among voters.[60]

In sum, though it remains a useful tool for individual legislators to be heard by their districts, the one-minute floor speech is popular with minority parties trying to address their collective concerns. Winning elections, shaping presidential politics (under certain conditions), and to a lesser extent protecting procedural rights are all important topics of one-minutes. Influencing policy may also drive speech-giving, since many floor statements address specific legislative issues, though ascertaining the exact degree to which that motivation is present is difficult.

What impact, if any, do these speeches have on the views of the public at large? In theory, it could be sizable. A floor speech could

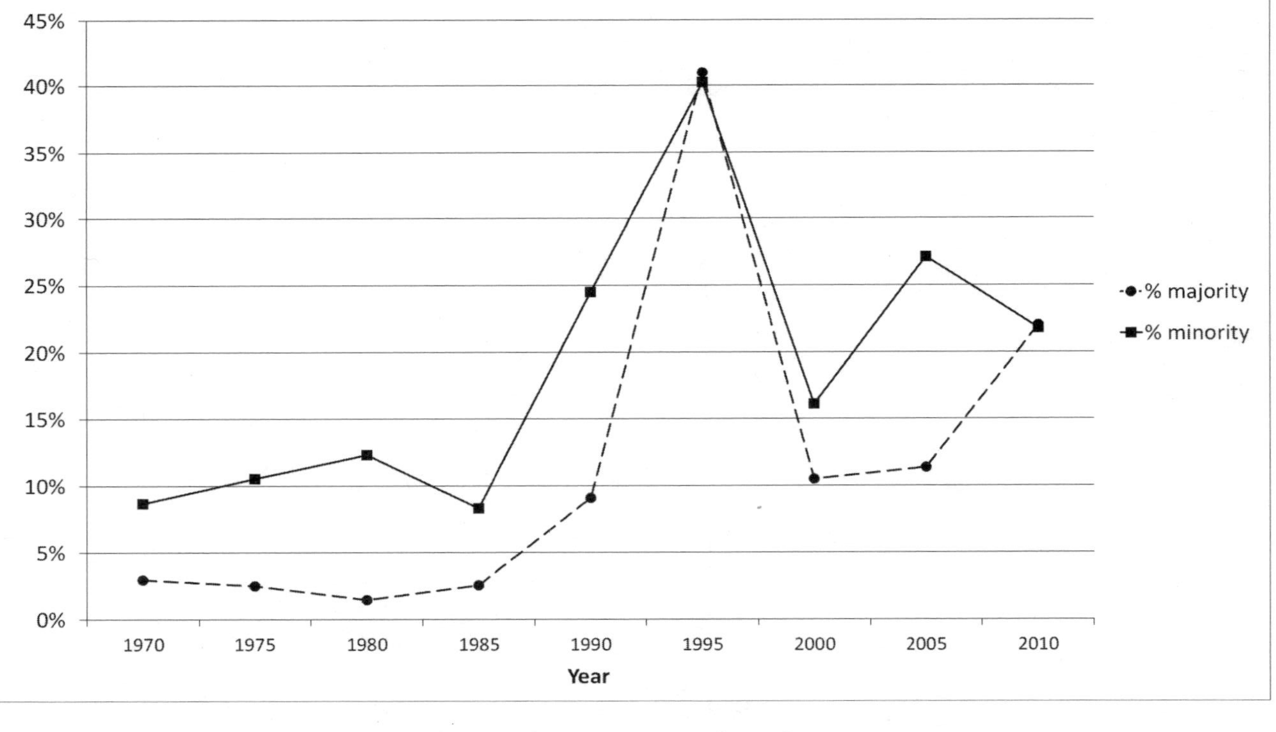

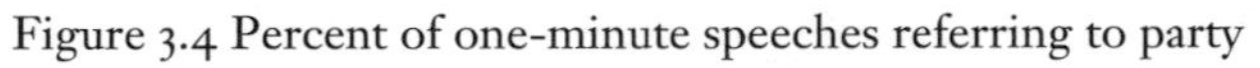

Figure 3.4 Percent of one-minute speeches referring to party

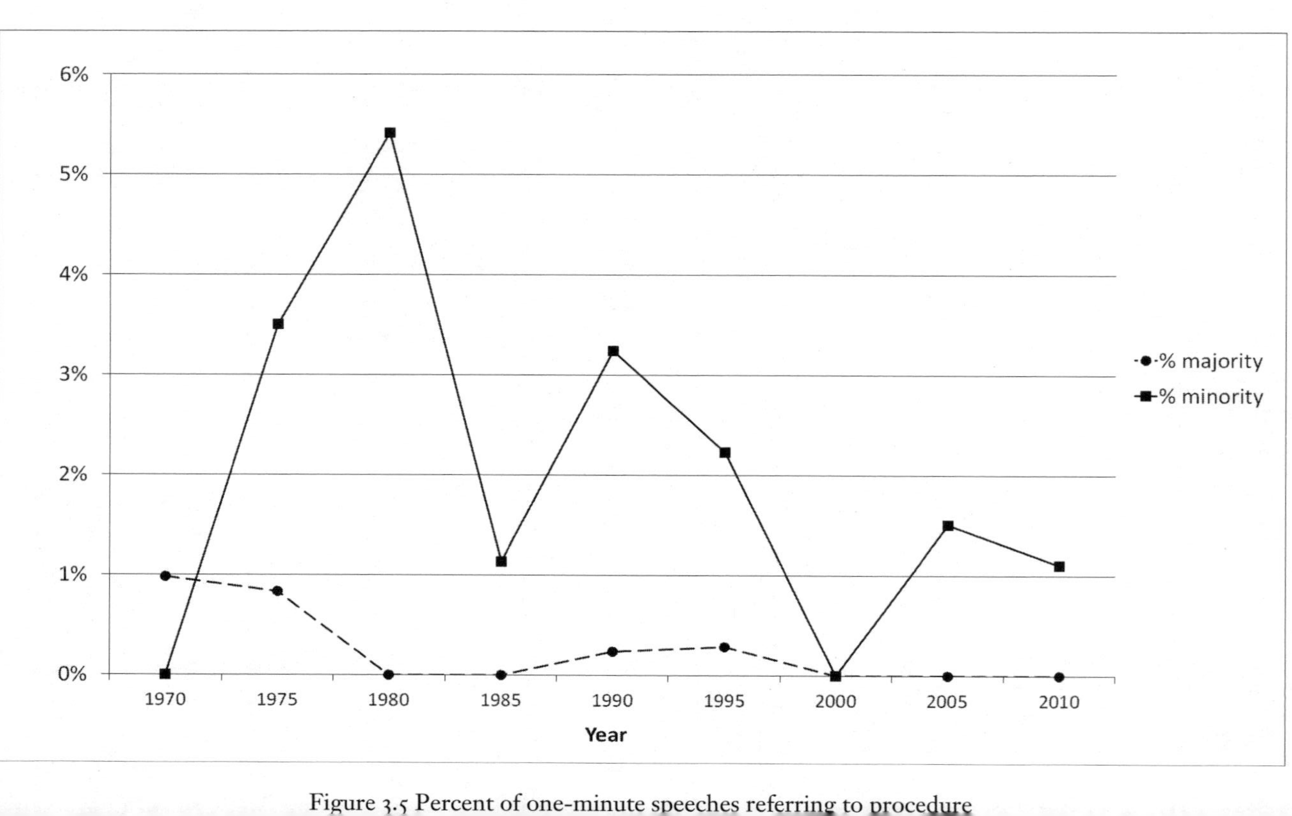

Figure 3.5 Percent of one-minute speeches referring to procedure

energize party activists, for instance; speculated one Republican when asked about the impact of special order speeches on the 2010 elections, "I think what we did was give voice to the frustration that later emerged across the land." And a speech could make national news if it is especially outrageous or provokes the majority to react, as happened when Tip O'Neill was reprimanded for his fiery retort to Newt Gingrich's provocative rhetoric. But the influence of such activity on public opinion at large is probably low, for C-SPAN is not watched by a large audience and the press rarely covers a floor speech.[61]

Illustrative of these speeches' likely influence on public attitudes is the case from July 2009, when House Republicans, in an impressive display of coordination and repetition, delivered hours of speeches that all asked the same catchy query, "Where are the jobs?" Despite using a smart, well-repeated sound bite, the speeches did little to move public opinion on Congress. In fact, they came *after* several months of slowly declining approval ratings for the institution, as shown in the last five rows of Table 3.2. And voters expressed virtually the same level of concern about the economy and jobs immediately following the event as they had right before, and significantly less about the economy than they had seven months prior (the bottom four rows of Table 3.3).[62] If delivering over an hour's worth of one-minute speeches on a single topic with a clever turn of phrase cannot move the public, it is hard to believe that one-minute speeches in general are a consistently effective tool for changing public opinion.

Media Messaging: The Press Conference

"Media coverage is the very lifeblood of politics," writes Doris Graber, "because it shapes the perceptions that form the reality on which political action is based." Floor speeches may help the minority party if they are heard by other lawmakers, policy-makers, and maybe even voters, but for a sizable transfusion of that "lifeblood of politics" the minority knows better than to rely on speeches alone. It needs the press.[63]

Table 3.2. Changes in Opinions of Congress following Messaging Events

Date	Polling firm	Results
April 1–4, 1995	CBS/NYT	30% approve
May 4–6, 1995	CBS	33% approve
August 5–9, 1995	CBS/NYT	31% approve
October 22–25, 1995	CBS/NYT	32% approve
May 8–11, 2008	Gallup	18% approve
June 9–12, 2008	Gallup	19% approve
July 10–13, 2008	Gallup	14% approve
August 7–10, 2008	Gallup	18% approve
September 8–11, 2008	Gallup	18% approve
April 6–9, 2009	Gallup	36% approve
May 7–10, 2009	Gallup	37% approve
June 14–17, 2009	Gallup	33% approve
July 10–12, 2009	Gallup	32% approve
August 6–9, 2009	Gallup	31% approve

Note: All poll questions were phrased as follows: "Do you approve or disapprove of the way Congress is handling its job?" Shaded rows indicate polls taken after the messaging event discussed in the text. All margins of error are ± 3%.

Table 3.3. Changes in Opinions about Congress and Certain Issues following Select Messaging Events

Date	Firm	Question	Results
July 14–17, 1995	ABC/*Wash. Post*	[Whom do you trust to do a better job handling the issue, Clinton or Republicans in Congress?]: protecting the Medicare system	53% Clinton, 36% GOP
September 28–October 1, 1995	ABC/*Wash. Post*	[Whom do you trust to do a better job handling the issue, Clinton or Republicans in Congress?]: preserving the Medicare system	54% Clinton, 37% GOP
May 31–June 1, 008	New Models (GOP firm)	Which of the following issues would you say is most important to you in deciding how to vote for Congress?	12% gas prices or energy
une 28–30, 008	New Models (GOP firm)	Which of the following issues would you say is most important to you in deciding how to vote for Congress?	9% gas prices or energy
July 2008	New Models (GOP firm)	Which of the following issues would you say is most important to you in deciding how to vote for Congress?	10% gas prices or energy

(continued)

Table 3.3. (*continued*)

Date	Firm	Question	Results
August 30–31, 2008	New Models (GOP firm)	Which of the following issues would you say is most important to you in deciding how to vote for Congress?	7% gas prices or energy
January 17–18, 2009	New Models (GOP firm)	Which of the following issues would you say is most important to you in deciding how to vote for Congress?	45% economy, 6% jobs
March 24–25, 2009	New Models (GOP firm)	Which of the following issues would you say is most important to you in deciding how to vote for Congress?	41% economy, 7% jobs
June 2–3, 2009	New Models (GOP firm)	Which of the following issues would you say is most important to you in deciding how to vote for Congress?	37% economy, 5% jobs
July 22–29, 2009	New Models (GOP firm)	Which of the following issues would you say is most important to you in deciding how to vote for Congress?	37% economy, 6% jobs

Note: Shaded rows indicate polls taken after the messaging event discussed in the text. The margin of error for all surveys is ± 3%.

Press conferences are the most direct way to get media attention and shape the daily news narrative.[64] Leaders and well-spoken members of both parties regularly organize news conferences and events designed to get the party's message out. However, there is no guarantee the public will hear that message. Reporters can ask embarrassing or difficult questions, report on only certain aspects of a press event, or even not show up at all. The Internet can circumvent traditional news outlets to some extent, but it has yet to surpass them in audience members. And, because reporters remain a boundary between politicians and citizens, they can not only distort a party's message but contribute to an impression of distance and inauthenticity that dilutes its effectiveness. Nonetheless, press conferences can and do get positive coverage in the national news media. The interdependent relationship between Congress and the press means that reporters need news as much as lawmakers crave coverage, and press conferences are a way to feed that mutual appetite.[65]

The 1970s and '80s were a time when members of Congress increasingly looked to the news media to get attention for themselves and their pet issues. By 1976 there were so many press secretaries on the Hill that they formed their own association. The number of reporters covering Congress also grew steadily, and by 2006 over seven thousand correspondents were accredited to the House and Senate press galleries. Press conferences in particular were evolving into significant media events. Republicans made a splash in the 1960s with "The Ev and Charlie Show," a series of joint televised conferences held by House Minority Leader Charlie Halleck and his Senate counterpart, Everett Dirksen. But it was not until the 1990s that leaders of both political parties regularly televised their conferences. Of course, the growth in media politics on Capitol Hill did not mean that party messages arrived unfiltered to the public. In the 1970s, and especially after Watergate, the national news media was becoming "harder, tougher, [and] more cynical." When the novelty of televised news conferences and other classic media tactics wore off, lawmakers and party leaders had to be more creative. Today, legislators will hold rallies, design eye-catching props, travel to strategic locations, conduct mock hearings, and many other things to make a press event worthy of coverage.[66]

As with one-minute speeches, press conferences can be held for any number of reasons that are not immediately self-evident.[67] To glean what the minority party hopes to get from using them, I examine press conferences in which the party's top leader participated. This approach makes sense insofar as party leaders not only get more press coverage than other members of Congress but are also seen both by reporters and fellow legislators as spokespersons for the party's collective interests. Here too I use content to infer purpose, coding lawmakers' opening statements from a randomly selected sample of news conferences by both parties from 2000, 2005, and 2010. Despite some imperfections, the data serve as a useful gauge of intent and differences in that intent (if any) between the majority and minority parties.[68]

The results appear in Table 3.4. Some are strikingly similar to patterns found in one-minute speeches. In two of the three sampled years (2000 and 2010), for instance, the minority used critical partisan rhetoric far more often than did the majority. Procedure is an infrequent topic, usually discussed more often by the minority party. (Not so in 2005, because majority Republicans were touting a relatively open rule for considering a bill at one of their conferences.) Criticism or praise of a president or presidential candidate, and requests for the White House to take some sort of action, dominate the press conferences of the party not in power in the Oval Office. (The word *president*, unsurprisingly, was popular in many conferences.)

Leadership press conferences, then, appear to address several minority party concerns, including winning elections (via partisan rhetoric), presidential politics (contingent on who controls the executive branch), and minority rights (on occasion). What about the party's interest in shaping policy, however? The common topics of press conferences suggest that electoral interests matter more: each party tends to discuss issues that play to their strengths (Democrats: social security, health care; Republicans: energy) or the other party's weaknesses (excessive spending, mishandling the aftermath of Hurricane

Table 3.4. Descriptive Statistics of Selected Press Conferences by Party Leaders

	2000		2005		2010	
	Minority party (D)	Majority party (R)	Minority party (D)	Majority party (R)	Minority party (R)	Majority party (D)
Common topics	Republican/ tax cuts, Bush/ education	Russia/ education, children/ health	Social Security, health care, Hurricane Katrina	energy/ refinery, Hurricane Katrina	spending/ Democrats/ Congress	Wall Street/ jobs/ health care
Most frequent words	tax (121), people (106), bill (93), Republican (79)	bill (121), people (111), children (99), thank (92)	people (88), security (49), president (48), bill (41)	people (41), bill (38), energy/ thank (26)	people (138), American (113), president (66), spending/ house (60)	people (89), thank (79), president (72), jobs (69)
% praising past or promising future party actions	69%	100%	87%	83%	93%	79%

(*continued*)

Table 3.4. (*continued*)

	2000		2005		2010	
	Minority party (D)	Majority party (R)	Minority party (D)	Majority party (R)	Minority party (R)	Majority party (D)
% criticizing other party	94%	38%	31%	33%	87%	24%
% praising or criticizing president(ial candidate)	63%	88%	74%	33%	80%	57%
% urging other party to take action	31%	0%	13%	17%	20%	0%
% urging president to take action	6%	63%	13%	0%	27%	0%
% commenting on procedure	25%	0%	0%	17%	7%	0%
N	16	8	15	6	15	14

Note: Data are all press conferences featuring the top party leader from twelve randomly selected weeks (three per quarterly period). Question-and-answer dialogue is excluded from the analysis. Common topics and word frequencies were determined using R packages *tm* and *topicmodels*; other categories were coded by the author.

Katrina). The word *people* is also among the most commonly used terms, an electorally useful word that helps the party connect what it is saying and doing with voters.[69] On the other hand, in 2000 and 2010 the minority party was more likely to ask, not demand, the ruling majority to act in a certain fashion. This makes for a useful campaign talking point ("We asked the majority to do something good, and it refused"), but if one hopes to influence policy, success is more likely to follow from a request than from open criticism. So we cannot entirely dismiss the possibility, however remote, that the minority hopes to influence policy with news conferences.

Though these media events could affect political outcomes in all kinds of ways, their impact is probably minimal. If party leaders can get reporters to give them favorable coverage, of course, that may help move the electorate. And the means by which the press covers Congress has been shown to create more polarized views of the institution among certain citizens. But reporters are a filter between lawmakers and the public, and they can be a thick and distorting filter indeed. A minority party with an ally in the White House is also largely helpless to control how the news media portrays it. One Republican lawmaker summed up the minority's plight best: "We can't make the press cover what we have to say."[70]

Refusing to Leave the Floor, Refusing to Stay

Less common than floor speeches or press conferences, but more dramatic as a form of partisan communication, is the use of the floor as a stage for mass protest. Sometimes this manifests itself as a refusal to exit the chamber when the House has adjourned for the day, but more often it means the party's members walk off the floor while the House is in session, usually during a roll call vote. Both are strongly symbolic forms of messaging. By refusing to leave, the minority party hopes to appear more responsible and willing to legislate and to imply that the majority has wrongly abandoned its work when action on policy is desperately needed. If the minority party leaves the floor, it can signal that the majority, if not Congress as a whole, is somehow acting illegitimately.[71]

Sometimes reporters will write stories about these events, but the primary audience for both kinds of activity is fellow lawmakers, not the broader public. Once the House adjourns or is in recess, C-SPAN coverage of the floor ends, and it is hard to easily televise a walkout unless the minority has scheduled a press conference to advertise it. By contrast, members of the majority party are well aware when these incidents happen.

Twice since 1970 have significant numbers of the minority party stayed in the chamber. The first occasion was in mid-November 1995, amid heated conflicts between majority Republicans and President Clinton over the federal budget. With several spending bills yet to be signed into law, the G.O.P. moved that the House go into recess, forcing Clinton to either sign the bills or face a partial closure of the federal government. A handful of House Democrats refused to depart, arguing for a compromise solution to avoid a government shutdown. As their number grew, the gathering transformed into an impromptu party meeting (moderated, appropriately enough, by the chair of the caucus, Vic Fazio). Democrats took turns giving lively partisan speeches defending the president, attacking Republicans, and praising the Democratic Party. C-SPAN's cameras were off, and Republicans had deactivated the chamber's sound system, but that did not deter the Democrats. Though they could do nothing about C-SPAN, recalled Democratic whip David Bonior, members cheered as one intrepid Democrat "went up to the balcony, opened up the box that controlled the sound, and turned it back on."[72]

The spontaneous event lasted only a few hours, but it allowed Democrats to claim they would not be responsible for a government closure, express their strong support for progressive policies, and stand up for the president. It also rallied Democrats together at a time that the minority, still wounded by its loss of the House in 1994, badly needed it. At one point, Barney Frank (MA) dryly remarked to the audience that the Democrats had considered passing a resolution "to make Newt Gingrich and Dick Armey honorary morale officers of the caucus," drawing laughter from his colleagues. The event, though not televised, was mentioned in news reports the next day, including a full-length story (with photo) in the *Washington Post*.[73]

The other refusal to leave the floor occurred in August 2008. Gas prices were the topic du jour: the average cost for a gallon of unleaded fuel surged past $4 in July, and Republican presidential candidate John McCain had called for more offshore oil exploration and development to increase gas supplies. As in 1995, the event was unplanned. As Tom Price (GA), who helped organize the event, later recounted, on the last day of the House's session before recess "we lined up, I think, thirty-five or forty people" to speak on gas prices while the chamber was still in session. But then Democrats unexpectedly adjourned the House. Price went on: "Mike Pence (R-IN) was standing at the leadership table. [I said,] 'We need to give our speeches.' And Mike said, 'Well, who're you going to give them to?' And I looked up at the galleries and said, 'We'll give them to them.' Westmoreland [a Republican congressman from Georgia] was ready to go with his first speech, and I said, 'Go ahead, give your speech.' And he kind of looked at me and said, 'Really?' . . . I'll never forget the look on [Majority Leader] Steny Hoyer's face. It was like, 'What are they up to?'" Another G.O.P. representative involved in the protest described what happened next. "We had a meeting that afternoon, and we said, 'Let's all come back next week.'" There was no plan to continue the protest for a month, and "we didn't know what kind of reaction we'd get . . . [Only] a group of about twenty of us pledged to come back." However, what started as a short-term effort "to crystallize a message and show a contrast" with the majority party developed into a monthlong campaign on the House floor, with Republicans giving speeches every weekday during the recess to complain about high gas prices and criticize Democrats for not considering a comprehensive, "all of the above" bill that included incentives for oil drilling. Many members of the party gave at least one speech during the unusually long protest.[74]

The event was salient to several collective party concerns: election success (opinion polls showed majorities in favor of offshore oil drilling, and the event was widely covered by the news media), policy influence (to the extent Republicans did, in fact, want to pass their energy proposal), and presidential (election) politics. It was also a reaction against a perceived lack of fairness by the majority Democrats—not just their quick adjournment, which cut off Republicans' speeches, but a Congress that had heretofore been full of slights and opportunities taken from them. As was explained later by one Republican who was involved with the extended sit-in, "So much had been denied to us [in that Congress] . . . Everything was a closed rule. [So] when they shut us down, we said, 'This isn't fair.'" Another lawmaker recalled that "many of us felt the rules had been changed in ways that had never been seen [before]." "Our guys had had it. They were just fed up," said a Republican leadership aide.

Like the 1995 sit-in, the 2008 "mock" session boosted the spirits of a minority party that had been recently kicked out of the majority. Wrote one reporter, its first day "energized" some Republicans and "had all the passion of a revival meeting," while another day's meeting was described by a different journalist as "a partisan pep rally." It was an event that Republicans recalled in interviews several years later with no small degree of pride.[75]

In contrast to the rare refusal to leave the House, mass departure from the chamber while it is in session is a little more common. When it deprives the majority of a quorum, it can delay legislative proceedings, but this seldom happens in the modern House: attendance by the majority party is usually more than adequate to meet the chamber's quorum requirement.[76] Rather, its utility is primarily symbolic: to show so much distaste for the work of the majority that the minority feels it can no longer remain present. Table 3.5 lists the seven prominent instances of minority party walkouts from the House that have occurred since 1970, including threatened, attempted, and realized walkouts, and the primary collective concern or concerns behind each of them.[77]

Distress about procedural rules and decisions that disadvantage the minority party is the most common precipitating cause of a floor walkout. The first mass exodus in May 1985 followed the decision of a Democrat-dominated task force to leave uncounted several absentee

Table 3.5. Walkouts from House Floor by the Minority Party, 1971–2012

ear (Date)	Minority party	Precipitating event	Result	Primary concern(s)
985 (May 1)	R	Democratic candidate from Indiana is given House seat	Walkout	* Majority status * Procedural rights, powers
987 (Nov. 21)	R	Gorbachev invited to give speech to Congress	Threatened walkout	* *Other*
992 (April 9)	R	House passes reform bill that GOP opposes	Attempted walkout	* Policy * Procedural rights, powers
998 (Dec. 19)	D	Vote on impeachment of President Clinton	Walkout	* Procedural rights, powers * Presidential party
000 (June 28)	D	Restrictive rule for considering Medicare bill	Walkout	* Policy * Procedural rights, powers
007 (Aug. 2)	R	Agriculture bill passed while voting clock still open	Walkout	* Policy * Procedural rights, powers
008 (Feb. 14)	R	Contempt citations issued against Bush administration officials, failure to renew electronic surveillance law	Walkout	* Policy * Presidential party

Sources: Black 1998; Carey 2000, 2008; *CQ Weekly* 1992; Katz and Taylor 1998; Plattner 1985; Richert 2007; Roberts 1985; Starks 2008; Towell 1987; Wallison 2000b.

ballots in a contested Indiana election. Republicans "went on the warpath," forcing an all-night session and later halting legislative activity for a day with a series of tactics organized by party leaders. When the House still voted to seat the Democratic candidate in that election, a "furious" Bill Thomas (R-CA) led his colleagues off the floor in protest.[78] In 1998, the refusal of majority Republicans to allow a vote to reprimand (instead of to impeach) President Clinton led House Democrats to storm out of the chamber en masse; a denial by Republicans to let Democrats vote on a Medicare prescription drug bill two years later led to another walkout. And a voting-clock snafu at the conclusion of a narrow vote to pass a contentious agriculture bill in 2007 led outraged minority Republicans to file off the floor.

Protecting the rights of the minority is not the only reason minority parties leave the House chamber. The contested election of 1985 angered Republicans not only because of how it was resolved, but because it robbed the party of a potential seat and suggested they would have to struggle even further to win back control of the House. Moves by the majority party that threaten, attack, or undermine the president have also motivated some walkouts, as in 1998 (the impeachment of Clinton) and 2008 (contempt citations against Bush administration officials). The minority may also be driven by policy concerns. Democrats in 2000 were deeply opposed to, and left the floor during consideration of, a Medicare prescription drug bill written by majority Republicans, and in 2008 Republicans badly wanted the House to vote on extending an electronic surveillance law they supported. In addition, emotional reactions to provocative moves by the majority are often what compel members like Bill Thomas to instigate, and other lawmakers to participate in, walkouts.[79]

Though walkouts, like refusals to leave the chamber, have as their primary audience the majority party, the minority sometimes tries to expand that audience. In 1985, for instance, Republicans left the House "to a score of waiting television cameras," while Democrats marched from the chamber in 2000 to a scrum of reporters while carrying umbrellas labeled "shame." Nonetheless, most walkouts are about minority party mistreatment, and lawmakers realize that voters rarely care much about that subject. As one Republican complained after an attempted walkout in 1992, which was intended to protest the Democrats' management of the House and their allocation of committee seats to the G.O.P.: "How many people do you have on the Rules Committee? People at home could care less." Furthermore, there is a risk that leaving the chamber makes the minority look petty and puerile. Explaining why the attempted walkout was opposed by so many party members, Republican Sherwood Boehlert opined that "people want us to act like adults."[80]

A walkout cannot hope to be effective or get attention without unanimous, or near-unanimous, participation. (It is no coincidence that Gephardt used his unity-building tactic of showing film clips, mentioned in Chapter 1, just prior to the walkout on a Medicare bill in 2000.) But dissent within the minority party over the effectiveness of walkouts and how they will be perceived is not uncommon.[81] As a consequence, while organizing an exodus can demonstrate unity or even help unify a minority party, it can just as easily expose tactical or ideological divisions within it. The 1987 attempted walkout was initiated by conservative Republicans unhappy at the news that President Reagan had invited Soviet leader Mikhail Gorbachev to address Congress; but when other House Republicans disagreed with the tactic, the plan was never carried out. The 2007 walkout over the voting-clock dispute did take place, but it involved only "more than half" of the party.[82] Even the 1985 G.O.P. departure over the contested Indiana election, though widely supported, led to publically aired disputes over what to do afterward. Republican leader Michel hoped it would "create public awareness of 'the autocratic, tyrannical rule of the Democratic majority'" and help get Republican challengers elected in 1986, but he did not want to press the issue too far lest it jeopardize Reagan's agenda. Newt Gingrich and fellow party activists, however, insisted that they would keep employing delaying procedures and other aggressive tactics in retaliation.[83]

As with one-minute speeches and press conferences, walkouts from the House floor and refusals to leave the floor appear to do little to move public opinion. If we consider the most high-profile instances of such floor stunts—for which the minority has usually tried to get outside media attention—it seems they made little impression on the typical voter. Take, for instance, the August 2008 sit-in by House Republicans over high gas prices. Despite getting fairly extensive news coverage, it led to no change in the approval rating of Congress and was actually followed by a slight decline in the percentage of voters mentioning gas prices or energy as their primary policy concern (the fifth through ninth rows in Table 3.2 and the third through sixth rows in Table 3.3). To be fair, however, the primary purpose of minority party walkouts and sit-ins is not to move public opinion, and these tactics may yield other political benefits. For example, the 2008 protest on oil prices was followed within a few weeks by passage in the House of a bill expanding offshore oil production. Though it was a largely symbolic measure, and perhaps would have been introduced without the G.O.P. protest (since gas prices were a presidential campaign issue), Republicans nonetheless took credit for pushing the majority to act.[84]

Conclusion

Messaging is perhaps *the* central activity of the minority party in today's House of Representatives. It is one of the only tools freely available to its members to address all four of the party's collective concerns: winning control of the House in the next election, influencing public policy, protecting party rights, and shaping presidential politics. It also helps the party by giving the rank and file opportunities to act and innovate, express their views and emotions, and create or demonstrate a unity of purpose. In fact, in today's media-centered political world members of Congress from both the minority and majority see partisan communication as an expectation, not merely an opportunity. One frequent speech-giver from the minority G.O.P. in the 2000s explained that "I just saw it as part of my job . . . I don't think I should be seen as a more active member. I think everyone should do it."[85]

There are, of course, many other ways for lawmakers to garner public awareness of their party besides the ones considered in this chapter. Interviews on national television allow prominent party members to draw attention to themselves and their party's message. Faux hearings give the minority a chance at the media advantages of official committee hearings without having the power to convene them. There are also a slew of non-messaging tactics the minority can use that also convey a message. But the kinds of messaging examined in this chapter exemplify nicely the politics and centrality of messaging as a strategy of the House minority.

As much time as it consumes, minority messaging appears to have only a minimal effect on public opinion. Surveys taken before and after selected messaging events suggest that attitudes probably shift little in the aftermath of coordinated one-minute speeches, press conferences, or walkouts from the floor. Similar communication-related campaigns also show a lack of impact. For instance, in September 1995 House Democrats used speeches and a rainy outdoor "mock" hearing to highlight their support for Medicare and to accuse Republicans of planning to cut it. Despite getting considerable news coverage, the campaign did nothing to deepen voters' pre-existing skepticism toward Republicans on the issue, and it did not noticeably shift Congress' approval ratings either (see the first four rows of Table 3.2 and the first two rows of Table 3.3).

This should, at some level, come as no surprise. The vast majority of citizens are part of the "inattentive public" and, in Walter Lippmann's words, "suffer from anemia, from a lack of appetite and curiosity for the human scene." Studies have found that messaging, and in particular issue-framing, tends to have at best a limited and short-term effect on public opinion, especially if there are competing messages on the airwaves. It is asking too much for minority parties to make more than tiny ripples in the great sea of media chatter or move voters in a substantive direction, especially if not even presidential rhetoric can change public opinion noticeably.[86]

These limited effects should not be taken as evidence that minority parties are foolish to pursue messaging tactics, however. Besides the fact that they may influence public opinion in ways that are difficult to capture, the minority's other collective concerns may be served through messaging. Getting good media coverage may induce other policy-makers to respond to that coverage, regardless of its impact on voters' views. One study found that if messaging by legislators gets picked up in the news, other lawmakers may legislate based on that coverage, though the effect may be greater for senators' rhetoric than for representatives'. In addition, the president's reputation or behavior could well be shaped by minority party messaging. Presidents and presidential candidates sometimes even adopt messages first developed by members of Congress, including their opponents. In his 2012 State of the Union speech, for instance, President Barack Obama used the term *all of the above* to describe his energy plan, a phrase that had been popularized by House Republicans touting their pro-oil-drilling energy proposal four years before.[87]

In addition to all this, messaging may be designed less to move public opinion than to associate the minority party with the direction the public is already headed. Consider the numerous "where are the jobs" one-minute speeches Republicans gave in July 2009. It was wise for the minority party to come out swinging against the ruling party when polls were showing sinking support for Congress (which, as mentioned previously, tends to translate into seat losses for the majority party). And if the minority had (also) been thinking of President Obama when it delivered them, it did so as Americans were souring on the president's economic policies. The four previous months of polls had revealed a steady drop in support for Obama on that issue, from 59% in mid-April to 52% in mid-July.[88]

In any event, both parties do messaging because their members have long believed that it matters. It is the way the two parties try to find lines of rhetorical attack or sell their policy initiatives to voters. And with the potential to influence politics in many ways, and in fashions difficult to trace, it is a belief that is unlikely to be dispelled any time soon.[89]

four
OBSTRUCTING

The problem with the minority is you get to spend your days
figuring out how to pour sand in the gears.
—former House Republican aide

It was not the usual sort of amendment one might see in the House of Representatives. Phil Gingrey, a Republican from Georgia, had just been recognized on the floor to offer the first amendment of the day to an agriculture spending bill. His amendment proposed cutting $50,050 from the office of the secretary of agriculture, a mere 1% of its total budget for the 2008 fiscal year.[1] After Gingrey gave a short speech defending the proposal, Connecticut Democrat Rosa DeLauro rose and announced that her party, the majority party in the House, would agree to the amendment. But that was not the outcome Gingrey and his fellow Republicans wanted. Instead of accepting DeLauro's offer, they began delivering five-minute speeches related only tangentially to Gingrey's amendment and critical of another bill, one that expanded federal health care coverage to qualified minors, which was supposed to come to the floor later. An hour of speeches and parliamentary inquiries passed. Then another Republican, Patrick McHenry (NC), proposed an amendment to Gingrey's amendment that doubled his cut to $100,100. Nine more of his colleagues took turns speaking for five minutes each (again, mostly on the children's health care bill) until Democrats finally gave up, ending debate on the spending measure for the evening. Three and a half hours had been consumed by debate, procedural motions, and points of order.[2]

Obstruction and delay are often seen as the scourge of legislative democracy: the abuse of parliamentary procedure by a minority seeking to subvert the will of the majority. If so, it is a scourge that has been with us long before the House Republicans' "filibuster by amendment" of the agriculture bill in July 2007. In the 1st century B.C., Cato the Younger was notorious for slowing down the Roman Senate. On one occasion, when the Senate considered granting Julius Caesar special dispensation to run for the office of consul, Cato spoke so long during debate that the chamber was forced to adjourn.[3]

In the U.S. Congress, individuals, groups of lawmakers, and minority parties have all found ways to slow down, if not stop, the legislative process. What gets the most attention by far is the Senate filibuster.[4] But the example that opened this chapter illustrates how the minority party in the House sometimes pursues dilatory tactics, too. Therein lies a puzzle: since the House's rules do not allow the minority party to delay legislation for more than a short period, and rarely does that delay lead to a bill's defeat, why does it bother with delaying tactics at all?

Answering this question requires looking beyond the decision calculus of individual representatives, the topic of choice for most scholars of legislative delay in Congress.[5] Since obstruction in the House has become increasingly organized and waged by the minority party collectively, it makes sense to examine the motives, methods, and consequences of party-wide obstruction—delays of House business pursued by party leaders or entrepreneurs with the party's interests in mind, usually supported by a majority of the minority party. Although obstruction is possible within committees, I focus on delay on the floor of the House, where dilatory tactics and lawmakers' support for them are most visible and often the most dramatic. It is not a common occurrence, but it happens enough, and certainly more than it did four decades ago, to warrant closer inspection.[6]

Identifying with certainty all instances of, and reasons for, legislative obstruction and delay is not easy. There are many ways to delay the legislative process, and with a little creativity dozens of procedures can be employed, alone or in combination, to slow things down. Amendments and extended debate, as Gingrey, McHenry, and other Republicans used against the agriculture bill, are but two examples. Table 4.1 lists fourteen procedures and tactics that have been part of the House minority's delaying "tool kit" since the 1970s, and

Table 4.1. Common Methods of Obstruction in the U.S. House of Representatives since 1970

	Immediate or principal effect(s) on floor proceedings			
ouse floor tactic or rocedure	Delay proceedings	Alter legislation	Kill legislation	None/ other
otion to adjourn	X			
equest for division vote[a]	X			
lotion to enter ommittee of the Whole[a]	X			
evotes on amendments the Committee of the Vhole	X	X		
ffering a large number of nendments	X	X		
asting/switching vote at id of voting time	X	X	X	
lotion to rise	X		X[b]	
econsideration of vote in ouse	X		X	
emand for a second[a]	X		X	
evotes when delegates ote	X			X
uorum call[a]	X			X
rolonged speeches/debate	X			X
aising question of rivilege	X			X
epeated parliamentary iquiries	X			X

a. Curtailed and/or eliminated by rules changes between 1961 and 2010.
b. If the motion recommends that the enacting clause be stricken.

there are others.[7] Most of these procedures can also be used to influence legislation or communicate a message, making intent difficult to discern. For instance, the minority party may offer large numbers of amendments to a bill because its members want the chance to revise it or take a position on an issue, not because they want to delay its passage. Or minority leaders may raise a question of privilege not to slow floor activity per se but to express unhappiness and "hold the majority party publicly accountable for its stewardship of the institution," as one scholar described it.[8]

As a result, measuring the frequency of real obstruction, not incidental or unintended obstruction, is sticky business. Just counting the number of times a procedure is used, or how many partisans vote for it, is not enough. Instead, I analyze select cases of obvious delay as well as aggregated instances in which the minority had a clear intent of slowing the legislative process. The former allows for more in-depth study of context, motive, and technique, while the latter permits a broader evaluation of obstruction over time.

I begin with three noteworthy instances in which delay was significant and obstruction was the minority party's clear intent, explaining why they happened and what benefits they yielded the minority, if any. I then examine two particular floor procedures that have been used clearly and consistently to slow down the House and whether they have had any impact on political outcomes. First, however, I briefly explain the politics of minority party obstruction in the House and the reasoning behind it, followed by a brief review of changes in House obstructive tactics and strategy since the mid-20th century.

The Politics of Minority Party Obstruction

To return to the question posed earlier: why would a House minority party waste its time trying to stop legislation when it is virtually impossible for it to do so? The answer, in part, is that the party pursues this seemingly futile approach because it can, at least in theory, help the minority address its core collective concerns.

Take the minority's most important objective, to become the governing party by winning elections. Voters may punish the current majority party if desired legislation is not enacted, or if passing it involves lengthy and messy procedural fights that make Congress look bad. Why vote for a party that seems helpless in the face of obstruction? Delay also draws attention to the minority and its platform, serving as a kind of advertising tool. Dilatory tactics are "much less about improving legislation and much more about communicating a message," explained a Democratic consultant, while one G.O.P. leadership aide noted that delay is an appealing strategy because "first, it causes a stink and allows us to tell people why we're doing it." It can also mobilize the minority's biggest supporters in anticipation of the next election. Obstruction, in short, is a plausibly powerful electoral gambit. After 1992, House Republicans believed it was important enough that they made "derailing Clinton's agenda" part of their three-prong strategy to win back Congress in 1994.[9]

Obstruction could be used by the minority party on behalf of its other collective concerns, too. Even just an hour or two of delay can change legislative outcomes if it buys time for minority leaders to build a winning coalition for a vote or postpone an urgent matter long enough that the governing party concedes on some policy matter. For similar reasons obstruction gives the minority leverage when negotiating for additional procedural rights. In 1993, for example, House Republicans succeeded in getting more bills to the floor under open proceedings after forcing a series of dilatory votes (though Democrats argued they would have done so anyway), and Republicans who blocked the agriculture bill in 2007 were in part worried that the majority party would limit their right to offer amendments to the children's health care proposal. Finally, delay can assist the presidential party by bringing attention to issues salient to Oval Office candidates or delaying bills that might hurt the minority's same-party president. House Republicans were willing to use dilatory tactics on behalf of the children's health care measure partly because it would have diverted funds from the Medicare prescription drug program that the Bush White House had shepherded into law three years before.[10]

Though it has its benefits, obstruction also carries with it many potential costs. By violating an expectation that both parties participate responsibly, if not constructively, in the legislative process, it can sully the minority party's reputation and perhaps its chances of winning more seats.[11] Majority parties seldom pass up the chance to make obstruction an issue during an election campaign or criticize the minority for dilatory tactics. (Analogies to juvenile behavior are a particular favorite—"Little League politics," "childish," "temper tantrum," "pouting," and so on.) Delay puts the brakes on *all* floor activity, including the passage of bills the minority party might like, and gives the majority extra time to lobby members on future votes. It also sours the majority on the idea of cross-party cooperation, and the party may retaliate by limiting the minority's rights altogether. After the Republicans' delay of the agriculture-spending bill, for instance, Democrats brought the bill back to the floor under a rule that made just twelve amendments in order and, for good measure, restricted the minority's ability to make one kind of delaying motion. Finally, same-party presidents and White House candidates risk being tarnished by the same dark brush of excessive obstructionism as the House minority.[12]

One way minority party leaders can reduce the costs of obstruction is to delegate it to individual members and keep a wide berth from them. That way, they have plausible deniability and are shielded from criticism by fellow partisans who might think the costs of delay outweigh its advantages.[13] These designated individuals often have extensive procedural knowledge and know how to employ delaying tactics adroitly.[14] They also must have thick skins and usually represent safe districts. Former representative Robert Walker (R-PA) recalled that, in retaliation for his partisan use of floor procedure, Democrats made "attempts to make [it] politically damaging to me in my district," but without success. Nonetheless, he added, "I got tremendous criticism from people in my own party . . . I had committee chairs [and] subcommittee chairs who were absolutely furious with me. I had committee staff who wouldn't speak with me." If leaders hear too much grumbling or believe the costs of obstruction are becoming too great, they may try to rein in overly zealous members who are gumming up the floor. Dan Burton (R-IN), for instance, was admonished by party members in 1993 for waging a solitary crusade of obstruction to protest restrictive procedures for considering bills, and at least one Republican urged his leader to have the "renegade" Burton work more closely with the G.O.P. Conference or the Rules Committee's ranking member.[15]

Sometimes the minority party ignores these costs and benefits altogether. A lack of alternative avenues to legislate can drive the party to "pour sand in the gears," as the G.O.P. aide put it, regardless of whether it is expected to help with collective party concerns or not. "As the majority continues to deny outlets for other perspectives," explained Illinois Republican Peter Roskam in 2009, "that energy goes somewhere." Emotion, especially frustration and anger, often precipitates delay. "If they [the majority] keep running over you, and running over you, you have to resort to those kinds of tactics," noted former Democratic whip David Bonior. Said one Republican staffer, "we're not going to be steamrolled and bullied around on the floor." "I don't have time to sit around feeling frustrated," declared Dick Armey (R-TX) to a reporter in 1986. "I'm too busy trying to stop Democrats' bills." Emotional motives may be particularly acute when the psychic wound of losing majority status is fresh, as it was for Republicans in 2007, or after an especially egregious or flagrant violation of legislative norms or rules by the party in power.[16]

Some obstruction only has a chance of working (or working well, anyway) if the minority is united behind it, but one reason to pursue delaying maneuvers is to *create* unity of purpose (and, often, boost party morale). An example of this occurred in the summer of 2009, when Minority Leader John Boehner exploited a House norm that each party's top leader may address the floor longer than his or her allotted speaking time. Boehner was recognized to talk for one minute, but he began a lengthy speech (later nicknamed the "fili-Boehner" by some) that took nearly an hour to finish. Recounted one leadership aide, "The floor was full of [Republican] members. They sat there, listening. It was really a nice moment, actually—it helped members understand the value of really articulating something." The staffer added that the event was "good for the members" of the G.O.P. and even "energized" them because "even before we lost the House, Republicans almost didn't remember why they ran . . . Members were really down on themselves."[17]

As previously noted, however, delaying tactics can be quite irksome to some minority party members, leading to more, not less, dissention within its ranks. Complaints tend to be fiercest from influential lawmakers and "institutionalists" who are invested in the House's regular order, or when delay occurs at inconvenient times. A dilatory motion "has a double edge to it," said erstwhile Democratic whip Bonior, "because it annoys some of your own members. Especially senior members. If you're senior, you want to get out of there. Life is short." Recalled former Gephardt aide Steve Elmendorf, "The minute that [a delaying motion] inconveniences them" they lose interest in obstruction. "Try doing a motion to adjourn when you've got California members trying to catch a 5 p.m. flight on a Friday," noted a Republican staffer. Irritation by minority party members over dilatory votes "happens not that infrequently," remarked a Rules Committee aide, and "[sometimes] half the members come down [to the floor] and they're mad."[18]

With the potential for internal opposition, the minority party usually employs delay judiciously. The politics of floor obstruction also tends to resemble a game of chicken or a "war of attrition" in which each party tries to outlast the other. A month before the G.O.P. delay of the agriculture spending bill, Republican dilatory tactics against a change in the House's rules governing earmarks led the majority to temporarily pull the bill being blocked, but—unbeknownst to Democrats—Republicans were not necessarily prepared to continue their delays much longer.[19]

Minority Party Obstruction in the House since 1958

Obstruction and delay have always been a part of House politics. In the modern chamber, however, obstructionism—concerted delay by members of the minority bothersome enough to elicit a reaction from the governing party—has its contemporary origins in the late 1950s. In the 86th Congress (1959–60), minority party Republicans began monopolizing a rarely used procedure requiring that an engrossed, or pre-published, copy of a bill be produced prior to its final passage, which usually took a day to complete. Unlike in the past, when the procedure was used by members of either party (and sometimes incorrectly), demands for an engrossed bill were now made primarily by the minority party and, while rare, could still be a serious nuisance for Democrats. For example, when a demand for engrossment was made before the vote to enact President Lyndon Johnson's 1964 anti-poverty initiative, for which Johnson had built a fragile majority coalition of support, some bill supporters had to cancel planned trips home to wait for the rescheduled vote.[20]

The next year, Democrats abolished the right to demand engrossed bills—what was then an unusual step of changing the House's procedures to stop minority party obstruction.[21] This move ushered in a new tit-for-tat pattern of procedural party politics in the House, whereby the minority sporadically delayed floor proceedings using a previously neglected rule; the majority then tightened up the House's procedures; and the minority subsequently delayed the House by some other means. Republicans made an extraordinary use of multiple quorum calls in late 1968 that used up over twenty-four hours of floor time (discussed below), and in 1970 Democrats eliminated one of the procedures used in that "mini-filibuster." After the 1976 elections, Democrats crossed a new partisan Rubicon, drafting and approving House rules without any input from Republicans at all. Though only a few of those rules were dedicated to eliminating minority party obstruction, the majority had embraced a "party cartel" model of governance in which it would monopolize the instruments of power in Congress, tinkering with the chamber's rule book after each election in order to "stack the procedural deck" in its favor.[22]

Restive and undeterred, Republicans continued to exploit other procedural options for delaying the House—sometimes to protest previous rules changes, other times to address various individual or collective party concerns, and other times out of simple boredom or anger. The minority also began taking tentative steps toward coordinating its dilatory tactics. It had long relied on self-designated floor watchdogs to ensure that House rules were used fairly, look out for opportunities to manipulate procedures to the party's advantage, and delay when deemed necessary. Such watchdogs included the irascible H. R. Gross (IA), the "House's great nay-sayer" who objected to spending bills he deemed excessive and measures that gave perks to lawmakers; the procedurally brilliant Robert Bauman (MD), who led the "Bauman Group" of legislators (which included John Ashbrook of Ohio and John Rousselot of California) willing and able to "harass Democrats at every opportunity;" and Robert Walker, a major irritant for Democrats who could be as tenacious as a bulldog in fighting the majority party, often using clever procedural devices.[23] Many of the younger activist Republicans elected in the late 1970s, like Newt Gingrich, went further, encouraging broader and more organized efforts to throw monkey wrenches into House proceedings. But their work was often frowned upon by senior party members and their leadership, exposing divisions within the party over the utility of obstruction. And the majority invariably clamped down Republican delays with more rules revisions.[24] Democrats also began taking advantage of the floor rule, the set of instructions by which a bill is considered. By having the Rules Committee craft more restrictive floor rules, the majority limited the minority's right to offer amendments or make certain motions or objections that might delay matters.[25]

The infamous 1985 seating of a Democrat in a contested Indiana election was marked by notable delays from angry Republicans (and a walkout from the floor, discussed in the previous chapter), and it helped bolster the conservatives' case that obstruction was a necessary response to majority party tyranny.[26] It was, recalled one Republican leadership aide, "kind of a turning point that radicalized the conservatives." But a further level of acceptance toward obstruction was reached within the G.O.P. after the 1992 elections. Republicans felt both stymied and unfettered by their party's complete exclusion from power, and with the help of new, confrontation-minded members the party sponsored a series of initiatives designed to expand its floor rights and help it win elections, including the targeted use of obstruction.[27]

The roles of the parties reversed in 1995, and some embittered and frustrated minority Democrats took a page from the Republicans' dilatory playbook. They also developed new ways to block the floor; especially popular were repeated motions to rise or to adjourn (discussed below). Representatives like Barney Frank (MA) and Harold Volkmer (MO) served as floor watchdogs and occasional participants in dilatory campaigns. Democrats also tried to coordinate and generate party-wide support for obstruction. In June 1995, for instance, minority leaders directed a series of delaying tactics to protest the G.O.P. giving party-switcher Greg Laughlin (TX) a new seat on the powerful Ways and Means Committee, and in September 1997 the Democratic caucus endorsed using delay to force campaign-finance reform onto the floor. But it took time for many Democrats to accept obstruction as a legitimate tool. This was not so much because the party was demoralized or divided, but because, as one former leader put it, "it was kind of something not in our DNA." The minority's members were simply more accustomed to governing.[28]

Republicans picked up right where Democrats left off when they were sent back into the minority in 2006. G.O.P. whip Eric Cantor formed a "floor action team" of members willing to be floor objectors and who could act independently, and Robert Walker, now no longer in Congress, offered his services as an occasional informal advisor to the party on the use of floor procedure. Republicans made creative use of a range of procedures, including motions to rise, motions to adjourn, multiple amendments, and requests to switch a vote. In 2007 and 2008 especially, the G.O.P. seemed to benefit from being a newly minted minority that still remembered how to trip up the governing party. But their obstruction also reflected serious frustration with the resurgence of House Democrats, and especially with the majority's decision to stop bringing appropriation bills to the floor under open rules—whereby members of both parties had had free rein to offer amendments—because of Republican dilatory tactics.[29]

Such is the recent history of obstruction in the House. To understand why the minority party uses obstruction and delay, illustrate some common features of obstructive politics in the House, and demonstrate how effective they can be, I turn now to three noteworthy cases of procedural delay by the minority party since the late 1960s.

Three Cases of Significant House Obstruction

1. Election Debate Bill, October 1968. Though it happened a few years before the starting point of my analysis, the October 1968 mini-filibuster mounted by House Republicans was so remarkable in its audacity that it is worth mention. It also illustrates how collective concerns apart from winning power can motivate minority obstruction.

With Richard Nixon ahead in the autumn polls of 1968, Democrats desperately hoped that a televised debate between Nixon and their own presidential nominee, Hubert Humphrey, might give their candidate a much-needed boost. They especially wanted the debate to include a third candidate, conservative southerner George Wallace, to bolster Wallace's share of the vote and draw support away from Nixon. Unsurprisingly, Nixon opposed that idea, and though he agreed to debate Humphrey he doubtless remembered how pale and sweaty he had appeared in his own televised tête-à-tête against John F. Kennedy in the 1960 presidential race. Regardless, for any debate to occur without the participation of "minor or splinter parties," Congress would have to approve a temporary suspension of the federal "equal time" rule, which mandated that networks grant equal broadcast time to all prominent candidates for federal office.[30]

As Election Day approached, House Democrats pushed forward on a suspension of the equal-time rule that had already been approved by the Senate. But the House's version of the suspension explicitly allowed for a three-candidate debate. If that became law, Nixon would be forced to debate both Wallace and Humphrey. Alternatively, he could reject a debate altogether, but his own polling suggested that doing so might hurt his image among as many as one in five Americans.[31] Bryce Harlow, a legendary Washington lobbyist and close Nixon ally, asked a young ambitious Illinois Republican named Donald Rumsfeld to help stop the House bill. Rumsfeld was serving his third term in Congress and had already proven himself an effective vote counter and aggressive procedural fighter. In 1965 he had helped engineer the overthrow of his party's leader, Charlie Halleck, and had since become the head of a band of activist, pro-reform Republicans known as "Rumsfeld's Raiders." Rumsfeld was happy to oblige Harlow. Fighting the bill would put his group in the spotlight whether he succeeded or failed. But more importantly, Rumsfeld was among many in his party who were indignant about "the Democrats' last-minute attempt to jury-rig the rules," as he later described it. Plus, if he managed to kill the bill, the young congressman might help Nixon win.[32]

On October 8, as the chamber prepared to consider the debate legislation, Rumsfeld stood up and demanded a full reading by the House clerk of the previous day's *Journal*, the official record of House activities. As the clerk began to recite it, the minority party took advantage of the fact that many Democrats were absent from Washington, campaigning in their districts. Republicans quietly filed out of the chamber while Rumsfeld made a point of order that a quorum (majority) of the House was no longer present. The presiding officer upheld the point of order and issued a quorum call, a thirty-minute endeavor in which the clerk read the names of every single Representative to see who was absent. The Republicans came back to answer the call, but when the clerk resumed reading the *Journal*, they left again, and one of their members made another point of order of no quorum.

This exercise was repeated for hours. Democrats, increasingly flummoxed, complained mightily: one decried it as the "children's hour," and others accused Republicans of playing partisan politics. Rumsfeld countered that the slowdown had nothing to do with the debate bill at all, but rather was an effort to bring congressional reform legislation to the floor before the House adjourned. Finally, Speaker John McCormack ordered the doors of the chamber to be locked to keep Republicans from leaving. The presidential debate bill eventually passed, but only after what had become an unprecedented blockade of House business: the chamber had stayed in continuous session for an exhausting thirty-two hours, thanks in part to a record-breaking thirty-three quorum calls forced by the minority.[33]

Only sixteen Republicans made motions, objections, or points of order to maintain the filibuster, and as few as forty-two minority party members were needed to deny the House a quorum that day. But there are good reasons to consider the incident as one supported by the G.O.P. at large, not just a handful of its members. Though "tradition conscious" members of the party looked down upon what Rumsfeld had done, G.O.P. leader Gerald Ford "stood apart and cheered us on," according to Rumsfeld, and Ford defended his colleagues on the floor during the mini-filibuster. Also, the vast majority of voting Republicans (83%) supported their party's motion to recommit the debate bill, which would have eliminated the provision that all three presidential candidates appear in the same debate.[34]

Rumsfeld did not achieve the goal of killing the bill in the House, but he later took credit for having bought some time for Senate Republicans to successfully stop the measure until Congress adjourned. If true, the obstruction could well have been a factor in Nixon's extraordinarily narrow victory over Humphrey that November. It also imposed minimal costs on Rumsfeld's party. The G.O.P.'s reputation seemed untarnished by the event, as it won seats in the House that year, though not enough to win back the chamber. The House did change its rules in 1970 to eliminate the right of any individual to demand a full reading of the *Journal*—the motion that began the mini-filibuster that October day—but it chose not to abolish the right to note the absence of a quorum.[35]

2. *Foreign Aid Bill, July 1997*. When the majority gets a little too eager to steal credit and opportunities from the minority party, it risks a backlash. That is exactly what happened in the summer of 1997 when a group of minority party Democrats began making a series of delaying motions to protest a restrictive rule, one that denied one of their own members the right to offer an amendment under her own name.

When the Appropriations Committee cleared that year's foreign aid spending bill, it was the job of the Republican-led Rules Committee to craft the floor rule that dictated what amendments could be offered to the bill on the floor. Pro-choice Democrats were unhappy that an amendment would be allowed that banned funds for organizations providing abortions in other countries. Nancy Pelosi (CA), then a member of the Appropriations Committee, asked Rules if she could offer a pro-choice alternative amendment. The committee agreed—sort of. The amendment could be offered, it assented, but three Republicans, not Pelosi, would have the right to offer it.

Furious Democrats saw this as the most egregious example yet of the Rules Committee ignoring the requests of prominent minority party members to offer amendments to bills. They chose to protest with delay. An agriculture-spending bill was the next item up for consideration on the House floor, and not long after debate on the measure began Pelosi rose to demand a recorded vote on whether to begin considering the bill for amendments (known as entering the Committee of the Whole). When that vote was finished, Rep. Barney Frank moved to reconsider the vote, and the Republicans moved to table Frank's motion. That required another recorded vote. Three different Democrats then each made a motion for the committee to rise, meaning that the House would temporarily cease debating amendments, and they all demanded recorded votes on their motions, consuming yet more time. Each time, large majorities of Democrats voted against the G.O.P. After over two hours of nothing but votes, motions, and debate over the Democrats' complaints, Republicans had had enough of their "legislative water torture," and on the third motion to rise they voted with Democrats to end debate for the day.

Both Republicans and Democrats on Appropriations complained about the Rules Committee's unsporting move, and Rules' chairman, the irascible Gerald Solomon (NY), was put on the defensive. One week later, his committee backed down and produced a new rule for the bill. Pelosi was permitted to offer an amendment of her own, albeit not precisely the one she had originally wanted to propose.[36]

3. Housing and Iraq Spending Bills, May 2008. Procedural innovation and creativity—discovering little-used rules or making novel use of existing rules—are important features of obstructive strategy. In May 2008, minority Republicans cleverly utilized a rule that allowed any lawmaker to cast or change his or her vote after the expiration of official voting time. The rule was presumably designed as a convenience to individuals of either party who come late to the floor, but the G.O.P. took advantage of it to extend a vote longer than usual.

House Republicans had a specific gripe. Democratic leaders, it was rumored, planned to draft a supplemental spending bill for the war in Iraq, send it to the floor without prior review by a legislative committee, and debate it under a closed rule prohibiting all amendments. The minority party was also upset more generally at the closed nature of the legislative process under the Democrats, which gave Republicans few chances to offer amendments or otherwise shape legislation—including appropriations bills, which were traditionally considered under open floor rules. As Minority Leader John Boehner later explained in a floor speech: "No amendments, no substitutes, no motions to recommit. Last night, we get rid of all the Special Orders. At some point, the majority has an obligation to treat the minority with respect. It is not happening, and that's why we're going to continue to wage this fight to be heard on this floor and represent nearly half of the American people that we're here to represent."[37] From the perspective of the majority party, however, time was running short to pass legislation before the November elections, and Republicans had already used many dilatory maneuvers against bills in the 110th Congress, hardly warranting any generosity on their part.

Just as Democrats had done in July 1997, Republicans picked the first target they could: in this case, a mortgage-assistance bill to combat the nation's emerging housing crisis. On May 7, as the House considered the floor rule for the bill and other proposals, Republicans made seven motions to adjourn, each subject to a fifteen-minute vote, and multiple requests to reconsider votes on various bills and resolutions that were each followed by a fifteen-minute vote to table the request. It was well past 5 p.m., with the House yet to debate the mortgage bill, when Rep. Tom Price of Georgia got up and made yet another motion to adjourn. This time, however, nearly sixty Republicans cast their ballots late or switched their votes. What would have been a fifteen-minute vote took nearly twice as long to finish. This last delay rankled Democratic leaders and prompted a sharp rebuke from House Majority Leader Steny Hoyer, who lamented an "abuse of process." Republicans, undaunted, offered three more motions to rise or adjourn before the House finally adjourned.[38]

The day's delaying tactics were clearly supported by the minority party and its leadership. Though less than a majority of the G.O.P. participated in the last-minute voting scheme, over half of them voted for Price's motion to adjourn, and an average of 83% of the party cast ballots in favor of the day's many motions to rise, motions to adjourn, and votes to table requests to reconsider votes. Minority Leader Boehner was among the G.O.P. leaders who voted for these motions and vocally supported them.

If Republicans hoped to open up the legislative process to grant their party more opportunities, the delaying maneuvers were a failure. Democrats continued to use closed or restrictive rules on legislation the rest of the year. The Iraq spending bill still went to the floor without consideration by a committee, and only three floor amendments, all endorsed by Democratic Party leaders, were made in order. But Republicans did succeed in delaying the housing bill overnight, and the Iraq bill was put off for a week (though conservative Democrats, unhappy with the measure for other reasons, were partly to blame). Republicans would also use strategic voting on an amendment to the Iraq measure to put Democrats on the spot. As for electoral consequences of the delay, there appeared to be none. Republicans lost seats in the November elections and most polls showed no significant change in attitudes toward Congress or either congressional party after the day's events.[39] Nonetheless, the Republicans' tactics did garner some negative press coverage, albeit for themselves. One of their motions to reconsider a previous vote, if passed, would have required a second vote on a resolution honoring the nation's mothers. The symbolism was too tempting for *Washington Post* columnist Dana Milbank to pass up; he described it as a Republican "assault on mothers" coming just before Mother's Day.[40]

The Use of Motions to Rise or Adjourn

Though most procedural motions in the House (or in any legislature, for that matter) may be used for more than one purpose, two motions in particular are unambiguous in having the primary effect of slowing down floor activity. These are the *motion to adjourn* and the *motion to rise*.[41] The motion to adjourn asks that the House end its deliberations. The motion to rise interrupts the House while meeting as the Committee of the Whole, when the chamber considers and debates amendments to bills. Both motions are effective delaying tools because they (a) are privileged under the rules, giving them precedence over other motions; (b) are subject to a recorded vote, which takes time to complete; and (c) threaten to temporarily halt floor proceedings should either pass.[42]

The solid line in Figure 4.1 tracks the number of recorded floor votes that were cast on motions to rise or adjourn, made by a member of the House minority party, from the 92nd Congress (1971–72) through the 112th Congress (2011–12). As can be seen, these motions became more common starting in 1991–92, at times reaching considerable heights (as in 1997–98 and 2007–8). But they have never dominated floor voting. Less than 6% of all recorded votes in a given

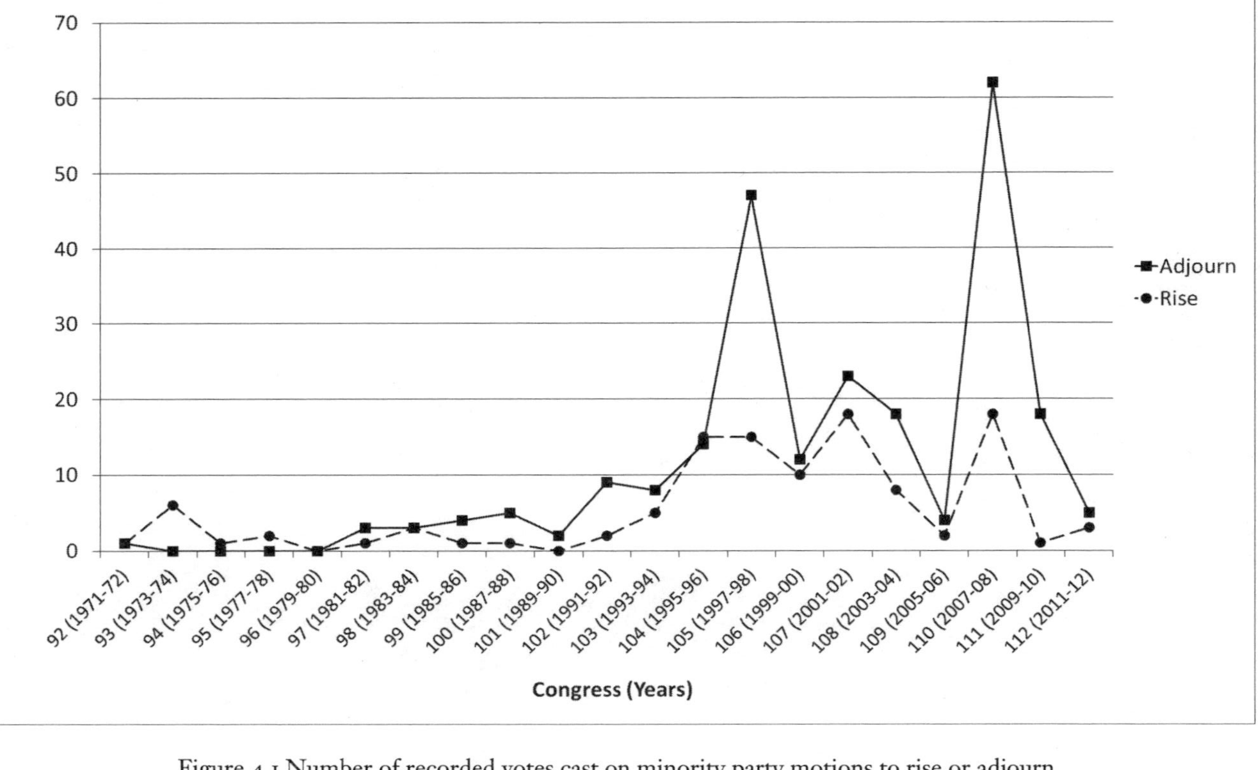

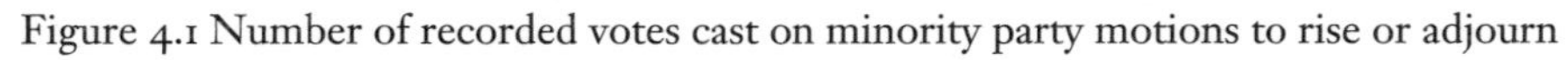
Figure 4.1 Number of recorded votes cast on minority party motions to rise or adjourn

Congress have been cast on these motions, and they fluctuate greatly in frequency from one Congress to another.

More important for delaying purposes than the overall number of motions is the extent to which they are clustered together to better slow things down. As shown in Figure 4.2, clustering became more common starting in the early 1990s. In the 111th Congress (2009–10), for instance, over eight in ten motions to rise or adjourn occurred within one day of another such motion. (Clustering did drop off precipitously following the Republicans' capture of the House in 2010, as did the number of motions overall, as minority Democrats' interest in the use of motions to rise or adjourn seemed to slacken.) Most of the time, this clustering occurs on a single event, issue, or point of conflict. Clustered motions to rise or adjourn are an example of what Don Wolfensberger, a scholar of House rules, coined the "procedural vote pummeling ploy."[43]

Motions to rise or adjourn may be made by a single minority party member for personal reasons, or on behalf of collective party concerns.[44] One reasonable way to tell the difference is to see how many party members vote for a motion. If a majority of the minority does so, one can reasonably infer that the motion is seen as representing the party's broader interests. Since 1991, 48% of these kinds of motions have fit this description or have otherwise been made by a member of the minority party leadership; their variation by Congress is shown in Figure 4.3.[45] Sometimes leaders take a hands-off approach to these motions, but other times they coordinate their use or, if they believe them to be counterproductive, try to get members not to offer them. As minority whip, Republican Eric Cantor would occasionally have to tell a lawmaker, "I know you're mad that Rules denied your amendment, but rather than making a motion to adjourn, why not quiz a vulnerable Democrat on the floor instead?"[46]

To figure out exactly which collective party concern (if any) is associated with motions to rise or adjourn supported by a majority of the minority, I look at the justifications offered by the sponsor of each motion. Over three-fourths (79%) were followed or preceded by the sponsor explaining his or her motive, either in the press or on

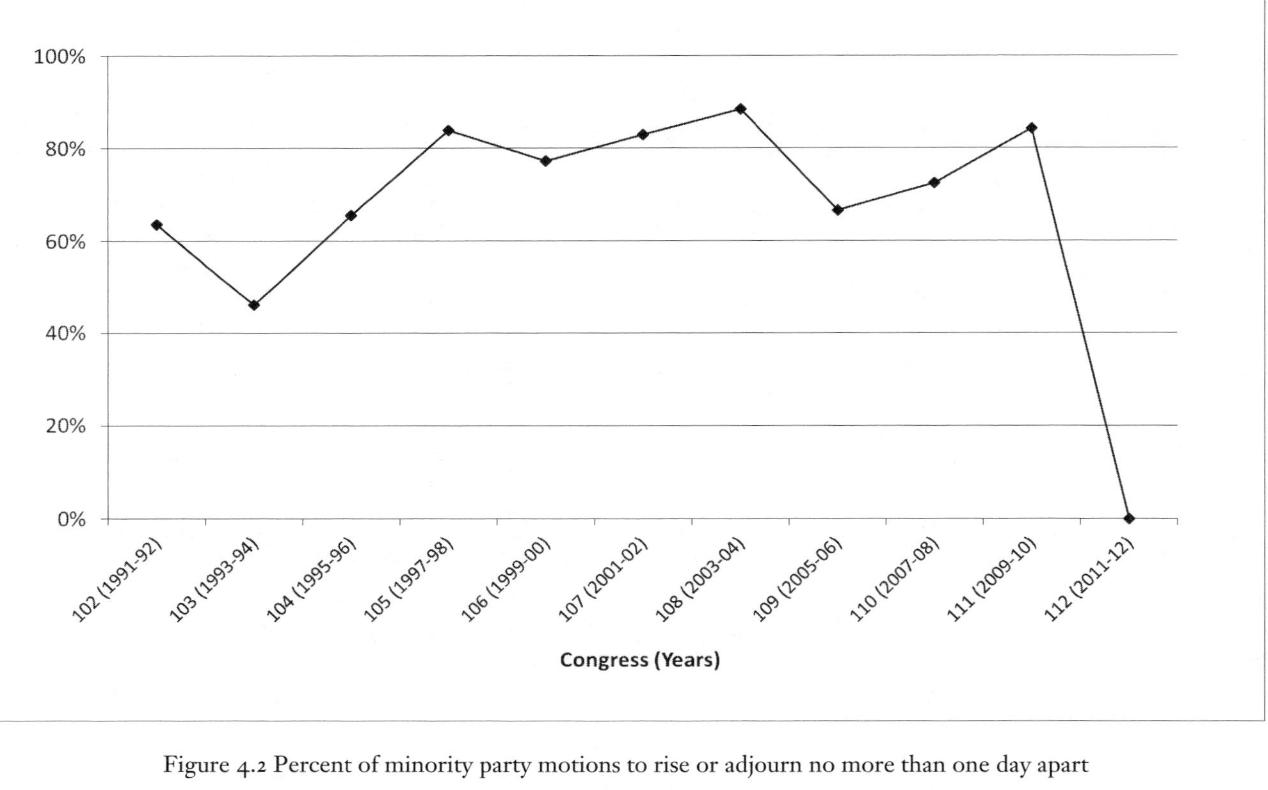

Figure 4.2 Percent of minority party motions to rise or adjourn no more than one day apart

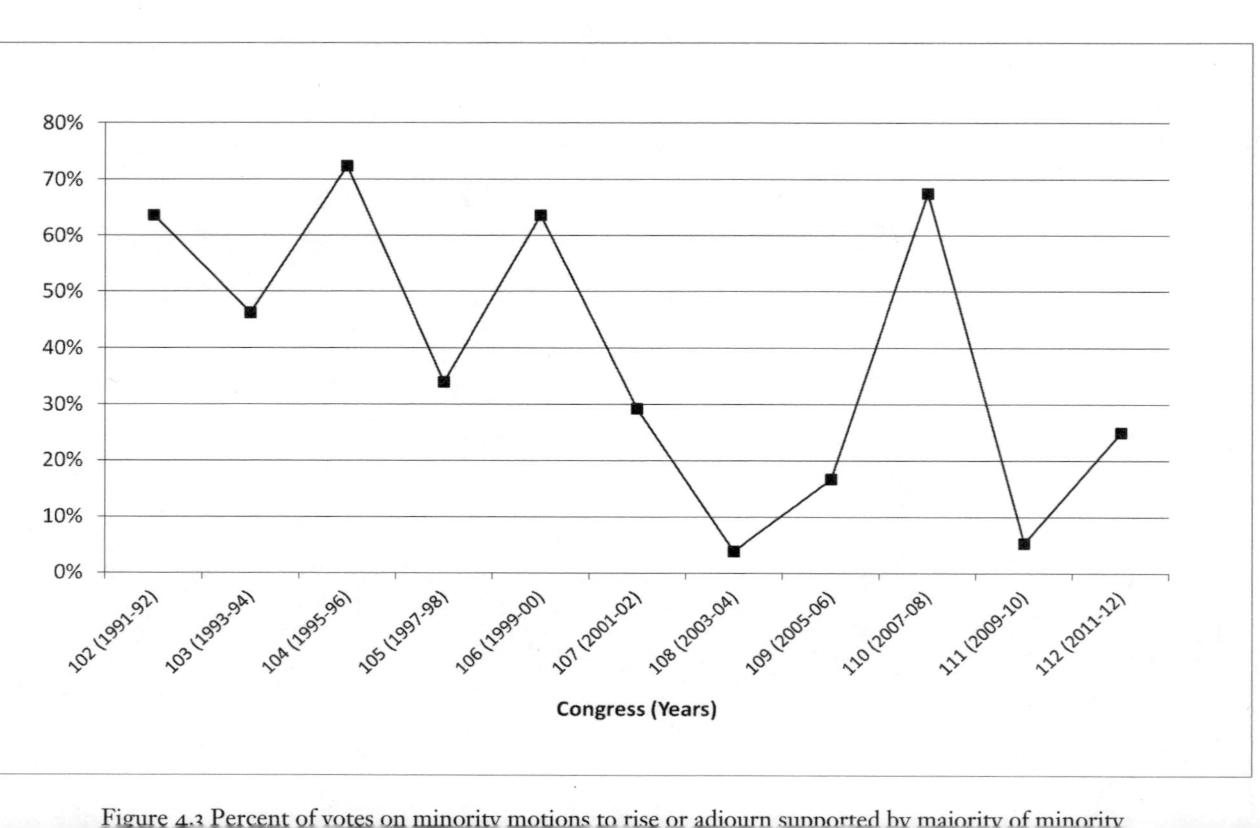

Figure 4.3 Percent of votes on minority motions to rise or adjourn supported by majority of minority

the House floor. Using these explanations has obvious drawbacks: a stated justification may differ from, or be only one facet of, the "true" reason a motion is offered, or might not explain why rank-and-file lawmakers vote for the motion.[47] But I believe such circumstances are too infrequent to disqualify this potentially revealing measurement.

Nearly all (93%) of the motions for which an explanation was offered fell into at least one of five categories (see Table 4.2).[48] Nearly half were a reaction against *a particular floor rule*, or the procedures

Table 4.2. Stated Reasons for a Motion to Rise/Adjourn and Their Connection with Minority Party Concerns, 1993–2012

	Minority party concern				
Explanation for issuing motion	Majority status	Policy	Procedural rights and powers	Successful presidential party	Percent (N)[a]
Unfair floor rule	Perhaps	Perhaps	Yes	Perhaps	48% (49)
Ignoring "regular order"	No	Yes	Yes	Perhaps	28% (29)
Other abuse of power	Perhaps	No	Yes	Perhaps	22% (22)
Majority's legislative agenda	Yes	Yes	No	Perhaps	9% (9)
Opposition to bill	Yes	Yes	No	Perhaps	7% (7)

Note: Counts only motions supported by majority of minority party or made by a minority party leader.

a. Excludes "other" (7%, or 7, of total); sum is greater than 100% because some motions (21 total) were accompanied by more than one explanation.

under which a bill was to be considered. A floor rule is a powerful tool in the hands of the majority party, since it can curtail the time permitted for debate, specify what amendments are allowed, and even enact legislation automatically, and its approval is considered a test of party loyalty. The complaint that a floor rule is restrictive or unfair is closely related to the protection of minority party rights: in this case, the right to offer amendments or speak on a legislative proposal. Depending on the rule and what minority party members hope to propose or discuss on the floor, obstruction so justified may be also relevant to the goal of winning elections (if the rule prevents what might be an embarrassing vote for the majority—although floor rules themselves are of little interest to the public, with rare exceptions).[49] It may also be relevant to the party's collective policy concerns (if the rule blocked a proposal expected to pass) or to presidential politics (if the underlying bill is related to the White House or a presidential campaign).

The next most common justification for these motions is *a failure to follow "regular order,"* meaning any instance in which the majority party violated (or was expected to violate) the spirit, if not the letter, of the rules of the House. Examples include breaking a pre-existing agreement of how a bill will be considered, scheduling a floor vote when many lawmakers will be absent or busy, or leaders revising a bill without committee approval. While unlikely to do much for the goal of winning elections, this kind of delay is related to policy-making (provided that the violation of regular order prevented a minority party preferred outcome), defending the rights of the minority party, and possibly presidential politics (again, depending on what the legislative consequences of irregular order might be).

Third, a complaint about *some other "abuse" of power* is associated with a number of motions to rise or adjourn. This is a claim that the majority party has misused or is likely to misuse its authority in some way, other than with floor procedure or the consideration of legislation on the floor. Examples include the questionable seating of a winner in a contested election, unfair reprimanding of a lawmaker, expanding the membership of a powerful committee to include a party-switcher, or threatening to change the rules in the majority party's favor. As with the first two categories, this sort of explanation most clearly involves the minority party's rights and powers in the House. While not directly related to the policy goals of the minority, these motions could also be motivated by presidential politics (depending on the issue at hand) or be seen as a way to improve the party's electoral fortunes by inspiring the minority's base supporters. If the abuse is considered especially egregious by outside observers, it could theoretically tarnish the reputation of the majority party as well.[50]

A small percentage of motions (9%) were used to *register opposition to the legislative agenda*.[51] These motions are best understood as attempts to either shape policy outcomes (by trying to get an alternative agenda to the floor) or influence the next election by bringing attention to the minority's policy agenda—or, if that agenda comes to the floor, forcing vulnerable majority party members to cast potentially difficult votes. By the same token, they can be used to help bolster the platform of the party's presidential candidate or remonstrate against a congressional attack on the White House, depending on the issue. (Democrats, for instance, used a motion to adjourn to protest the impeachment of Bill Clinton in December 1996, and Republicans used it twice in 2007 when the majority sought contempt resolutions against Bush White House employees.) Minority parties are not accorded agenda-setting powers in the House, so these motions are not offered to protect existing minority rights.

Finally, a handful of motions are explicitly justified as part of the minority's *opposition to a specific bill*. These are closely related to the minority's goal of enacting its preferred policy over that of the majority, as well as the goal of majority status (if the public agrees with the minority's opposition). They could help the presidential party, depending on the bill that the House is considering, but they are not related to the minority's procedural rights.

In short, the House minority party's collective concerns can explain why it uses and endorses most motions to rise or adjourn. Though achieving majority status is goal number one for the party, that goal cannot explain some important instances of minority delay.

Of course, as already noted, legislators may not be fully honest about why they make these motions. Many could be quietly inspired by opposition to the substance of a bill. It is unlikely, for instance, that Democrats were protesting only the procedures for considering a G.O.P. prescription drug plan in 2000, since they also detested the underlying bill; or that in May 2007 Republicans objected solely to the process for debating a children's health care bill they so deeply disliked. There is also an intriguing correspondence between the frequency of delaying tactics and the degree of legislative activity of congressional majorities, such as in the 110th Congress. The minority may sometimes be trying to impede an assertive majority party for its own sake, irrespective of the specific issue, whether out of hopes for electoral or policy gains or simply to halt the majority's momentum and rebuild a sense of unity and confidence.

In fact, the desire to increase party unity is an important reason for offering motions to rise or adjourn. After all, they give every member of the party an opportunity to express himself or herself via a recorded vote and give activist members something to do to register their opposition. Certain issues, like the violation of "regular order" or the abuse of power, are good opportunities to improve internal party morale and harmony because they indict the majority with committing especially galling or unfair behavior. Democrats' use of these motions after Greg Laughlin was given a new seat on Ways and Means in 1995, as one journalist wrote, "brought new unity" to the party, and Rep. Richard Durbin (D-IL) explained that "being in the minority, we need events to inspire and mobilize us. We've just caught a second wind."[52] But as noted before, an excessive or poorly timed use of motions to rise or adjourn can also lead to dissention and grumbling among the party's ranks. On the motion to adjourn, for instance, one House Republican warned that it "aggravates everybody. Everybody suffers when that's done . . . You don't make friends and influence people by making motions to adjourn."[53]

How well do these motions work in helping the minority address its collective concerns? Table 4.3 summarizes the political outcomes that followed each of the 134 motions to rise or adjourn between 1993 and 2012 that was offered by a minority party member and supported by a majority of the minority party. Fully 38% (51) of those motions were immediately followed by some outcome that favored the minority party, such as a more open floor rule, a significant delay (or even the defeat) of a bill, or a change in the agenda. Since a number

Table 4.3. The Consequences of Motions to Rise/Adjourn Supported by Majority of Minority Party, 1993–2012

Outcome	Percent of individual instances (N)	Percent of sets of motions (N)[a]
Bill altered	6% (8)	2% (1)
Bill defeated	1% (1)	2% (1)
Bill delayed	13% (18)	8% (4)
Change in agenda	1% (2)	4% (2)
Change in schedule	3% (4)	2% (1)
More debate time provided	2% (3)	4% (2)
More open rule/ amendments allowed	6% (8)	6% (3)
Rules/rights of minority protected	5% (7)	2% (1)
No change	35% (47)	60% (31)
Unclear	27% (36)	12% (6)
TOTAL	134	52

a. Each set is defined by one or more motions to rise or adjourn occurring at a proximate time period and used to achieve the same political, procedural, or policy outcome. A set is counted as being supported by a majority of the minority party if at least one motion in the set was supported by a majority of the minority party.

of these motions were clustered together, it might be more reasonable to look at outcomes by sets of motions, with each set defined as the group of all minority-offered motions to rise or adjourn that occurred on or near the same day, that had the same stated objective, and that included at least one motion supported by a majority of the minority party. For all 52 such sets (which range in size from 1 motion to 16), a somewhat smaller but still non-trivial percentage (28%, or 15) led to political outcomes favorable to the minority. Even taking into consideration that the outcome may have been less than, or different from, what the minority wanted, and that a causal relationship cannot be proven by this data alone, the finding still suggests that collectively supported minority party dilatory motions in the House may change political outcomes.[54]

Conclusion

Minority party delay, as we have seen, is not unique to Congress' upper chamber. In the House of Representatives minority parties also consult the rule book for ways to impede the legislative process as a means of getting what they want. Their collective concerns, not to mention the need for action—especially in response to frustrating or infuriating situations, as the minority often finds itself in—explain a good deal of why we see obstruction in the House. And even though it cannot kill bills nearly as easily as in the Senate, obstruction does sometimes bear fruit for the minority party. This is especially so if used when the majority is eager to wrap up its work before adjournment. The Rumsfeld-led ploy to use quorum calls in October 1968 is one example of the importance of delay coming late in the congressional calendar; in another example from 1978, Robert Walker demanded a full reading of a bill that would have created the Department of Education, and, joined by Republicans filing almost one hundred amendments to the bill, he forced Democrats to pull the measure.[55] The House's rules may prohibit these two particular gambits today, but both examples, along with others discussed in this chapter, suggest that a determined minority party may always find means to successfully block or postpone votes in the House.

In fact, the use of dilatory tactics, particularly motions to rise and adjourn, has become more common in recent years. But the reader should not infer that obstruction or delay by the minority party has come to dominate House politics. Minority parties do many other things besides obstruct, and the amount of obstruction in the chamber is a far cry from what it was in the late nineteenth century. Still, the data and analysis presented here suggest that minority parties are readily willing to draw from their procedural toolbox to slow down Congress. They raise questions about how fairly majority parties govern the House, as well as how much stake minority parties should have in a well-functioning legislature—questions I explore further in the concluding chapter.

five
LEGISLATING

Any time any member of the Committee wants something,
or wants to get a bill out, we get it out for him . . . Makes no
difference—Republican or Democrat. We are all
Americans when it comes to that.
—Member of the House Public Works Committee, late 1960s

Republicans are just going to have to get it through
their heads that they are not going to write legislation!
—Speaker Thomas P. "Tip" O'Neill to John J. Rhodes, 1970s

Legislators are supposed to legislate. But no legislative body gives all its members equal power to do so. In the House of Representatives, it is the members of one group—the majority party—who are granted disproportionate say in the lawmaking process. While this may make sense in terms of efficiency and democratic theory, it is also the core source of frustration for the minority party. It largely explains why the minority today focuses far less attention on shaping the law than on its other collective concerns, and why it has become especially eager in recent years to wrest control of the House from its partisan opponents.

In the early 1970s it was not unreasonable to expect individual members of the House minority party, if not the party as a whole, to have some opportunity to make policy in a meaningful way. Certain committees, like Public Works and Armed Services, had members from the majority who shared the sentiment expressed in the epigraph above that one's party affiliation made "no difference" in eligibility to participate in committee decisions. Floor proceedings were relatively open, allowing any individual of either party to offer amendments to bills with the hope of influencing national policy. And some of the nation's most significant laws were the result of new ideas and initiatives by minority Republicans in the 1970s and early '80s. The quintessential example from that era was President Reagan's dramatic 1981 budget proposal to cut taxes and social programs. His proposal not only passed the House over majority Democrats' opposition but was the culmination of legislation first introduced in 1977 by a member of the minority, Jack Kemp (R-NY), beginning a major shift in the Republican Party's platform toward an emphasis on tax reduction.[1]

Yet even in the late 1970s legislative opportunities were starting to shrink for congressional Republicans. And the House today is not a place where the minority party can expect to have much say in policy-making. The right to offer amendments is frequently limited, minority party bills rarely see the light of day, and majority party leaders insist that their members vote against the minority on principle.[2] Speaker O'Neill's admonition to Minority Leader Rhodes, it seems, expresses a belief that is all too prevalent.

Nonetheless, minority members of the House still introduce bills, offer amendments, and propose legislative alternatives. Why? For today's minority party, legislative tactics are seldom about making laws. More often they are an effort to convey symbolic messages, bolster the status of the White House or a presidential candidate, protect the minority party's rights, or create a public record for the next campaign. But members of the minority are also expected to legislate and often genuinely want to. And evidence suggests that the House minority can wield policy influence using several legislative tools at its disposal: most often to kill bills, but sometimes to pass or modify bills to its liking.

Before turning to that evidence, I first review the basic politics of minority party legislating and how the party's lawmaking activity has changed since 1970 as its opportunities to shape legislation gradually diminished. I look next at some of the essential legislative procedures and tactics available to the minority to bring about change both positive (i.e. passing bills) and negative (i.e. blocking them). These include introducing bills and amendments, voting on the floor, offering a motion to recommit (often called the party's "last bite at the apple" to change a bill), and introducing a discharge petition (to eject legislation from committee). The latter two procedures are used almost entirely by the minority party and are relatively protected from infringement, and thanks largely to the innovations of the minority have transformed in use and purpose since the 1970s.[3]

The Politics of Minority Party Legislating

The most obvious reason why the minority party tries to legislate is to influence policy: to make new laws or keep potential laws off the books. There is always the prospect, however slim, that the minority might kill a majority party bill or pass a well-written amendment or bill of its own. But there are other ways that successful legislating can benefit the party. A legislative win gives it the chance to tout its success in the next election. If unexpected, it could (in the words of Congressman Henry Waxman) "force the other side to have to fall back and regroup, in the process sowing doubt and discord in its ranks." Legislation may occasionally touch upon or be related to the minority's privileges in the chamber, and some legislative procedures treasured by the minority may be used to ensure they are not eliminated due to neglect. The minority can also vote to sustain a same-party president's veto or stop initiatives that would politically damage him or a presidential candidate.[4]

Legislating comes with some risks, however. Procedures that successfully trump the policy goals of the majority party are tempting targets for removal or curtailment. In 2009, for instance, House Democrats banned motions to recommit from being phrased in a way that could covertly kill a bill after Republicans used them for that purpose numerous times (discussed below). There is also a potential trade-off for the minority between legislating and achieving electoral goals. Even when marginal changes in policy are the best the minority party can hope for, noted Charles O. Jones, "victories of this type [may] result in general satisfaction with the performance of the majority." And the minority often acquires more influence at the expense of losing bragging rights with voters. "It's amazing how much you can get done if you don't care who gets the credit," as one House Republican observed in the mid-1980s.[5]

The prospects to shape policy through legislating have become more remote for the House's out-party since the 1970s. True, there are always potential pockets of influence available within certain committees or on issues about which the majority cares little. But on the floor of the House the governing party routinely crafts special floor rules that exclude the minority from offering amendments, permit only "safe" amendments, shield bills from points of order, or structure voting so as to reduce the number of defections. For its part, the minority party is less likely to offer bills or amendments because it expects them to pass. Rather, it does so to convey the party's position to voters, draw attention to minority party rights, raise issues salient to the White House or a presidential election, force majority party members to cast politically hazardous votes, or bring disagreements within the majority out in the open.[6]

Whether a minority party tries to make policy, send political messages, or both via the legislative process is contingent on a slew of factors that vary by issue and by Congress. The size of the minority party, its degree of internal ideological agreement, the kinds of issues that divide both parties, the House's agenda, what matters most to the minority's members or core constituents, and the opportunities afforded to the minority under the rules of the House all determine the minority's legislative leverage and what it will do with the procedures available to it. Minority parties with legislatively minded members, or with little hope of winning back power, may be more drawn toward legislating if circumstances permit. An aide to one moderate Republican recalled that his boss had some sway over legislative outcomes in 2007 and 2008 because Bush was still president and his party, though in the minority, was fairly large. After the 2008 elections, however, "all of it went away. And I don't mean most of it—I mean *all* of it." The House, he added sardonically, "became a pretty desolate and wonderfully boring place to work." The desire to legislate proved to be a particularly big problem for House Democrats after the 1994 election ended their forty-year-long monopoly on power. One former Democratic leader recalled that his colleagues "needed to get beyond the premise that had moved them to run in the first place: to govern and to legislate." Even ten months after the election, many had not made that psychological adjustment. When Republicans put together a bill in the fall of 1995 that would trim Medicare costs, some Democrats argued that their party had to come up with a Medicare bill of its own. Complained a Democratic staffer at the time, "We have a problem in trying to convince our members that their mind-set has to change . . . Republicans are not interested in any alternatives we come up with."[7]

The behavior of other players in the political arena matter, too. The president, an integral part of the legislative process, is especially important. If a same-party president is in office, he may be able to help the minority win votes by using the bully pulpit and lobbying lawmakers on his party's behalf. Meanwhile, the minority party's primary legislative mission with a chief executive of the same party is usually to support the president's policy agenda. In his first speech to the G.O.P. conference after being selected party leader in December 1980, Robert Michel declared that "our bottom line has got to be the enactment of the Reagan program." In the next Congress, with the help of Rep. Trent Lott's (MS) impressive new vote-counting operation, House Republicans followed Michel's exhortation "to help strategize and execute commando raids for votes from the other side on specific pieces of legislation." Especially heartening for a minority party is if its proposals become the basis for the president's agenda, as happened to Jack Kemp's tax-cutting plan of the late 1970s.[8]

The role of supporting player to the president is not always easy for the minority party to perform. Under divided government, a minority party president often makes deals with the congressional party in power—deals that can be distasteful to the minority. The result is an unpalatable choice for the minority's members between disloyalty to the White House and compromise on policy principles. Lott, for instance, felt compelled to whip on behalf of President Reagan's 1985 tax bill despite his own deep dislike for the measure. Five years later, George H. W. Bush broke his "no new taxes" pledge to craft a major deficit-reduction package with majority Democrats, splitting the House G.O.P.; many Republicans voted against it, contributing to its initial defeat. Five years after that, minority party Democrats "went ballistic" when Bill Clinton proposed cuts to future Medicare spending. California Democrat Pete Stark complained that "I've been jumping off a bridge every night for" the president, but "when I jumped this morning, somebody forgot to tie my bungee rope to the bridge." Many minority Republicans detested George W. Bush's 2008 emergency economic bailout bill, and because scores of them (plus some Democrats) voted against it, the bill failed, sending the stock market into a panic. During the difficult 2011 negotiations between President Obama and Republicans over raising the debt limit, Democratic leaders in the House were often left out of the discussions and complained, with some justification, that Obama was surrendering too readily on liberal priorities. Yet Minority Leader Nancy Pelosi admitted to Obama that he had an advantage, for "you are our president, and we are in a time of crisis."[9]

Minority party unity, particularly voting unity, is often essential to the successful deployment of legislative tactics. Frank Wolf (R-VA) put it best in a 1993 speech begging his colleagues to oppose a Democratic bill allowing federal workers to participate in more political activities, to which no amendments were permitted: "If we do not stick together as Republicans, then we will not have any self respect . . . If you do not have the courage to vote to defeat this bill whereby a member of the minority can have an opportunity to offer an amendment, then I want to tell you something: we are always going to be in the minority because we will never, never stick together."[10] One reason unity is so important is the leverage it provides against both the majority party and the president, particularly if the majority party is unlikely to go along with the chief executive. Minority Leader Pelosi angrily warned the White House in July 2011 that because so many Republicans (particularly its Tea Party freshmen) were willing to default on the debt, Obama had to negotiate with House Democrats to get enough votes to pass a debt limit increase. Democrats would eventually play hardball with a G.O.P. desperate for votes to pass the final debt-limit plan: Pelosi did not whip on its behalf, Minority Whip Steny Hoyer initially refused to promise more than twenty-five Democratic votes for it, and the minority party withheld its support until the very last minute.[11]

Innovators and entrepreneurs within the minority are also an important source of successful legislative proposals, strategies, and tactics. In addition to Jack Kemp, lawmakers whose ideas managed to become law despite hailing from the minority include Henry Hyde (R-IL), whose proposal to ban federal funding for abortions has been adopted by Congress every year since 1976, and Dick Armey, whose initiative to divest the military of excess facilities was mentioned in Chapter 1.[12] Subgroups within the minority also innovate. The Republican Study Committee (RSC), which includes the G.O.P.'s more ideologically right-leaning members, has as one of its primary missions "to enact conservative policy into law" (in the words of a top RSC aide), which sometimes means coming up with unorthodox ways to legislate. It was the RSC that originated a plan to strategically vote "present" on an amendment to a 2008 spending bill that provided funds for the war in Iraq, forcing anti-war majority party Democrats to either vote for the war funding (angering their liberal constituents in the process) or let the amendment die and face criticism for abandoning American troops in mid-deployment. As might be expected, however, innovators with strong views on policy matters can be as much a problem for party leaders as an asset. The RSC, for instance, staunchly opposed President Bush's 2008 bailout package, complicating efforts to pass it. The year before, when one RSC staffer e-mailed Republicans on the floor to warn about revenue increases in a pending G.O.P. motion to recommit, "you start[ed] seeing some clustering of members, pointing to their BlackBerrys," recalled a staffer, "and all of a sudden you start[ed] seeing Republicans switch from yes to no." The motion was defeated, to the annoyance of minority party leaders.[13]

Minority Party Legislating since 1971

By many accounts, the House minority party had at least some share of policy-making influence in the early 1970s. Naturally, it was not to the degree that the majority party could boast of. Writing in 1970, Charles O. Jones observed that as a rule "minority party leaders will have to settle for victories that are not dramatic, victories that come in subcommittees and committees, in having clarifying amendments adopted, in minor concessions in conference committees." "We had success at the sufferance of the Democrats," explained one G.O.P. staffer for Minority Leader Gerald Ford. "They were willing to consider some watering down of ideas in order to not have drag-out fights on the floor . . . It was frustrating, but it was the way the system worked." Nonetheless, bills were largely open to floor amendments and "minority members on most committees share[d] in the decision making in all its stages," wrote David Mayhew in 1974.[14] Cross-party voting was not uncommon either. And minority party leaders since at least the mid-1960s had been actively looking for ways to develop what Ford called "constructive Republican alternatives" on policy. The House Republican Policy Committee, first formed in 1949, was responsible for developing and proposing these alternatives, though in 1971 it had no paid employees and "a borrowed staff of four."[15]

Legislative opportunities began to vanish in the latter half of the decade as majority Democrats became increasingly liberal, granted their leaders and party organizations more power over procedure and lawmaking, and put greater emphasis on internal cohesion. They eliminated certain House procedures like the quorum call that could delay proceedings, robbing the minority of a bargaining tool and a way to buy time to build winning coalitions.[16] More significantly, the G.O.P. lost influence on legislative committees. The majority party began issuing specific directives to committees and put the party caucus in charge of determining committee assignments, and when the caucus voted to remove three chairmen for disloyalty in 1975, it became crystal clear to the remaining chairs that they were to obey the dictates of the Democratic majority. That same year Democrats reversed their agreement from the year before to guarantee Republicans one-third of all investigative staff on committees and ban a committee chair's use of proxy voting by absent Democrats. Perhaps most crippling to the minority was the growth of special floor rules that could block amendments, limit debate time, and set up votes so that the majority could win more easily. Some of these moves targeted not Republicans but conservative Democratic troublemakers and defectors,[17] but others were a direct response to the minority exploiting the rules in ways that slowed down debate and improved its chances of policy victory. For instance, the number of amendments offered on the House floor nearly doubled from the 92nd Congress (1971–72) to the 93rd Congress (1973–74), and the percent of those offered by the minority party increased from 29% to 44%. Regardless, this more restrictive environment augured ill for the minority party's future as a legislative player, as the above quote by Speaker O'Neill bluntly spelled out.[18]

One way Republicans tried to overcome these hindrances was by improving their methods for rounding up votes. In the 1970s, G.O.P. whip Bob Michel began employing computerized calls and a team of members stationed at the chamber's doors to instruct legislators on floor business and lobby for support, and Michel used these new techniques to help defeat a major Democratic labor picketing bill in 1977. When Trent Lott became whip in 1981, he revamped the whip system so that it was, in his words, organized "like a battle group of Napoleon's army," and Republicans soon began whipping on more recorded votes than in the past.[19]

With creativity, persistence, sufficient disunity in the majority party, and the right political issue (and, if available, lobbying help from a friendly White House or outside interest groups), Republicans could find ways to shape policy or at least force politically helpful matters to the floor. The passage of the 1981 Reagan budget bill, which required defeating a restrictive floor rule and adopting a new, more amenable rule, was one example. The surprise approval in 1984 of a Republican motion that enacted President Reagan's crime bill, a measure that had been bottled up in committee, was another. The G.O.P. needed some votes from Democrats to win these gambits, however, and starting in the 98th Congress (1983–84) the majority party voted with greater unity than the minority, a trend that has continued ever since (see Figure 5.1).[20] More exasperating to the minority was when Democrats violated accords with Republicans or bent the House's rules to benefit themselves. A vivid case in point was the passage of a welfare bill in October 1987 that required a creative, temporary "adjournment" of the House and a quarter-hour extension of the voting clock, during which time an infuriated Lott "pounded the rostrum in the well of the House until it bent." Conference chair Dick Cheney (WY) later replayed footage of the event to his colleagues because "it really gets the troops whipped up again," he explained, but Lott had had enough: he left the House to run for a Senate seat.[21]

Meanwhile, the percent of floor rules that significantly limited amendments and alternatives to Democratic bills jumped steeply from 20% to 50% after 1990, as shown by the bar graph in Figure 5.1.[22] This tightening noose constricted the Republicans' ability to use legislative tools and conduct debate on the floor to achieve party objectives. Members of the minority decided that, whereas they "could once win half a loaf by dealing with Democrats," wrote Connelly and Pitney, "now they had to settle for crumbs." The expectation that the congressional G.O.P. should support a Republican president hindered to some extent the minority's ability to fight constrictive floor rules. In mid-1991, for instance, party members chose not to challenge a restrictive rule on a civil rights bill because George H. W. Bush (and Republican leaders) endorsed the measure. But the 1992 election put the party into the "deep minority" and ended twelve years in which, as Minority Leader Michel later put it, "the White House position was automatically considered the Republican position."

The G.O.P. passed new party rules designed to increase internal unity and strengthen its leadership.[23] It also improved its tactical coordination; for instance, Republicans mounted a campaign against

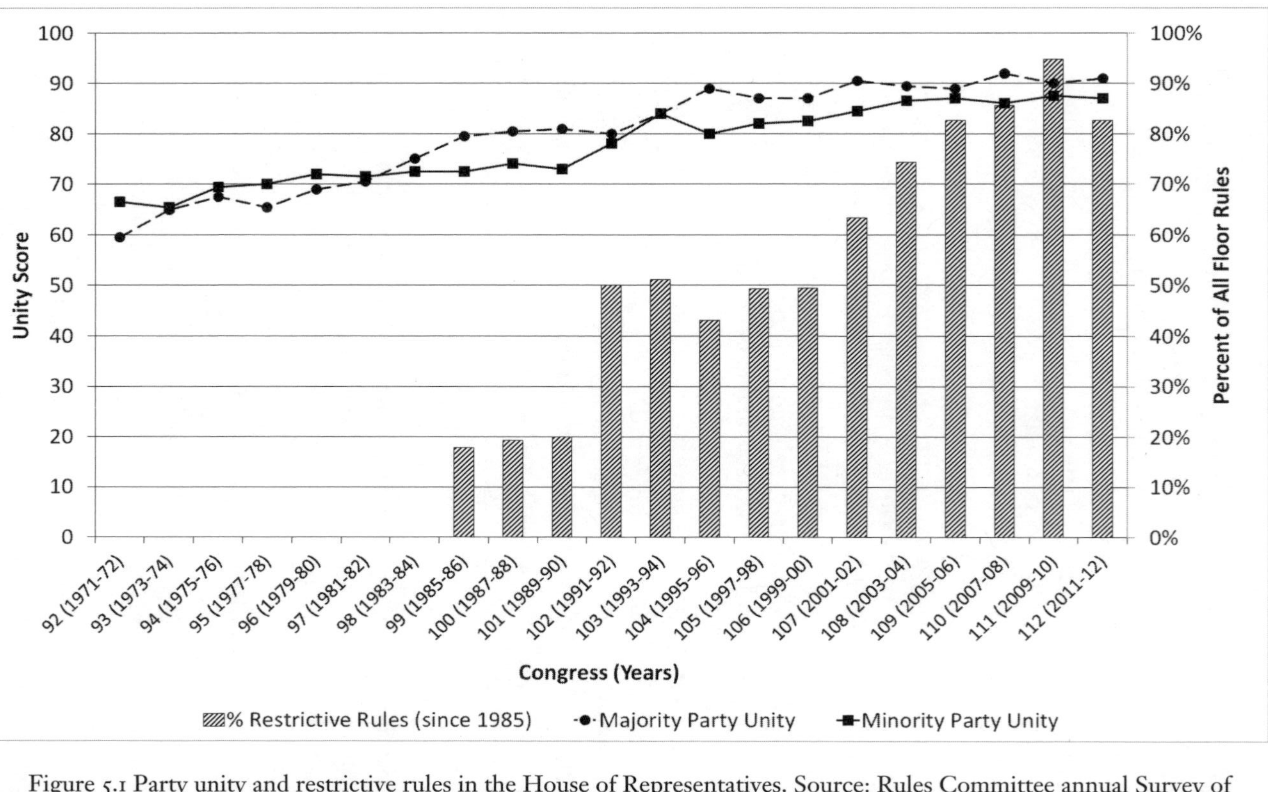

Figure 5.1 Party unity and restrictive rules in the House of Representatives. Source: Rules Committee annual Survey of

restrictive rules and employed a combination of delaying procedures and messaging to raise public awareness of them.[24] Michel continued to emphasize legislative influence in Congress, writing to party members in early 1994 that "every task, no matter how worthy . . . must flow from our fundamental duty to craft, implement, and win victories for our legislative policies." However, the G.O.P.'s policy-oriented members, including Michel, were being crowded out by new, more confrontation-minded partisans. The exhortations of Minority Whip Newt Gingrich and consultant Bill Kristol to oppose, rather than modify or suggest alternatives to, Bill Clinton's health care bill became the catalyst of a legislative approach that would become increasingly popular with House minority parties: zero compromise with the majority and total opposition to an opposite-party White House, with the goal of kicking the ruling party out.[25]

Fewer opportunities, greater voting unity, an emphasis on legislating for its messaging value, and deeper coordination within the minority continued as each party took its turn out of power. Democratic leaders had traditionally showed deference to committee chairs, but after 1994 a concentration of power within the party's leadership was the order of the day. The new Democratic minority quickly voted to allow its leaders final review of all motions to recommit, the minority's final amendment to a bill (discussed below). The rate of restrictive rules fell slightly in the 105th Congress, then climbed back up (as seen in Figure 5.1), and minority Democrats found it more and more difficult to amend legislation on the chamber floor. Majority Republicans one-upped their predecessors' aggressive exploitation of chamber procedures when, in November 2003, they held open a vote on a prescription drug bill for nearly three hours to eke out a victory. The G.O.P. also informally adopted the "Hastert Rule," named after Speaker Dennis Hastert, under which only items supported by a majority of the majority party could be brought to the House floor. Meanwhile, Pelosi became increasingly firm in insisting that Democrats vote against all major Republican bills.

Under Democratic majorities in 2007–10, both parties became still more unified internally, and even more restrictive floor rules were used—including, for the first time, on most (if not all) appropriations bills.[26] The percent of restrictive rules declined somewhat in 2011 and 2012 after incoming speaker John Boehner promised to bring more open rules to the floor. Nonetheless, the rate remained well above what it had been a decade before.

Minority Party Bills and Amendments

Despite the minority party's dwindling chances to legislate on the floor, its members have always had the right to offer or cosponsor bills and often, albeit not routinely, the opportunity to propose at least some changes to legislation via amendments. These classic vehicles for making law sometimes succeed in passing the House of Representatives. But the minority increasingly views them more as messaging tools than as direct instruments of policy change.

Take the introduction of bills. Some measures sponsored by minority party members do come to the floor of the House and are enacted; others do not yet still set the terms of debate or become the foundation for other bills that become law. However, most bills are crafted not to win bipartisan support or move policy but to make a political point. During the 109th Congress (2005–6), for instance, minority Democrats introduced 2,855 bills (44% of all bills proposed in that Congress) of which 92 were cosponsored by a majority of the minority party, a good sign that they were perceived as representing party-wide preferences. Eleven of the 92 passed the House, of which 7 became law—not a large number, but certainly more than zero.[27] Yet a great many of the remaining 81 bills were "messaging" measures, codifying proposals popular with the public or party loyalists and crafted for position-taking purposes. They included bills expanding Medicare to cover younger citizens, increasing the minimum wage, protecting labor union organizers, and reducing greenhouse-gas emissions.[28] A handful were also related, at least tangentially, to presidential politics: the prevention of voting machine irregularities, a leftover from the contentious 2000 presidential election; an investigation of the federal government's response to Hurricane Katrina; a ban on executive-branch surveillance of bookstore purchases; and an investigation into the abuse of Afghani detainees.[29] It is not surprising that these bills never made it out of Republican-controlled committees. After 2006, minority Republicans similarly used legislation for its symbolic electoral value. Under the leadership of Tom Price (2009–10), the RSC offered what one aide called "positive solution [bills] that said, 'this is how we would do things if we were in the majority'; and, you know, they're real bills, but in the minority *they're for messaging purposes*."[30]

It should be noted that cosponsorship of a bill by a majority of the minority party is itself a strong signifier that the legislation has messaging, not policy-making, import. Minority party lawmakers know that the best way to get something approved in Congress is to avoid the appearance of partisanship and let the majority party take credit, whereas for measures of high symbolic partisan significance their leaders will work hard to maximize the number of minority party cosponsors. Leaders will also do their best to keep their members from cosponsoring bills proposed by the majority party. Nancy Pelosi in particular pressed this code of conduct upon Democrats as minority leader, and others in her party adopted it. For example, when one Democrat in the 109th Congress (2005–6) cosponsored a bill introduced by Republican Nancy Johnson of Connecticut, other Democratic staff complained about this seemingly minor crossing of party lines to the legislator's own top aide.[31]

The messaging value of floor amendments for the minority is also much greater than their policy-making value. Some amendments are offered in the hopes of changing legislation, and some are "killer" or "grenade" amendments designed to defeat the underlying legislation if they pass; and these sorts of amendments do sometimes triumph. But the bulk of them are what some call "press release" amendments, and they are increasingly seen as serving the needs of the party as a whole as opposed to the individual lawmakers who sponsor them. Party leaders have accordingly sought to control their content. By 2006, minority Democrats were expected to forward all proposed amendments to bills to their leaders for review, and in early 2011 they were encouraged by party leaders to "rein in the number of amendments that they offer and focus them on jobs, the party's No. 1 talking point," according to one news story. The messaging content of amendments is a result of (and perhaps a reason for) the growing difficulty the minority has of actually getting its amendments approved: in the 1970s a quarter or more of minority party amendments might pass, but the rate dropped in the 2000s to 10% or lower.[32]

Floor Voting

Another way the minority party can try to legislate is by voting on the House floor. Voting matters greatly because it is the final determinant of outcomes. As one former congressman bluntly observed, "Votes are the only thing that counts around here. Everything else is bullshit."[33] Coordinated minority party voting does not happen on every vote; for most legislation the stakes are low and interest is slight, so minority leaders will "let the dogs walk" (in Hill-speak) and allow party members to vote their districts or their consciences. But in some circumstances the minority party eagerly pursues one of four major voting strategies to address its collective concerns.

The first minority party voting strategy, relevant when the House is trying to override a veto by a minority party president, is to sustain the veto by garnering the ballots of at least one-third of the House. With Gerald Ford in the White House, John J. Rhodes used this method "whenever Rhodes could make a reasonable case that a Ford veto was justified." Lott's whip machine often did the same for President Reagan, as did David Bonior's for Bill Clinton and Eric Cantor's for George W. Bush. Policy concerns and presidential politics are generally behind this strategy. Second, the minority can strive to reverse a vote outcome desired by the majority party. Any of the minority's four collective concerns may be behind this approach, depending on the issue and the expected political consequences of the vote. Third, the minority may hope to keep the majority's margin of victory as narrow as possible in order to garner leverage in negotiations with the ruling party or, if the Senate has passed a more desirable version of the bill by a large margin, give the Senate an advantage during conference negotiations. Finally, the party can vote unanimously on a measure (usually against it) to maximize the vote's significance for the next election. Sometimes the objective of this is to make the majority scrounge for support among its electorally vulnerable members. Such scrounging, even if successful, can make a vote look messy and generate headlines of majority party disarray. At other times the electoral goal of this unanimity is to distinguish the two parties: to create a "message vote" that puts blame for a bill entirely on the majority's shoulders "so they [party leaders] can have the purity of saying not a single [minority party member] voted for this piece of junk," observed one former G.O.P. aide. The hope, in the words of journalist Matt Bai, is to "introduce a reasonable doubt . . . into the jury box of public opinion" of the bill's merits.[34]

What makes it more likely for a voting strategy to work—particularly one (like the first or the second) designed to defeat the majority outright? One of the most important preconditions is division within the majority party. Sometimes division occurs on specific bills; other times, like in the 1970s, early '80s, and early 2010s the divisions are deeper and the potential for defections is greater on more issues.[35] Divisions can be exploited with strategic voting—that is, minority party members casting ballots contrary to their true preferences, usually by surprise—forcing the majority to scavenge for votes within its own ranks. Minority party leaders can also help turn potential divisions into actual voting defections by quietly lobbying legislators from the other side of the aisle for support. Such was the case with the passage of several of President Reagan's initiatives, including his 1981 budget. G.O.P. whip Lott assigned a Republican congressman the task of wooing southern conservative Democrats to get their votes on those initiatives, and some majority party legislators even became "unofficial members of the [minority whip] team." Reagan's own contribution to lobbying efforts on his proposals underscores the extent to which presidential help can be essential to the construction of winning cross-party coalitions. Gary Cox and Mathew McCubbins found that when the majority in the House was defeated on final passage votes, it usually corresponded with heavy involvement in the legislative process by the president (who was usually, but not always, of the opposite party), who bargained with the governing party or created political conditions that forced House leaders to bring certain bills to the floor.[36]

However, it has become far more difficult in recent years for the minority party to convince members of the ruling party to defect. When minority Republicans tried to woo moderate Democrats to oppose President Obama's health care reform bill, they came up short,[37] and an effort in late 2009 to have lobbyists recruit Democrats against banking regulation also failed.[38] In general, the greater ideological polarization of Congress and the disappearance of moderates from both parties have reduced the number of targets for defection within the majority party. And as lawmakers have come to see the White House in partisan terms, the power of presidents to win over converts from an opposite-party majority has greatly weakened. Majority party defections that do happen may occur in spite, not because, of minority party lobbying, as happened after 2010 when some majority Republicans voted against their leadership on bills they deemed insufficiently conservative.[39]

Minority party leaders today can arguably do more to achieve the other primary precondition for winning a floor vote: minority party unity. Unity denies the majority the votes it might need should it face internal divisions that jeopardize a win. An impressive example of the power of minority party unity occurred in the autumn of 2013, when House Republicans refused to fund the federal government unless President Obama agreed to defund or delay implementation of his signature health care law. Obama and the Democratic-led Senate rejected their demand. As the government remained largely shuttered, and a deadline to increase the nation's debt ceiling approached, Republicans became increasingly anxious over their party's plunging public support and divided over how to proceed. Minority Democrats, meanwhile, remained steadfastly in favor of reopening the government without preconditions, insisting (correctly) that enough House Republicans would vote to do so if given the chance. Unable to find enough votes in his own party to pass an alternative funding bill, Speaker Boehner finally relented, allowing the House to approve a largely "clean" short-term spending measure and debt-limit increase with the unanimous support of Democrats and the votes of a minority of Republicans, with little to show for it besides the worst approval ratings for Congress and the G.O.P. ever recorded.

Voting unity, then, is often essential to securing a policy victory for the party. But voting unity is a critical component of all four of the minority's voting strategies, since it is not only a prerequisite for winning a vote but also heightens the vote's symbolic value. Voting agreement is helpful even if the minority is unsure whether it wants electoral or policy benefits from a vote. In a memo sent to fellow Republicans shortly after their party's loss of the House in 2006, Whip Roy Blunt argued that "if we hold our Republican Members together, these Democrats [from conservative districts] will either show themselves for who they really are and demonstrate that they don't represent their district, or they will vote with us, and Nancy Pelosi will lose on the floor. *Either way, we win*."[40]

Granted, it is not always an easy task to build voting unity. The majority has traditionally had a larger and more developed whip organization;[41] it can offer bills appealing to moderates in the minority; and restrictive rules can be written to structure vote choices in ways that compel vulnerable legislators to join the majority party lest they risk their own reelection. "We were trying to gain members, not lose members," explained David Bonior, former Democratic whip, when asked why he did not press for unity on votes that could put his vulnerable colleagues in electoral danger. Some minority party members may also see voting unity as pointless if it will not change a vote outcome. "Why are you holding me to this?" some Democrats would ask Bonior if he urged them to vote with the party. "I'm in the minority."[42]

Still, minority party leaders can try to overcome these hindrances in several ways. They often develop or enhance intra-party whip operations.[43] If they are asking legislators to vote no on a bill, they may offer a positive alternative on the floor (via an amendment or motion to recommit) so fellow partisans can appear constructive and avoid looking like members of "a nihilistic party of reactionary opposition."[44] Rallying the troops is sometimes used. Minority Leader Gephardt's movie screenings prior to the vote on the G.O.P. prescription drug bill in the summer of 2000 is an example of this. On one day, Gephardt showed his caucus a scene from the film *Apollo 13* in which Ed Harris dramatically declares to fellow NASA scientists that "failure is not an option!" and the next day he screened a violent battle scene from the movie *Braveheart*.[45] Pelosi, Gephardt's successor, was willing to use more aggressive means of building unity. In 2003 she gave a "dressing down" to Rep. Steve Israel (NY) for supporting, and thus helping narrowly pass, a G.O.P. bill extending Medicare to cover prescription drugs. Israel later diplomatically reported that "it was not the happiest conversation I've had in politics." A friendly White House may also assist, since the heightened partisanship of presidential politics has improved the ability of presidents to keep their own congressional partisans loyal. Peer pressure can be a formidable tool as well; as one Democratic leadership aide put it, "*All* [party] members get angry at the Democrats who defect."[46]

It should also be noted that however it is achieved, minority party voting unity can, besides helping a voting strategy succeed, contribute to a greater sense of harmony and allow the minority to establish a stronger sense of collective purpose.[47] Naturally, its effects on party morale are greater if it results in defeating the majority on a vote. In 2011, for instance, minority Democrats became fed up at being excluded from the bill-making process, yet repeatedly expected to provide the winning margin of victory on the floor because of voting defections by the Republicans' large rebellious conservative faction. All but six Democrats voted against a disaster-relief bill in September that year, unexpectedly defeating it even though a majority of Republicans had voted yes. It was a "major morale boost" for a House minority that had lost majority status less than a year before, and Minority Whip Hoyer confronted Majority Whip Kevin McCarthy with a pointed query: "You're going to call us *now*, aren't you?"[48]

Finally, besides capitalizing on defections within the majority party and maximizing its internal unity, the minority party occasionally turns to procedural innovation to circumvent the majority's numerical and organizational advantages in floor voting. Billy Pitts, a G.O.P. floor staffer, gave his party crucial advice on how to pass legislation by using neglected or underappreciated House rules, contributing to the passage of Reagan's 1981 budget bill and 1984 crime bill. In 1993, Henry Hyde managed to pass an anti-abortion amendment even though it violated House rules by writing a key provision in the passive voice and getting the chamber to first reject a seemingly unrelated procedural motion. Hyde's victory caught pro-choice Democratic women off guard; infuriated, one complained that "I feel like we were raped on the House floor today."[49]

The conventional wisdom is that these efforts rarely, if ever, result in minority party voting victories. The most common measure of minority success is the frequency of *majority rolls*, or final passage votes in which the minority party manages to pass a bill over the opposition of a majority of the ruling party. As can be seen by the solid line in Figure 5.2, less than 5% of recorded final passage votes since 1971 have resulted in a majority roll, and in recent years the majority roll rate has been quite low: no more than 1.1% since 2000. This scarcity, along with the much higher rate at which the minority party is rolled, is cited by Cox and McCubbins as evidence for their claim that the House majority party is a powerful cartel that can prevent unwanted bills from coming to the floor.[50]

But this statistic is somewhat misleading. For one thing, many final passage votes are on routine or less-than-consequential matters for which the minority may not even be trying to roll the majority. On major initiatives, however, the minority has had some remarkable successes. Reagan's 1981 budget, the authorization of military force in Iraq in 1991, the North American Free Trade Agreement in 1993, new campaign-finance regulations in 2002, funding for the second Iraq war in 2007, and expanded government surveillance powers in 2008 were all enacted as the result of majority rolls in the House. And the majority was rolled no fewer than five times in the first ten

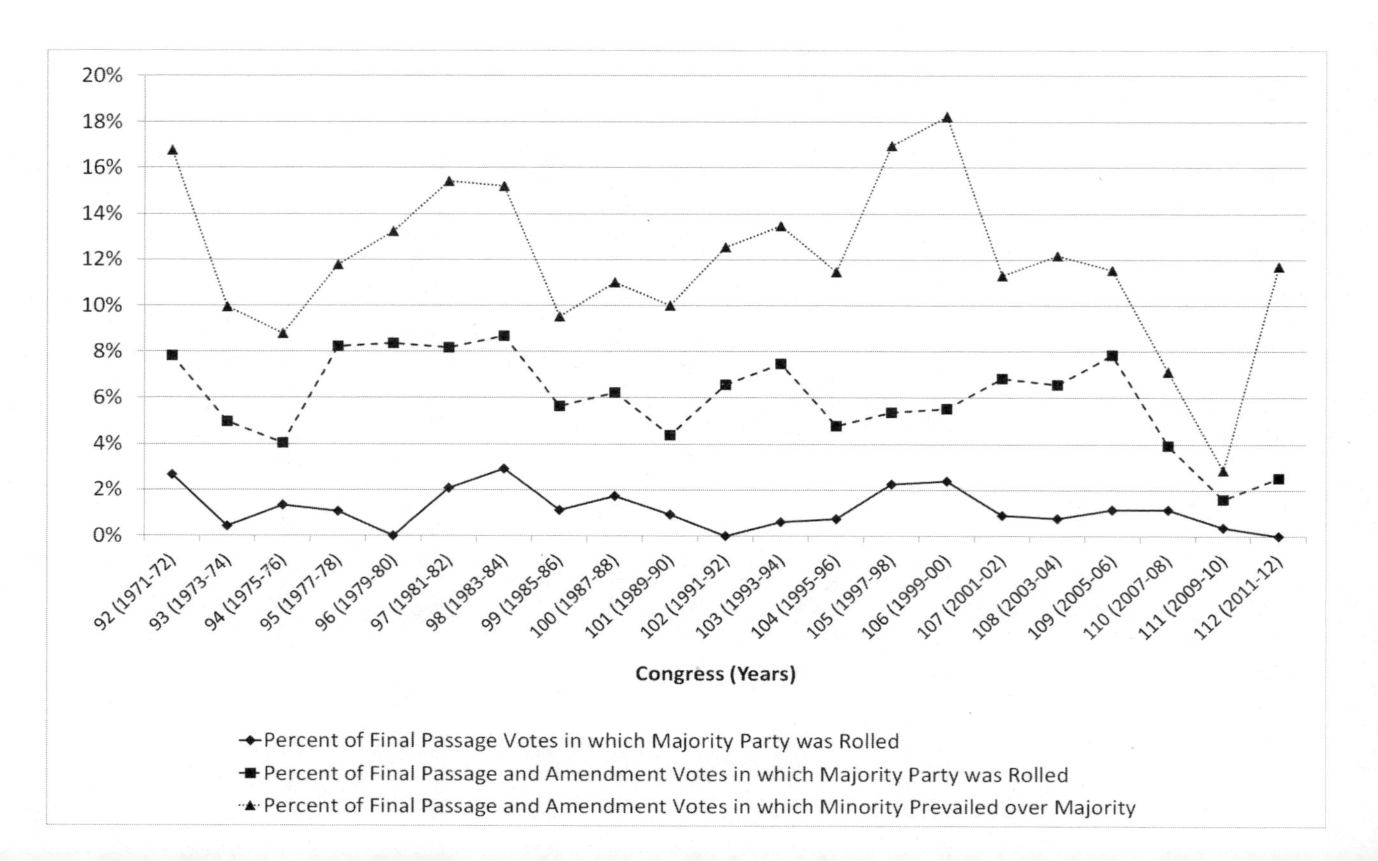

20%
18%
16%
14%
12%
10%
8%
6%
4%
2%
0%
92 (1971-72)
93 (1973-74)
94 (1975-76)
95 (1977-78)
96 (1979-80)
97 (1981-82)
98 (1983-84)
99 (1985-86)
100 (1987-88)
101 (1989-90)
102 (1991-92)
103 (1993-94)
104 (1995-96)
105 (1997-98)
106 (1999-00)
107 (2001-02)
108 (2003-04)
109 (2005-06)
110 (2007-08)
111 (2009-10)
112 (2011-12)
Congress (Years)
Percent of Final Passage Votes in which Majority Party was Rolled
Percent of Final Passage and Amendment Votes in which Majority Party was Rolled
Percent of Final Passage and Amendment Votes in which Minority Prevailed over Majority

months of 2013, resulting in laws that raised income taxes, provided relief funding for the victims of Hurricane Sandy, renewed the Violence Against Women Act, provided protection for historic battlefields, and raised the federal debt limit while ending a prolonged shutdown of the national government. One study found that majority roll rates on all votes deemed "significant" since the mid-1870s are much higher: from under 2% to 10% or more, depending on one's definition and measurement of "significant."[51]

Furthermore, the minority "gets its way" versus the majority in other ways and on other kinds of floor votes besides final passage. Its success rate increases appreciably (to an average of 6%) when one includes recorded votes in which a majority of the majority party opposed yet failed to defeat an amendment (the dashed line in Figure 5.2). It grows even more—to 12% on average between 1971 and 2012—when considering votes in which the minority successfully *defeated* or passed a bill or amendment despite the votes of a majority of the majority (the dotted line in Figure 5.2). (When the minority defeats a majority-supported bill, this is sometimes known as a "disappointment" vote as opposed to a roll.)[52] The minority defeats the governing party still more often when including matters that require a supermajority to pass, like constitutional amendments, veto overrides, and bills on the suspension calendar. These votes also cannot capture the times that majority parties, anticipating defeat at the hands of the minority, opt not to bring measures to the floor at all.[53]

To be sure, the majority party does not always mind being beaten. It may know that a bill is likely to be killed in the Senate or vetoed by the president, in which case getting rolled is costless from a policy perspective. Its leaders may even want to be rolled. By scheduling a vote on a bill or amendment popular with the public or an interest group yet unpopular with a majority of its members, and then hoping (or trying to arrange) for the minority party to provide needed votes to pass it, majority party leaders can help both their party's image and the political needs of their members. "Must pass" measures, like spending bills and debt-limit increases, are also strong candidates for this strategy when the majority party dislikes them but realizes their failure would lead to catastrophic policy outcomes.[54]

On many occasions, however, the majority party does not want, and may not expect, defeat by the minority. Even if the majority sees political benefits in letting the minority party win, it is nonetheless surrendering on its policy preferences, which is an important loss for the majority. It is also hazardous for the ruling party to pursue rolls deliberately, for it risks creating the appearance, particularly to its base, that it does not govern. Plus, counting on the minority to provide political cover makes the majority party vulnerable to strategic voting. In 1990, for instance, a majority of Democrats wanted to support a strong reform amendment to a campaign-finance bill, but their leaders feared the amendment was too extreme. When Republicans unexpectedly voted "present" on the proposal, leaders had to scramble for "no" votes among their rank and file. As already noted, Republicans used the same gambit on an Iraq funding proposal in 2008. In mid-2011 Democrats voted "present" on a conservative budget plan that a majority of Republicans wanted to support but that would, if approved, replace their leadership's official budget resolution; G.O.P. leaders quickly had to convince many of their conservative members to reverse their "yes" votes.[55]

The Discharge Petition

Voting matters, but there are also certain legislative procedures available to, and used primarily by, the minority party to address its core collective concerns. One procedure is designed to circumvent committees as the principal gatekeepers of Congress. Most bills, once introduced, are sent to committees and never return, but a tool that can overcome this hurdle is the *discharge petition*. If a discharge petition is signed by a majority of the entire House (218 members), it forces a specified bill out of the hands of whichever committee is considering it and brings it directly to the floor for debate and vote.[56]

Petitions are neither common nor regularly successful. Though thousands of bills are proposed in every Congress, a mere thirteen petitions have been filed per Congress, on average, since 1971.[57] And getting 218 signatures requires securing at least a handful of supporters from the majority party—and most majority members, fearing the wrath of committee chairs, party leaders, and their colleagues, are loath to sign petitions. Nonetheless, the occasional discharge petition does receive sufficient signatures to bring a bill to the floor. Other times a petition gets close enough to 218 signatures that the majority acts on the bill (or one similar to it) lest it be forced to do so. Petitions also offer position-taking opportunities for the minority party, a chance to show support for popular proposals and criticize the majority for failing to consider those initiatives.[58]

Both the position-taking and legislating advantages of discharge petitions have long been present, but they were enhanced in 1993 when the House began publishing the names of every legislator who signed a petition regardless of how many signatures it had received. (Previously signatures were confidential unless the petition was signed by 218 members.) This change, which was pushed for successfully by minority Republicans, allowed outside groups who endorsed a petition to easily identify and pressure non-signers, and it made petitions useful platforms for broadcasting the preferences of lawmakers and the minority party.[59]

Enterprising individuals from both the majority and minority have offered petitions for their own pet causes. However, since 1971 discharge petitions have gradually become a procedure used exclusively by the minority party on behalf of collective interests.[60] Forty percent of petitions in the 92nd Congress (1971–72) were introduced by a member of the minority party, but by the early 2000s minority party members were initiating all discharge petitions (as shown by the solid line in Figure 5.3). In addition, after the 1998 elections virtually all petition signers hailed from the minority (the solid bars in Figure 5.3) and petitions were usually signed by at least half of the minority party (the dotted line in Figure 5.3). The 112th Congress (2011–12) did show some variance from this trend of greater minority party exclusivity (one of the six petitions filed was by a majority party Republican, for example) but it is yet unclear whether this marks a

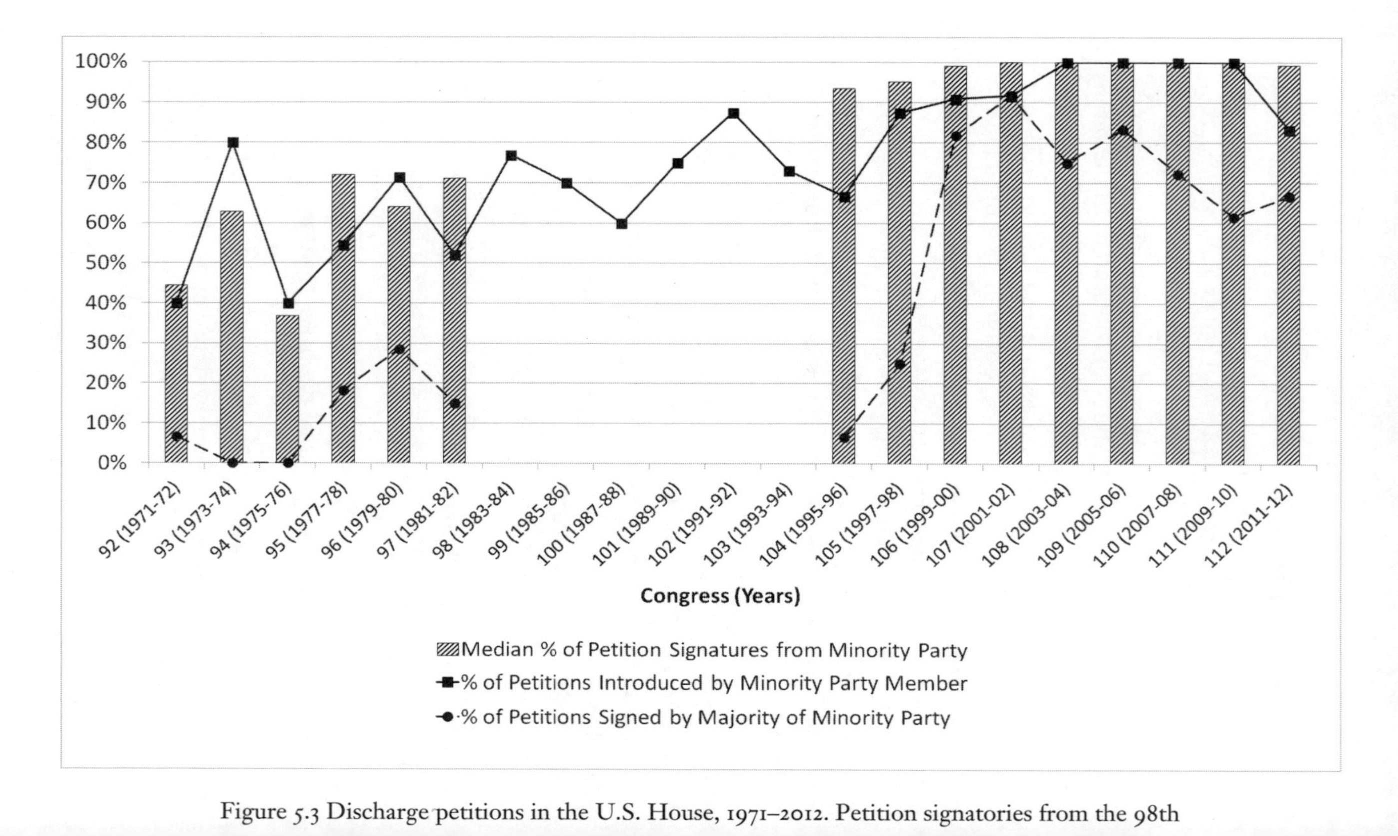

Figure 5.3 Discharge petitions in the U.S. House, 1971–2012. Petition signatories from the 98th

new trend or was an aberration caused by the large and unruly Republican freshman class in that Congress.

By far the most dominant purpose of petitions for the minority party, at least since the late 1990s, has been to achieve electoral goals through messaging, not to free bills from their committee captors. Certainly the topics of legislation subject to petitions signed by a majority of the minority, listed in Table 5.1, strongly suggest this.[61] Many petitions targeted bills on hot-button issues opposed by the majority party but not necessarily by voters, such as reinstating school prayer, raising the minimum wage, and providing health care assistance to seniors. Measures that highlighted scandal, ineptitude, or the need for reform—aspects of governmental competence, the sort of "valence" issues that commonly precede major electoral shifts in power—have also been popular.[62] Other bills fell into the category of "agenda advertising" whereby the minority seeks to garner attention for a new idea or plan, such as the Kemp-Roth tax bill. Even if the minority party was serious about getting these bills out of committee, it is quite likely that its goal was as much to force members of the majority to cast difficult votes as it was to enact a new law.[63]

As if to underscore the messaging import of discharge petitions, House Republicans after 2006 introduced a new "carpet bombing" petition technique. Choosing an issue with electoral salience that unified their party, they repeatedly filed and signed petitions on bills related to that issue. In 2008, for instance, just over half of the petitions signed by a majority of the G.O.P. in that Congress (seven of thirteen) targeted bills that would expand oil production, and all were filed in conjunction with other messaging efforts on energy, when national gas prices were at their summer peak.[64] In the next Congress, Republicans filed and signed en masse three petitions for bills that repealed, all or in part, President Obama's health care law, which was deeply opposed by conservatives and Republican voters.[65]

Besides winning elections, there is evidence that petitions have been used to address the minority party's other concerns. Virtually no bills related to procedural rights are subject to discharge

Table 5.1. Discharge Petitions Signed by Majority of Minority Party, 1971–82 and 1995–2012

Congress (Years)	Number/% of petitions signed by majority of minority party	Subject(s) of the petitions
92nd (1971–2)	1 (7%)	Prayer in public schools
93rd (1973–74)	0 (0%)	—
94th (1975–76)	0 (0%)	—
95th (1977–78)	3 (27%)	School busing, Kemp-Roth tax cuts, Panama Canal
96th (1979–80)	4 (29%)	School busing, Supreme Court discretion to hear cases, economic-growth package, anti-trust laws governing soft drink industry
97th (1981–82)	3 (15%)	School busing, lifting of age cap for surgeon general, balanced-budget constitutional amendment
104th (1995–96)	1 (7%)	Increase of debt ceiling
105th (1997–98)	2 (25%)	Campaign-finance reform, patient bill of rights
106th (1999–2000)	9 (82%)	Campaign-finance reform (2), patient bill of rights, school construction, minimum wage, Medicare prescription drugs (2), senior citizens programs, health insurance discrimination

Congress (Years)	Number/% of petitions signed by majority of minority party	Subject(s) of the petitions
107th (2001–2)	11 (92%)	School construction, energy regulation, campaign-finance reform, domestic steel industry, jobless benefits, Social Security reform, corporate overseas taxes, investor protection/corporate fraud (2), prescription drugs, hate crimes
108th (2003–4)	12 (75%)	Veterans compensation, jobless benefits, corporate overseas taxes, Social Security benefits, military spousal benefits, Medicare prescription drugs, energy regulation, low-income housing, patient bill of rights, Democratic appropriations bills (2), business reauthorization bill
109th (2005–6)	15 (83%)	Medicare prescription drugs (4), veterans compensation, military spousal benefits, Hurricane Katrina investigation (2), withdrawal of troops from Iraq, energy prices, minimum wage, FAA labor management, veterans benefits, Social Security benefits, farmer disaster assistance
110th (2007–8)	13 (72%)	Support for combat troops, enforcement of earmark rule, fairness doctrine, immigration reform, intelligence surveillance bill, energy production (7), D.C. gun rights

(*continued*)

Table 5.1. (*continued*)

Congress (Years)	Number/% of petitions signed by majority of minority party	Subject(s) of the petitions
111th (2009–10)	8 (62%)	AIG bailout, greenhouse-gas-emission regulation, posting of bill content in advance, prisoners at Guantánamo Bay, environmental regulations for California water system, health care repeal (3)
112th (2011–12)	4 (67%)	Foreign currency devaluation, insider trading by lawmakers, campaign-finance reform, taxes

Note: Though the subjects of petitions filed between 1983 and 1994 are publicly available, as of this writing data on signatories from those years are closed to the public.

petitions.[66] However, presidential politics does underlie some minority party petitions. One filed in the 97th Congress (1981–82) supported by a majority of the minority would have brought to the floor a bill to raise the age limit of the surgeon general; President Reagan's desired nominee, C. Everett Koop, was too old under existing law to be confirmed. In the summer of 1998, Democrats signed a petition to release legislation that provided protections for patients of managed health care plans, an initiative proposed by President Clinton.[67] Republicans in the 110th Congress (2007–8) also initiated petitions on measures salient to the White House, including a bill preventing a cutoff of funds for the Iraq war and another protecting the intelligence-gathering powers of the executive branch.[68] In the next Congress they used a discharge petition to draw attention to a bill limiting the transfer of accused terrorists from Guantánamo Bay, Cuba. Republicans believed the issue gave them a natural partisan advantage while exposing a political vulnerability of President Obama's.[69]

Finally, there have been occasional petitions that successfully brought bills to the floor and that may well have been introduced and signed in an effort to achieve party policy goals. One report tallied twenty-seven petitions between 1971 and 2002 (13% of the total) that either forced bills to the floor by getting 218 signatures or that otherwise led to "floor action of some means," even if they did not get enough members to sign them. Some petitions, like one targeting a school-prayer constitutional amendment in 1971 and another in 1979 that forced a vote on a school-busing amendment, have gotten 218 signatures only after long and intense campaigns to get majority party signatories.[70] Only in recent years have petitions regularly failed to garner close to 218 signatures—a sign not only that crossing party lines on petitions has become taboo for the majority but that petitions are used more than ever for election-oriented messaging, not to actually force bills to the floor.[71]

The Motion to Recommit: Last Bite at the Apple

Long protected by House rules and practice is one other important minority party legislative procedure: the *motion to recommit*. Offered prior to the final vote on a bill, the motion, if approved, sends a bill back to the committee that cleared it. If it comes without instructions (a "straight" motion to recommit), it effectively kills the bill; if it comes with instructions, it amends the bill.[72]

A motion to recommit may be offered by any individual opposed to the bill. Sometimes it is proposed with little or no support from the minority party. Nonetheless, the motion is best thought of as a tool that is used on behalf of the minority party as a whole. The right to offer it is by precedent and custom reserved to the minority party and to its leadership.[73] Even in the less partisan congressional world of the early 1970s, House Minority Leader Gerald Ford described the motion as part of his party's "technique of laying our program out in general debate."[74] By the late 1980s, wrote one observer, the motion had "the reputation of being the minority motion, and it is disfavored for majority Members to vote for it." Codifying its party-wide significance, House Republicans adopted an internal rule requiring that motions to recommit be cleared first with party leaders, a move Democrats replicated after being banished to the minority in 1994.[75]

John Rhodes described the motion to recommit as "probably the best weapon that the minority has." There are few limits on what can be included in it, and the right to offer one is largely sacrosanct. The minority is not required to tell the majority party in advance if it will offer a motion or what that motion's instructions might be, giving it the advantage of surprise.[76] A motion to recommit even buys the minority a little extra time (usually ten minutes of debate) should it have strategic motives to delay a final vote on the underlying bill.[77] For these reasons the minority has long treasured its ability to offer motions to recommit, and whenever the majority has tried to place limits on them—as Democrats did from the mid-1970s through the early 1990s—the minority party has complained vociferously.[78] The motion has become even more precious to the minority as other opportunities for legislating have diminished. For example, Republicans were able to propose amendments to President Carter's energy bill in August 1977 via a motion to recommit, even though those amendments had not been permitted under the bill's structured floor rule.[79]

Like an amendment, the motion to recommit is a procedural vessel that carries several potential, sometimes overlapping, purposes. One is to influence the next election. Motions with this collective goal in mind come with instructions so that their message is clear, and the minority often uses debate time to explain and defend them.[80] An extreme example of this occurred when Republicans offered over a dozen recommittal motions to different bills in 2008, all with instructions related to energy prices—a clear effort to promote the issue of high fuel costs. Sometimes the minority has even deliberately offered motions impermissible under the rules, like ones that include instructions with language not germane to the underlying bill, for the mere opportunity to make a brief floor speech on an issue.[81] Especially key is for a motion with instructions to be subject to a recorded vote so that the minority can take collective credit for the motion and attribute blame to the majority for its defeat. In the 110th Congress (2007–8), minority Republicans even occasionally offered motions with language redundant or unnecessary to the bill but which nonetheless forced lawmakers to take public stands on issues of high salience, like gun control or the prosecution of child sex offenders. On at least eight occasions in the following Congress, the majority offered to accept a minority motion to recommit without a recorded vote but was rebuffed by the minority, which did not want to pass up the chance to put legislators on the record.[82]

Besides scoring political points for the next election, the motion to recommit can influence policy. It can do so in at least three ways. First, the instructions accompanying a motion can be crafted to win enough votes from the majority party to pass. Second, the motion can impose "negative" change by killing the underlying bill. The standard way of attempting this is to recommit a bill without instructions. Until 2009, the minority could also kill a bill by including instructions that were not implemented "forthwith." Absent that word, the motion would in effect defeat the underlying bill because it required the measure to be revised and approved in committee and be scheduled for the floor at a later date. Third, the motion may slow down proceedings just long enough for the minority to round up votes against the bill being considered.[83]

Of course, if a motion to recommit shapes legislative outcomes it can also have electoral consequences—allowing the minority to claim credit for new policy, for instance. The motion is not purely and solely for electoral position-taking, however. Even "just the chance that you might win," one lawmaker remarked, "is encouraging. It keeps the morale up." And the power of a well-written motion is that it can address either policy or electoral concerns. If it includes language that puts vulnerable majority party members on the spot, either those members vote for the motion (perhaps in enough numbers to pass it) or they go on record opposing something that election challengers can exploit. On several occasions in 2007–8 Republicans proposed motions with appealing but "non-forthwith" instructions, tempting Democrats to vote yes and thus kill the underlying bill altogether, which gave Democratic leaders considerable headaches.[84] To limit the voting dilemma these motions impose on their members, majority party leaders have occasionally curtailed them with restrictive rules or banned certain uses of the motion altogether (as Democrats did against "non-forthwith" motions in 2009). More often, they simply insist to their members that all recommittal motions are meritless tomfoolery that should never be voted for.

The minority's concern with presidential politics is also behind some motions to recommit. From 2005 to 2012, for instance, between 5% and 19% of all motions offered by a member of the minority party were related in some significant way to White House politics.[85] Many brought up malfeasance by an opposite-party administration or raised issues expected to play well in the next presidential election.[86] Some included legislative text that was part of a same-party president's agenda, such as one in 1981 that required a committee to consider President Reagan's proposed cut to the federal legal services program and another in late 1984 (which passed) that contained Reagan's crime bill.

As for the minority's concern with its rights and powers, every once in a while a motion does contain text that would protect or enhance the party's rights.[87] Also, sometimes the minority deliberately offers motions that are out of order to make a point about the unfairness of floor procedures. Several times during the 108th Congress (2003–4), for instance, David Obey (WI) offered recommittal motions to spending bills, knowing they were impermissible under the rules, as an opportunity to complain about those rules. Even the regular use of the motion itself helps preserve it as an important and valued right of the minority.[88]

Minority parties in the early 1970s, it should be mentioned, did not exploit recommittal motions as partisan tools to the same degree they do today. In the 92nd and 93rd Congresses (1971–74), less than three-fifths of all motions were supported by a majority of the minority party. But after the 1974 elections the proportion rose to over 80% and has remained high ever since, sometimes even reaching 100% (the solid bars in Figure 5.4).[89] The inclusion of instructions in a motion also went from being an occasional event to a near certainty, as shown in Figure 5.4 by the closing gap over time between the total number of motions offered and those offered with instructions (the solid and dotted lines, respectively).[90] At around the same time, a greater percentage of motions were resolved with a recorded vote than by voice vote (the dashed line in Figure 5.4). Initially, it seems, the minority party viewed the recommittal motion as a pro forma procedure rather than an opportunity to change policy or create new ammunition for the next election, but gradually discovered that the motion had real utility as a position-taking mechanism.[91]

Finally, the reader's eye is likely drawn to the sudden spike in Figure 5.4 in the number of recommittal motions in the 110th Congress (the solid line).[92] In that particular Congress the minority Republicans' creative and aggressive use of the motion bore unexpected fruit, encouraging its frequent use. In early 2007, the G.O.P. began drafting motions designed to make moderate Democrats fearful of going on the record against them. Democratic leaders decided to allow its vulnerable members to cross party lines on those motions. "That was a huge procedural mistake," as one Republican leadership aide later explained; "they suddenly made the motion to recommit real." Some conservative interest groups, realizing the motion could actually pass, began asking minority party leaders to offer recommittal motions with legislative language they desired.[93] Then, on March 22, 2007, Republicans offered a motion to a voting-rights bill for the District of Columbia that prohibited certain gun restrictions in the District—a proposal attractive to many conservative Democrats with pro-gun constituencies—and that was not implemented "forthwith."[94] Facing certain passage of the killer motion, Democratic leaders pulled the voting-rights bill, but the damage had been done: it "reinforced the Republicans' belief that they could sink legislation the other side was pushing." A whopping 42% (52) of all motions offered by the G.O.P. in 2007–8 included instructions that

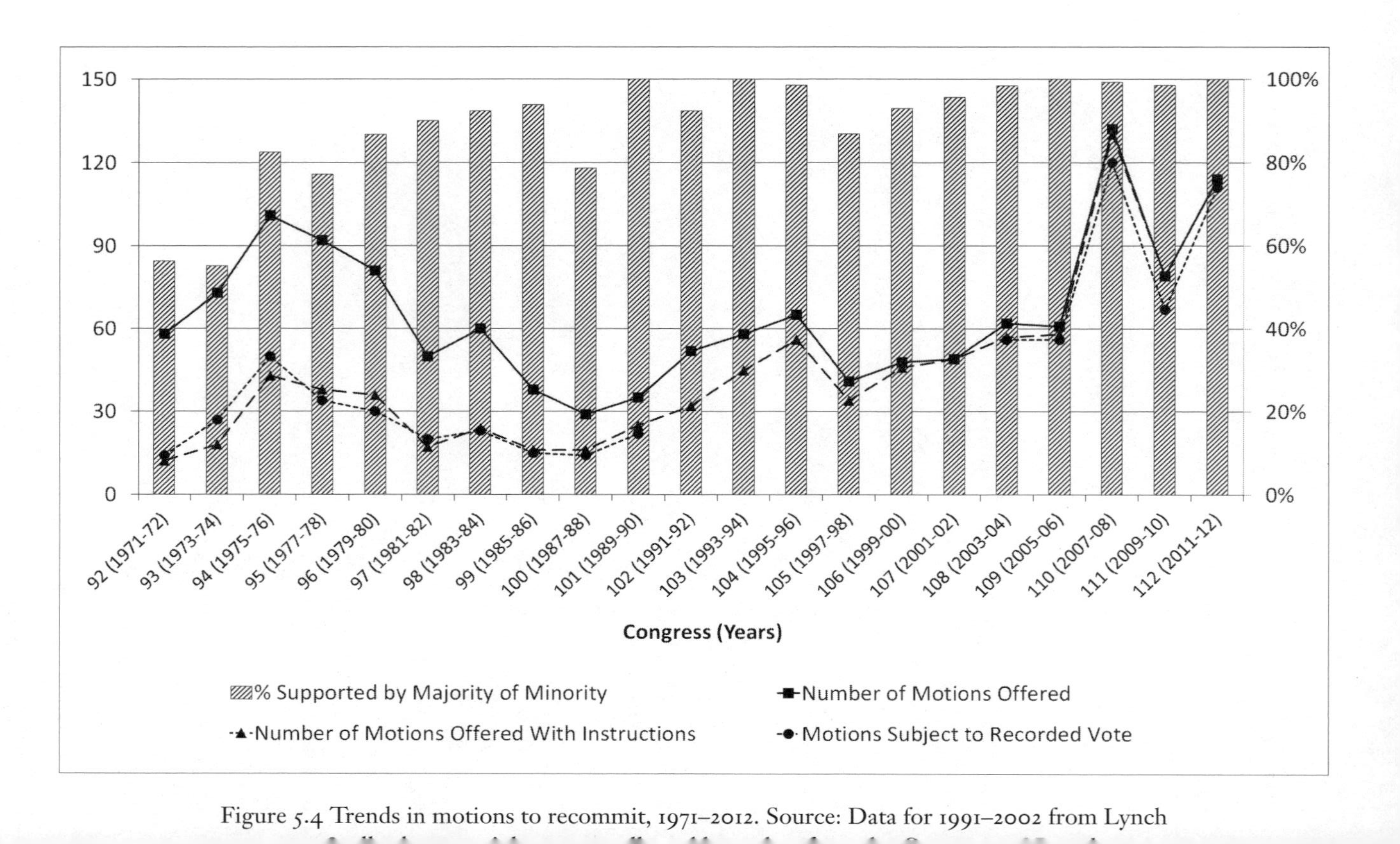

Figure 5.4 Trends in motions to recommit, 1971–2012. Source: Data for 1991–2002 from Lynch

did not require the "forthwith" return of the bill from committee, far more than the 10% offered by the minority in the previous Congress. As noted, the Democrats banned non-forthwith instructions from motions altogether in 2009.[95]

Granted, while the motion to recommit is the minority's most important amendment-like procedure, it does not pass often. Of the 1,064 motions offered by a member of the minority from 1971 to 1990 and from 2003 to 2012, only 92 (8.6%) were approved either by recorded vote or by a non-recorded (voice or division) vote. Almost half of those passed in just two Congresses, the 110th and 111th (2007–10), when Republicans adeptly used the motion to exploit policy divisions within the Democratic Party.[96] Nonetheless, some that did pass had major policy ramifications. As noted, Republicans managed to force the adoption of President Reagan's crime bill in 1984 via a motion to recommit that passed "to the surprise of nearly everyone." And the March 2007 motion on gun rights in the District of Columbia showed how motions can come so dangerously close to passing that they force the majority to revise the underlying bill, pull it altogether, or force some of its vulnerable members to take tough votes against them.[97]

Conclusion

In principle, legislating poses a difficult dilemma for minority parties in the House. If the party uses legislative tools to shape policy as best it can, it is often forced to compromise and it loses the chance to attack the opposition. But if it uses those tools to make political points for the next congressional election, it throws away opportunities to shape policy and may encourage the majority to weaken whatever legislative influence it has.[98]

Starting in the 1970s, the ruling party made that a less difficult choice for the minority. When House Democrats increasingly limited Republicans' ability to shape legislation on the floor and get its bills or amendments approved, the minority used many of the legislative tactics at its disposal toward the goal of influencing the next election, hoping to paint the governing party into a corner or advertise the G.O.P.'s agenda to the outside world. Republicans eventually demonstrated an equal lack of charity to the minority when it took control of the House, and Democrats similarly exploited legislative tools to make symbolic electoral attacks.

Nonetheless, the minority still can shape policy with legislative tactics. It can and does occasionally win floor votes, get amendments and bills approved, pass motions to recommit, and employ discharge petitions to release bills from the majority party's grip. Nor has this chapter explored all of the ways the minority can influence policy legislatively. There are times, after all—even in today's highly partisan and polarized Congress—when both parties share some common ground on policy and work together to enact legislation.[99]

But while the minority legislates more frequently than is supposed, it would be going too far to suggest that it utilizes legislative tools primarily for that purpose. In recent decades the minority party has principally taken advantage of them as vehicles of symbolic import, conveying messages to the electorate (even when these vehicles legislatively fail) that the minority hopes can be converted into votes at the polls. Amendments raise important election-year issues regardless of whether they pass or not. Rejected motions to recommit still contribute to a useful campaign narrative. Unified opposition to a bill that still passes may make the vote more salient and increase its potential as a partisan weapon in the next campaign.[100]

Whether this exploitation of legislative tools to achieve minority goals other than policy is healthy or harmful to American democracy is a topic I discuss in the next, and final, chapter.

six

THE MINORITY PARTY AND AMERICAN POLITICS

Politics is like trench warfare. Defense wins.
—Bruce Gyory

The opposition is indispensable. A good statesman, like any other sensible human being, always learns more from his opponents than from his fervent supporters.
—Walter Lippmann

The minority party in the House faces a strategic problem: how do you respond when given only a small slice of the legislative pie? Do you accept the slice you've been given, bargain for more, or use every means at your disposal to win the right to cut the pie yourself? It is this problem, and how the minority party chooses to solve it, that underlies the logic of minority party politics in the House of Representatives.

I have argued that there is no straightforward solution to this difficult conundrum. The belief that minorities respond by doing whatever will get them more power—the right to recut the legislative pie, to continue the analogy—is too reductive. Minority parties do not just fight for the right to become majorities; they also seek to influence policy with the powers they do have, try to preserve or even expand their procedural rights and powers, and attempt to shape presidential politics. To address these core collective concerns, the minority party uses a combination of electioneering, messaging, obstructing, and legislating tactics.

The previous chapters suggest that, in deciding when and how to use these tactics, the minority generally follows one or more central political strategies. One is to *negotiate* with the majority party or other political players (especially the president) to get what it wants.

The minority may even threaten to use tactics like press conferences, motions to recommit, or obstruction to bring the majority to the bargaining table. Another common strategy is to *distinguish* the minority from the majority in the eyes of the public, using votes, speeches, campaign agendas, or other tools to make the case that the minority is different and better (or would at least be a better choice for voters). A third is to *outcompete* with the majority for resources, candidates, voters, and media attention. Finally, the minority can *pressure the majority party* by forcing tough votes, lobbying its swing members, entrapping its members with tricky motions to recommit, spending heavily against its election candidates, or putting the obstructive squeeze on it—perhaps to force it down a certain path, roll the majority on a floor vote, or maybe make the majority's members more electorally vulnerable.

One important theme of this study has been that the minority is not a group that always or necessarily evaluates its goals and objectives rationally before it acts. There is often uncertainty over what tactics might yield the desired results; sometimes the minority chooses a path of action out of emotion, not reason; and on occasion the minority acts simply because it is preferable to taking no action at all. And if this is true of the minority, it is worth considering the extent to which it is true of the majority, too. Majority party members can certainly succumb to emotion: frustration at minority party tactics, arrogance that comes with the warrant to govern, fear that their party will lose the next election. Any of these can spur the majority party to make a decision—even a foolish, seemingly irrational decision—to use a particular tool or tactic. And morale and unity of purpose are important elements of an effective majority party just as they matter to the minority.

It should also be noted that while this has been a study of the House minority party, not every tactic documented here is unique to the minority. The majority and minority, for instance, both worry intensely about winning elections, and both have employed messaging tools to a greater degree in recent years. Nor may every tactic I have discussed be used in equal measures by Republicans and

Democrats. The two parties have long diverged in their constituencies, leaders, and perhaps even cultures, facilitating or encouraging differences in tactical and strategic decision-making. Also important are the differing conditions under which each has served in the minority. In particular, the House Republicans' forty years of minority status bred deep resentment and strong identity as a minority party that translated into the assertive and savvy use of maneuvers to trip up majority Democrats. Those same four decades, by contrast, inculcated among House Democrats a governing mentality, making it hard for them to adjust to powerlessness after 1994 and inclining many toward compromise with the ruling party in order to influence policy. The Democrats' shockingly large election losses in 1994 and 2010 likely exacerbated their difficulty in accepting minority status. Nonetheless, while it has not been possible to fully control for these competing variables, the data presented here are compelling evidence that the House minority should not only be considered distinct from the majority party but that the Democrats and Republicans have had much in common with each other when relegated to the minority.

Regardless of the reasons the minority party does what it does, over the past four decades it has repeatedly shown that is not helpless in the face of superior numbers. Even as its formal authority to bring about change has diminished, it has found other ways to meaningfully shape political outcomes. Like an insurgency group, the minority party tries to successfully exploit the opposition and its fixed position of power; and when it has resources on its side, such as votes, campaign dollars, good candidates, presidential influence, the attention of the media, it has an advantage.[1] Though it is often hard to draw a causal relationship between a minority party tactic and what follows its use, some tactics outlined in previous chapters are associated with an outcome beneficial to the minority's interests anywhere from 6% of the time to 30% or more—evidence consistent with the argument that the minority party possesses at least some degree of political influence. Those tactics may also produce long-term and indirect effects not documented in this book. So while the House majority party does exercise disproportionate formal control over the chamber's agenda and rules, the "cartel" model of congressional politics attributes far too little influence to the minority party in the contemporary House of Representatives.

Bruce Gyory's observation, however, is a wise one. Much (though not all) of what the minority does effectively is defensive and reactive in nature: blocking legislation, criticizing the majority's agenda, proposing motions to recommit to bills it did not write. "We need stuff to react to," admitted one aide to Minority Leader Richard Gephardt in 1997. "We can only be proactive to a point." In fact, it seems that the minority often succeeds politically less because of what *it* does than from what the *majority* party does, especially when the majority commits unforced errors or draws minority party members together into strong, unified opposition. Thinking back to his party's years in minority status under Speaker Nancy Pelosi, one Republican leadership aide recalled that Democrats "did so many things wrong, it just gave us golden opportunities to unify our troops."[2]

Specific examples abound. By being publicly admonished in 1984 for harsh language against Newt Gingrich, Speaker Tip O'Neill "put Gingrich and Co. on the map," as two journalists wrote, while Democrats' brash move the next year to award a contested Indiana seat to their party's candidate "brought new converts to [Gingrich's] cause." Speaker Jim Wright's tough partisan approach to politics "has made our minority status more painful," remarked G.O.P. whip Dick Cheney in late 1988; "he has reminded us why we should be dissatisfied." In 1994, House Democrats unexpectedly failed to pass the floor rule for a major crime bill, conveying an image of ineffectiveness, and then alienated southern constituents by including assault weapons restrictions in the final version of the legislation. President Clinton's unpopularity also dragged down his party that year, along with a White House memo leaked just before the 1994 elections that implied the president would soon propose tax increases. In March 2005, House Republicans rushed to pass a bill that would keep alive Terri Schiavo, a young Florida woman with severe brain damage. One G.O.P. Hill aide recalled it as "kind of the last straw for right-of-center voters, business conservatives, swing voters, and conservative-leaning Democrats" who saw it as overly intrusive and an obvious pander to the religious right, and Republicans lost their much-needed support in the 2006 elections. After Hurricane Katrina hit the Gulf Coast in 2005, missteps by the Bush White House created an opening for minority party Democrats, and they eagerly reiterated their theme that Republicans cared more about power than helping people. Tom DeLay's indictment that same year became the House minority's Exhibit A of Republican corruption. As a majority party four years later, Democrats passed new rules that unintentionally allowed Republicans to offer motions to recommit that included non-germane, potentially treacherous amendments. In 2009 the Democratic majority passed liberal bills on health care and the environment that galvanized G.O.P. opposition.[3]

In previous chapters we have seen the basic elements of the minority party's underdog politics: how and why the House minority campaigns, communicates, obstructs, and legislates, and the apparent impact of these activities on political outcomes. But what are the greater implications of this activity and the party's relative freedom of action for the U.S. Congress—and, by extension, for American democracy?

The Minority Party and the Future of Congress

Perhaps the minority party in the House should have more political influence. Perhaps it already has enough. Or maybe it even has too much, given that it failed to win the votes of a majority of congressional districts. Regardless, it is clear that the minority today does not *believe* it has enough influence—or, more accurately, enough of an opportunity to participate in the legislative process.

If we take 1971 as our starting point, it is obvious that the House minority party's formal legislative opportunities have dwindled considerably. Starting in the middle of that decade, the House's partisan regime—what parties did, what they could do, and what lawmakers believed the parties should do—began to change fundamentally. Elections started to bring new kinds of people to Congress, people reared on modern campaigns who believed less in compromise and more in partisan victory. The "truculent" Democratic class of 1974, as former Minority Leader John Rhodes called it, was followed by an "almost as truculent" Republican class of 1978 whose members had often won "rough and tumble" campaigns and who adopted that same style as legislators. Gradually, House members' activity became more centralized and directed by party leaders, the two parties became more adversarial, and the scope of conflict between them expanded. Majority Democrats found it useful to limit the occasions available to the minority to amend bills—to prevent embarrassing votes, to make the House more efficient, and to maximize the time available to campaign. The hindrances to party loyalty in Congress that David Mayhew witnessed in the early 1970s gradually evaporated, replaced by an expectation of team play.[4]

Is it so bad if the minority party has fewer chances to make law? A strong case can be made that it is. For one thing, the minority represents the views of tens of millions of Americans. To exclude it is, in effect, to disfranchise those citizens from having a say in policy.[5] Also, as Walter Lippmann observed, the minority party's ideas, arguments, and proposals can improve legislation. Bills written without input from the minority may be qualitatively worse than those with such input.[6] In addition, genuine participation increases the odds of intelligent and enlightened debate as opposed to the partisan jeremiads that characterize so much of Congress' public rhetoric. "It is very much in the interest of the majority to give the minority a fighting chance," said one witness at a House hearing in 1992, "because what it does, it improves the quality of the debate in the House. It makes it exciting. It makes it interesting." Wrote Edmund Burke in 1790, "He that wrestles with us strengthens our nerves and sharpens our skill. Our antagonist is our helper." By contrast, warned one congressional scholar in 1987, "when the minority feels obstructed or the majority feels thwarted . . . incivility is more likely to occur."[7]

Finally, excluding the minority party encourages it to stress its electoral concerns over all others, since it sees majority status as its only chance to be a serious legislative player. Virginia Republican

Tom Davis put it this way: "When you get the majority, the leadership team sits around the table, and the first question the winners ask, sitting in this ornate room, is 'How do we stay in the majority?' . . . And the minority, by the way, sits in a little less ornate room . . . and they say, 'How do we get it back?'" As Newt Gingrich told journalist John Barry in the late 1980s, "You're fighting a war. It is a war for power . . . What is the primary purpose of the political leader? To build a majority." Needless to say, this is not the kind of balanced role for the minority party implied by the term "loyal opposition."[8]

The emphasis on winning power over all other collective party concerns—further encouraged by the inability of either party to amass a large and durable majority in Congress—has led to some particularly disturbing developments. The most obvious is the growth of obstruction and delay by the minority party. To be sure, such delay, at least in the House, is a far cry from the level of obstruction in the U.S. Senate, let alone the daily paralysis the House suffered in the 1880s or the infamous delays imposed by Nazi and Communist deputies that helped bring down the German Reichstag in the early 1930s. Even so, it is not healthy for any legislative body to be beset with excessive obstruction. "Obstruction militates not only against the right of the parliamentary majority to decide but against the parliaments themselves as institutions," noted one early 20th-century scholar. The political scientist Clinton Rossiter warned that "few politicians in the ranks of the minority pay careful attention to the rough line between responsible opposition and irresponsible pugnacity. Yet it is a function that we could do ill without." A minority party that perceives itself as a besieged army is bound to ignore that line and see excessive delay as a legitimate tool, "laying siege to the majority" and conducting "guerrilla warfare," as one congressional aide described it.[9]

A heightened emphasis on power—which, as Tom Davis aptly noted, now consumes both the majority and minority parties—has had other deleterious effects besides encouraging obstruction. Manufactured conflict fills the halls of the House; "debate" consists of monologues full of rhetorical jabs and innuendo, often with little basis in fact. The minority openly blames the majority for its poor treatment, yet too often it acts just as tyrannically when it is in power, making both parties look hypocritical. Minority Republicans, for instance, bitterly denounced House Democrats for daring to pass health care reform in 2010 through a self-executing floor rule (which would have shielded lawmakers from having to vote directly on the measure), but two years later used the same procedure to pass a major budget measure over Democrats' opposition. Even press releases are part of the grand battle to beat the other party: one study found that over a quarter of press releases issued by senators in the mid-2000s contained partisan taunts, and it seems highly likely that House members do the same. The media hungrily devours this sort of conflict, resulting in a magnification of the "sage-chicken dances" and "pseudo-events" that suggest trivial and superficial politics have swallowed up Washington.[10]

Even more seriously, campaign politics have subsumed the legislative process. Lawmaking has become subject to the needs of messaging rather than the other way around. Legislators flagrantly vote against their own personal and constituency interests merely to try to cripple the other side in the next election. Time is wasted with votes designed to score political points, not make national policy. Noted freshman Republican and onetime prosecutor Trey Gowdy (SC): "You're voting on things in the middle of the night that you know have the same chance of becoming law as my son taking [supermodel] Kate Upton to the prom. Actually he may have more of a chance . . . So why do you do it? You do it because the jury's watching. And instead of viewing this as a mini-trial, it's a piece of evidence in a trial." Congress has long done things to appeal to the "jury" of American voters, but what was once relatively minor activity oriented toward one's own district has become partisan, nationalized, all-consuming, and far more negative. Perhaps most alarming of all, "the permanent campaign" has made compromise, the essence of what allows our political system to function, an anathema.[11]

These disorders of Congress extend well beyond the ubiquitous complaint that the institution is too polarized. Many scholars argue that a widening gap in ideological differences between the two parties is the cause of an ever-growing frequency of party-line voting.[12] There is much truth to this account (and considerable evidence for it), and the House especially seems more and more willing to pass major bills with the support of only the majority party. But this view arguably misses the nature and source of Congress' deeper ailment. My examination of the institution through the prism of minority party politics in the House—and the many things that party members do to address collective concerns—makes clear that far more than ideology or voting choices separate the two parties and fuel conflicts between them. An obsession with power—using it without regard to the other side, seeking it by any means necessary—ratchets up the partisan rhetoric, turns rules and procedures into armaments, and poisons the legislative well. Perhaps the two parties' core beliefs are too distant for them to reach compromise on major issues, but it is also true that neither party treats the other in a way that makes compromise much of a possibility.[13]

It may be that these developments are only temporary or have reached their limits. William Connelly argues that our constitutional system of government distributes power among so many institutions that it "precludes the formation of a 'government' or an 'opposition' . . . At all times both parties are both government and opposition." If so, a minority party that insists on playing the opposition role to the hilt, as increasingly seems to be the case, will always be checked by a competing impulse to act as a governing party. Overreaching and oppressive majority parties may also have a short shelf life: "partisan majorities," Connelly observes, "naturally tend to fall apart."[14]

At the micro level, however, serious and meaningful steps can still be taken to improve the way the two congressional parties treat each other and reduce the toxicity of Congress' political atmosphere. The most obvious path to reform is for one party to become so electorally dominant that the minority sees no immediate path to winning power. Under such circumstances, the minority party is likely to seek reconciliation and policy compromise with the majority rather than wage a futile battle to win majority status. Such was the case in the years during and after the Great Depression, when Democrats developed a seemingly unbreakable hold on the House of Representatives and many congressional Republicans saw cooperation as the only reasonable strategy available to them. At the state level, some legislatures today have very small minority parties; not surprisingly, they "aren't the partisan combat zones that Congress has become, and their lawmakers find ways to work cooperatively on issues."[15]

Short of dooming one party to decades of minority status (which seems neither preferable nor very likely, given our closely divided national electorate) the public could create an impetus for both political parties to behave differently. Members of Congress do believe that elections carry messages, and an obstructionist minority or bullying majority might change its tune if it is punished at the polls. However, citizens have few realistic choices at the ballot box, and an election's message is usually open to interpretation. Our delegate system of representation also means that once lawmakers are elected there is only so much the public can do to realistically affect how they behave in office. More importantly, procedural fairness and interparty relations within Congress have almost never been especially salient matters with the American public. Some politically engaged voters may even relish the partisan conflict they see on C-SPAN.[16]

We are left, then, with those who are in Congress. It is ultimately their responsibility to remember, in the words of one historian, that "institutions can be no better than the men who embody them." The majority party, which has the capacity to change House rules and practice far better than the minority, must be the first mover. If appeals to the integrity of the House do not sway the majority's members to treat the minority better, then naked self-interest should. It is not easy to govern with an ornery minority that threatens, that blockades, that opposes reflexively, that converts every legislative tool into a messaging weapon. Continually clamping down on obstruction can turn the chamber into little more than "a voting machine" that treats all lawmakers as automatons, and even then "a determined minority will resort to methods contrary to the rules" to delay matters.[17] Petty partisan bickering, internal squabbles over procedure, and confusing delays tarnish the image and reputation of the House, and studies have shown that come election time, a poorly regarded Congress tends to cost the majority party seats.[18] Furthermore, the odds of losing power have become so great for the majority party that it makes logical sense for it to follow the Golden Rule. "Smart majorities," in the words of one former Republican congressman, "give minorities opportunities."[19]

Each party has occasionally toyed with restoring some degree of amicable treatment toward the minority. In 1996, for instance, aides to Minority Leader Gephardt privately considered a plan to reach out to Republicans and improve interparty relations if Democrats won back the House that year, albeit under the assumption that its majority would be too small and divided to govern without minority party support. In 2011, Speaker John Boehner tried restoring the practice of having open rules for appropriation bills, a time-consuming process that nonetheless may have helped defuse potential unrest from minority Democrats. Sadly, though Boehner seemed dedicated at least publicly to a more open House despite incentives to abandon that path, majority parties in the past have either given up such efforts or never even tried them. They instead follow the path described by John Dingell who, while still in the minority in the mid-2000s, lamented that "when we get done we're not going back to the fair way of doing things. Democrats will say [to Republicans], you did it, now you bastards enjoy it." And the majority is often encouraged to do so by the minority party, which too often finds it easier to convert opportunities to legislate into opportunities to obstruct and embarrass.[20]

Many issues divide our country, and people expect their representatives in Congress to advocate for those issues with passion. And giving the minority a fairer shake is hardly a cure-all for an election-oriented Congress: expensive campaigns, polarized voters, and the modern media all feed the desire for lawmakers to be extreme in their rhetoric and employ symbolism over substance. But better treatment of the minority party—and the minority's more tempered use of the influence it has—may, even in a small way, make the House a more responsible, responsive, and reasonable institution. If we believe that a viable opposition is what makes for a healthy democracy; if we believe it serves as a critical check against an ethic of "might makes right;" if we believe that even an opposition party should take some responsibility for governance; if we believe that lawmakers, regardless of their party affiliation, are the legitimate spokespersons for the constituents they represent; then reversing the trend of the last four decades of governance and party relations in the House of Representatives is the best way forward.

NOTES

Chapter One. The Politics of the Minority Party

Epigraph 1. Billings 2003a.

Epigraph 2. Trollope 1969 [1869], 158.

1. Interview with National Republican Campaign Committee (NRCC) aide, August 26, 2011.
2. *Congressional Record*, September 9, 1988, 23295, 23298–99; *Congressional Quarterly* 1988; Manning 2005; McCutcheon, Towell, and Barron 2000; Towell 2000.
3. Cox and McCubbins 1993, 2005; Rawls 2009, 39–51. Notable recent studies on the Senate and the filibuster especially include Binder and Smith 1997; Koger 2010; Lee 2009; and Wawro and Schickler 2006.
4. See e.g. Mann and Ornstein 2006, 2012.
5. This point has been made by others (e.g. Krehbiel and Wiseman 2005). Connelly 2010 and Evans 2000 do offer recent treatments of the subject and Klinker 1994 examines the politics of the presidential out-party.
6. Jones 1970, 11–19. He did note one factor shaping strategic flexibility that varies within a given Congress: whether it is early or late in the legislative process (19).
7. Eric Schickler (2001) argues that collective *interests* motivate institutional change, but I prefer the term *concern* over *interests* when describing the minority party's actions because the former implies a greater sense of worry and immediacy that would motivate behavior. My theoretical approach also has some similarities to those found in Robert Dahl, "The American Oppositions: Affirmation and Denial" and "Patterns of Opposition," from Dahl 1966; Jones 1970; and Smith 2007.
8. Examples of major studies in one or more of these categories include Cox and McCubbins 1993 and 2005; Jones 1970; Lebo, McGlynn, and Koger 2007; Rohde 1991; Sinclair 1995; and Smith 2007.
9. Smith 2007, 214; see also Jones 1965, 1.
10. *Federalist Papers* 10 and 58; Foord 1964, 3; Mill 1991 [1861], ch. 7; Tocqueville 1969 [1848], 252; see also Madison 1910, 180, 528. For a history of the development of majority rule, see Heinberg 1926.

11. Minority groups or parties in a legislature are not quite the same as minorities in society, of course. Nonetheless, I would argue that the basic concerns of political theorists about the role and rights of the minority in society apply to a legislative minority, too.
12. See e.g. Chambers 1963, 80; Elkins and McKitrick 1993; and Nichols 1967, esp. 171 and 292. The story of party development is not only one of creativity born from opposition, however. As a majority party, the Hamiltonian Federalists helped create the first American party system in the 1790s by building a broad coalition to support their program of internal improvements (Chambers 1963, 191). Also, some historians, like Chambers and Richard McCormick (1966), argue that party development was more haphazard and uneven, and undertaken with much less foresight, than implied by this account or others (e.g. Aldrich 1995). Though mass parties first showed up in the United States, organized opposition in the House of Commons had emerged over a hundred years earlier (Johnson 1997).
13. Chambers 1963, 5–7; Elkins and McKitrick 1993, 224, 693–94, and ch. 7; Foord 1964; Matson 1958, 334; Selinger 2012. Nancy Rosenblum identifies two philosophical objections to parties: they divide society into parts and foment political conflict. Both were, and to some extent remain, the foundation for anti-partyism in the United States. Rosenblum 2008, chs. 1–2.
14. Burke 1770, 110; Chambers 1963, 9–10; Elkins and McKitrick 1993, 265; Hofstadter 1969, quote 249; Leonard 2002; Matson 1958, 334–35.
15. Eigen and Siegel 1993, 367; Johnson 1997; Strong 2011; U.S. Constitution, Art. 1, Sec. 5. William Nisbet Chambers (1963, 145) makes a similar point about the two challenges associated with opposition parties.
16. Committee on Political Parties 1950, 18; Eigen and Siegel 1993, 478, 488; Luce 1972 [1922], 5; Rhodes 1995, 237.
17. Chambers 1963, 14; Connelly and Pitney 1994, 160; Johnson 1997; Rossiter 1960, 46.
18. Connelly and Pitney 1994; Eigen and Siegel 1993, 361; Johnson 1997, 498–99. For a recent analysis of congressional politics that considers the "government or opposition" dilemma of both parties, see Connelly 2010.
19. Smith 2007, 4–5; quote from Aldrich 1995, 23; see also Sjöblom 1968, 68. The scholar most responsible for popularizing the goal-oriented approach to studying the U.S. Congress is Richard Fenno (1973). Some have argued that since a goal is not itself a cause of action, a more ac-

curate descriptive term is *motivation*. Edelman 1971, ch. 8; Eulau 1984; and Frisch and Kelly 2006, 70.

20. This is not exactly a groundbreaking claim; see e.g. Dahl, "The American Oppositions," from Dahl 1966, 34; Gamm and Smith 2003, 8; Jones 1970, 22; Smith 2007, 25.
21. See e.g,. Agar 1950, 689–90; Sindler 1966, 7. Some distinguish between parties that seek votes versus political office; see Kaare Strøm and Wolfgang C. Müller, "Political Parties and Hard Choices," from Müller and Strøm 1999, 5–6, 8–9.
22. Nyhan, McGhee, Sides, Masket, and Greene 2012. The consequences of winning a majority are far more transformative and potentially reconstitutive for the minority than for the majority. If the latter retains power, the result is largely the status quo, but if the former wins the party's formal power increases considerably and its new members may help alter the party's platform, legislative strategy, and internal culture—though new majority members can also change their party, as happened for example to House Democrats after the 1974 election.
23. G.O.P. minority leaders John Rhodes and Robert Michel both opted to leave their leadership posts in part because they faced some unhappiness—stoked by Newt Gingrich, an ambitious rival—from among party members, though not necessarily because of the party's continual minority status (Rhodes 1995, 235–36; Smith 2005, 255–56).
24. Dahl, "The American Oppositions," from Dahl 1966, 34; Gamm and Smith 2003, 8; Jones 1970, 23–24; Strøm and Müller, "Political Parties and Hard Choices," from Müller and Strøm 1999, 7–8; Smith 2007. Charles O. Jones describes this as an "expectation" of the minority to "behave 'responsibly' in the policy process" and get legislation enacted (23). I would argue that Jones describes not a party *goal* but a concern with the *consequences* of appearing irresponsible (e.g. unpopularity among voters, a tarnished reputation, losing future congressional elections).
25. Fenno 1973; Mayhew 2005, 130–31; Schickler 2001; Sindler 1966, 7–8; Smith 2007.
26. Gamm and Smith (2003, 8) suggest that parties also have a collective goal of ensuring a strong public reputation (see also Cox and McCubbins 1993, 110–12). But a positive reputation is, I would submit, the means to another and more central end—winning election—rather than an end in itself.
27. Jones 1968. One could think of the minority as having a *goal* of greater procedural rights, but if so it is a goal that tends to be salient only when

the party's rights have just been curtailed. There is, however, a broader and more durable *concern* that the party's existing rights be protected *and* that any recent curtailments of rights be rolled back. On party conflict in the U.S. Senate over procedural issues, see Lee 2009, ch. 6.

28. Luce 1972 [1922], 5; Mayhew 1974; quotes from Jefferson 1997 [1812], Sec. 1, §283 and U.S. House 1983, 312. In his 1983 quote Dingell was referring to bureaucratic procedures, but it applies just as well to Congress' procedures for considering legislation.
29. Burns 1963.
30. Dahl, "The American Oppositions," from Dahl 1966, 34; Lee 2009, 10 and ch. 4; quote from Connelly and Pitney 1994, 14–15. This particular goal can be seen as sharing some kinship with the model of parties as office-seeking. Strøm and Müller, "Political Parties and Hard Choices," from Müller and Strøm 1999, 5.
31. Rhodes admitted he would consider resigning as leader if he felt compelled to vote for impeachment. Smith 2005, 124.
32. Pianin 1987; interview with former Democratic leader, September 15, 2011. Michel made similar remarks about George H. W. Bush; see Connelly and Pitney 1994, 32.
33. See e.g. Bibby and Davidson 1972, 153 and Edwards 2012, ch. 10.
34. See e.g. Connelly and Pitney 1994, 105–6, 114; Ford 1979, 89; Koszczuk 1995; and Stanton 2011a.
35. So warned former Speaker Newt Gingrich to minority House Republicans in 2009 (Bai 2009).
36. Quotes from Balz and Brownstein 1996, 147; and Connelly and Pitney 1994, 156 (see also 33). See also Jones 1965, 129–30.
37. Balz and Brownstein 1996, 135–40; Connelly and Pitney 1994, 119–22; Feulner 1983; Woodward 2011; interview with David Bonior, July 3, 2012. On the incentive for minority parties to oppose their own president to get more media coverage, see Groeling 2010. Majority parties can, and sometimes do, revolt against same-party presidents, too; see e.g. Vande Hei and Babington 2005.
38. Johnson 1997; Jones 1970, 3, 24.
39. Brownstein 2007, 139; Cohen 2002; Connelly and Pitney 1994, 9; "House Counsel," June 12, 1980, from Robert H. Michel Papers, Leadership Box 2, Folder 96th Congress Leadership Contests, 1980(1); Mercurio and Wallison 1998, Vande Hei 1997d; interview with former House Republican leader, December 7, 2011; quote from Smith 2007, 40; see also Connelly and Pitney 1994, 22–24. Majority party leaders

can also have preferences and goals that differ from their parties' (e.g. Green 2010).

40. Interview with former Republican leadership aide, September 15, 2011.
41. Drew 2009; Hume 1888 [1739], Book 2, Part 3, Sec. 3, 415; March and Olsen 1984. Edelman (1971, 56–57) argues that emotion cannot be readily accepted as a cause of action.
42. Connelly and Pitney 1994, ch. 4; interview with former House Republican leader, December 7, 2011.
43. March and Olsen 1984, 742; Montaigne 1958 [1580], Book 2, ch. 8 ("On the affection of fathers for their children"), 139; interview with Steve Elmendorf, September 30, 2011. The term *autonomous motivational dynamic* comes from de Waal 2011, 156. On accretion in decision-making, see Weiss 1980.
44. March and Olsen 1984; interview with Republican House member, October 14, 2011. Michael Oakeshott defined "rational" behavior not as advance knowledge of an outcome, since that is impossible, but from how consistently certain behavior is followed given its suitability for a particular situation (Oakeshott 1981 [1962], 101–2).
45. Evans (2000) identifies three kinds of minority party tactics used to win elections: voting against majority party proposals (which I define as *legislating*), obstructing, and proposing alternatives (such as campaign agendas, one kind of *electioneering*). One category of tactics I do not examine in depth is the exposure or accusation of ethical violations by the majority party (see e.g. Lee 2009, ch. 5). Another, more defensive category is to defend, contain, or root out malfeasance or embarrassing behavior within one's own party. A variant of messaging also unexplored here is to seek changes to House rules to make a political point, à la the Pledge of Allegiance example that started this chapter. Finally, every once in a while minority parties may try to force a change in the majority's leadership or weaken its procedural control over the chamber (see e.g. Barry 1989; Farrell 2001, 631).
46. See e.g. Smith 1989, 155–58; Strøm and Müller, "Political Parties and Hard Choices," from Müller and Strøm 1999, 10. In late 1987, for instance, Minority Leader Bob Michel distanced himself from Gingrich's controversial tactics of confrontation by telling a reporter: "I from time to time have problems with [Gingrich's] methodology," adding that it "certainly is not my agenda." Gingrich was unhappy with Michel's remarks, however. He sent to Michel a copy of the news story that printed them, along with a handwritten note that read in part, "I am deeply

disappointed. I have taken the risks. I thought you could at least have been positive." Michel Papers, RHM Staff, Kehl Box 12, Folder Republican Party-House (3).

47. Many argue the collective-action problem can be severe (see e.g. Olson 1966 and Smith 2007, 26–30); Lee 2009 (13–18) argues the contrary.
48. For more on sustaining vetoes, see Chapter 5. For an example of this emphasis of unity on procedural matters, see Sinclair 2006, 177. On the electoral utility of unity, see Grynaviski 2010, 76–92, 104–7. Unity can sometimes be an end in itself; minorities often believe that a unified party wins elections. But I believe it is best thought of as a necessary precondition to acting collectively. For more on the consideration of unity as a distinct party goal, see Sjöblom 1968, 85–87.
49. Hulse 2009b; Weisman 2007. According to one Republican staffer, Boehner's lobbying was less influential in getting Cao's vote than the congressman's own concerns about how the bill would affect accessibility to abortion. Interview with Republican leadership aide, April 7, 2010.
50. See e.g. Koopman 1996, 141. On the divisions that can exist within a minority party along other dimensions besides policy, see Connelly and Pitney 1994, ch. 2. Unity between parties in the House and Senate can also yield legislative and electoral benefits, but it can be hard to come by (Connelly and Pitney 1994, 106–7). The reader will encounter occasional examples in the book of such agreement and coordination of tactics between both chambers, though it is not a central focus of this study.
51. Connelly and Pitney 1994, 4; Davidson, Oleszek, and Lee 2012, 165–66; Peabody 1976, 106; Sinclair 2006, 175–76, 179–80; Vande Hei 1997a, 1997c; interview with Cal Dooley, September 8, 2011. The inability of the minority to reward sufficiently the contributions of its rank and file can be thought of as a nonsimultaneous exchange problem. Strøm and Müller, "Political Parties and Hard Choices," from Müller and Strøm 1999, 16.
52. Connelly and Pitney 1994, 46; Durkheim 2001 [1912], 157; Evans 2000; Farrell 2001; Sinclair 2006, 176–77; Wegner 2001; interview with former Democratic leader, January 6, 2011; Hoyer quote from Sinclair 2006, 176–77.
53. Billings 2003a; Draper 2012, xviii; Wallison 2000c; interview with David Bonior, July 3, 2012; quote by Willis Gradison (OH), from Connelly and Pitney 1994, 5; see also Jones 1970, 192. In 1992, for instance, Lawrence Coughlin (R-PA) made a "surprise announcement" that he would leave

the House because of "40 years of control by a now-tired majority" that displayed an "arrogance of power." Foerstel 1992.

54. Connelly and Pitney 1994, 122; Rosenblum 2008, 54; see also Allen and Bresnahan 2010; CNN 2002; and Davis 2006.
55. Ignazio Silone, from Crossman 1965, 100; interview with Democratic leadership aide, August 1, 2003; interview with Cal Dooley, September 8, 2011; interview with former Democratic leader, September 15, 2011; interview with Steve Elmendorf, September 30, 2011; interview with Democratic House member, October 27, 2011.
56. Woodward 2012, 22; interview with Republican leadership aide, October 18, 2011.
57. Allen 2004; comment by former representative Robert Walker (R-PA), Wilson Center 2010; acceptance speech by Robert Michel to House Republicans, December 8, 1980, 8 (http://www.dirksencenter.org/images/RHMichel/rhmleader1980.PDF).
58. Hinckley 1971, 115; Smith 2005, 91; "Gephardt Speech to Freshmen Orientation," Richard A. Gephardt Papers, Box 835, Folder 23. Lawmakers and scholars alike have likened American political parties to teams. See e.g. Brownstein 2007, 123–24; Downs 1957, 25; Edwards 2012; Grynaviski 2010, 210; and Lee 2009.
59. Bader 1996; Balz and Brownstein 1996, 116–19, 142–47, quote 118; Connelly and Pitney 1994, 8, 26, quote 58; Rhodes 1995, 235–36; Roberts and Smith 2003; Smith 2005, 258; interview with John Feehery, August 31, 2011; interview with Democratic leadership aide, September 28, 2011; interview with former House Republican leader, December 7, 2011.
60. Berman 2001; Fenno 2000; Kabaservice 2012; Karol 2009; Koopman 1996, 136–39; Lee 2009; McKee 2010; Noel 2014; Poole and Rosenthal 1997; Rae 1989; Sinclair 2006; Smith 2005, 277; see also Connelly and Pitney 1994, 154–55.
61. I use the term *entrepreneur* loosely here. For more on political entrepreneurs and innovators, including those in Congress, see Arnold 1990; Bader 1996, 88–99; Dahl, "Patterns of Opposition," from Dahl 1966, 344; Koopman 1996; and Bruce Miroff, "Leadership and American Political Development," from Skowronek and Glassman 2007.
62. Lowi 1963; but see also Jones 1970, ch. 9. Fear of losing power can also drive innovation (see Chapter 2) and political parties that lose elections at the state and presidential level tend to innovate as well; see Klinker 1994, 1–2.

63. House Republicans, for instance, lost many of their promising members during their long pre-1994 stretch in the minority to jobs elsewhere, including Mel Laird, Don Rumsfeld, Dick Cheney, and David Stockman (all to the executive branch); Jack Kemp (who ran for the presidency); Trent Lott (to the Senate); and Vin Weber (to the private sector). See Connelly and Pitney 1994, 14, 113.
64. Heberlig and Larson 2012, 187; Koopman 1996, 141; Mayhew 2000, 25, 127–28; Smith 2007, 30; interview with Republican leadership aide, October 18, 2011. Consider for instance Gingrich's undermining of Rhodes' leadership; he later employed the support of more junior members to successfully force Robert Michel to retire in 1994 (Balz and Brownstein 1996, 148; Rhodes 1995, 235; Smith 2005, 74). There are certainly examples of strong minority party leaders, such as Leslie Arends and Nancy Pelosi, who have discouraged entrepreneurship within their parties, perhaps out of fear of such rivalry.
65. Trent Lott noted that as a member of the Conservative Opportunity Society he was in part "just keeping an eye on Newt's guys. The leadership was concerned that they would rise up on some issue and cause problems" (Lott 2005, 93–94). See also Roberts 1979 and Roberts 1980, 287.
66. Bai 2009; Baker 1981.
67. For recent treatments of the subject, see Bawn, Cohen, Karol, Masket, Noel, and Zaller 2012; Cohen, Karol, Noel, and Zaller 2008; Karol 2009; and Masket 2009.
68. For another approach to studying collective party activity, see Jones 1970, 6.
69. See e.g. Jones 1970, 19; Sinclair 1995; and Smith 2007, 41–42.

Chapter Two. Electioneering

Epigraph 1. Jackson 1988, 187.

Epigraph 2. Anonymous interview, September 29, 2011.

1. Jacobson 2009, 97; Kolodny 1998, 9.
2. Kolodny 1998, 11. Since the cost of protecting an incumbent is roughly double that of funding a challenger, it can be quite debilitating to a minority if it has many endangered incumbents. Interview with former DCCC aide, September 29, 2011.
3. Bacon 2010; Jacobson 2009, 89; interview with NRCC aide, August 26, 2011. On social learning in politics, see also Hershey 1984, 69–79. Brooks

Jackson described this replication of campaign tactics as "reminiscent of the technological competition between armor and artillery; an advance on one side inevitably led to a compensating innovation on the other" (Jackson 1988, 154).

4. Certain kinds of campaign activity could strengthen internal unity by instilling a sense of obligation to the party for campaign help, or rewarding loyalists with more resources. The party could also try getting new lawmakers elected who are more likely to agree with their partisan colleagues. But minorities care first and foremost about having a majority, regardless of how "loyal" its members are to the party platform, and will give help even to rebellious incumbents if they are in electoral trouble (Parker 2008, 124–28). Sometimes unity of purpose emerges when the minority realizes that it cannot regain the majority without tolerating members who can win a diversity of districts (Wallison 1999a).
5. Jacobson 2009, 119, 249–52.
6. Kolodny 1998, 111, 116–17.
7. Herrnson 2012, 91–92; Jackson 1988, 34, 43–44; Kolodny 1998, ch. 5.
8. Jackson 1988, 53–54, 70–75, 181, quote 54; Kolodny 1998, 132–33.
9. Jackson 1988, 55–56, 60, 68–70, 98–101, 142–66; quotes 52, 56, 288. For more on the growth of business and other PACs and how they shifted from Republicans to Democrats after Coelho's aggressive solicitation, see Jacobson 2009, 67–72 and Sorauf 1992, 102–3.
10. Bruck 1995; Currinder 2009, 120; Glasgow 2002; Heberlig 2003, 2007; Heberlig and Larson 2012; Henry and Burger 1996; Kolodny 1998, 148–50, 186; Larson 2004. The DCCC also rushed to establish a national fund-raising program after 1994, supplementing its earlier and narrower Washington-based fund-raising model. Interview with former Democratic leader, September 15, 2011. Ed Rollins, who was co-chair of the NRCC in 1989–90, may have helped develop the NRCC's more targeted donation strategy. Whalen 1990. For more on how Paxon improved and professionalized the NRCC's operations, see Balz and Brownstein 1996, 47–48 and Kolodny 1998, 200–202.
11. Kucinich 2010c; quote from Herrnson 2012, 97.
12. Herrnson 2012, 97; Jacobson 2009, 79–80; interview with former NRCC aide, September 30, 2011; interview with former Democratic leader, September 15, 2011; interview with former Democratic leader, December 4, 2002. The NRCC chair is elected by all House Republicans, while the DCCC chair is appointed by the party's top leader. For

examples of some of these techniques as used by DCCC chair Rahm Emanuel, see Bendavid 2007, 66, 77–80, 124–25.

13. Bendavid 2007, 79; Currinder 2009, 179; Eilperin 2006, 24, 71–74; Heberlig and Larson 2012; Henry and Burger 1996; Herrnson 2012, 98–99, quote 99; Kucinich 2010b; Nather 2006; Newmyer and McArdle 2010; interview with former Republican leadership aide, June 6, 2003; interview with former Democratic aide, August 29, 2011. Democrats tend to press for dues throughout a cycle, while Republicans employ periodic fund-raising campaigns (McArdle 2010).
14. Bendavid 2007, 14; Curran 1991; Walsh 1985; interview with former Democratic leader, September 15, 2011; interview with former DCCC aide, September 29, 2011.
15. Interview with former Democratic aide, August 29, 2011 (and follow-up e-mail); interview with former DCCC aide, September 29, 2011. Congressional staff are also looked to as sources of information that might be of help in a campaign.
16. Bendavid 2007, 131; Carney 1999; interview with former Democratic leader, September 15, 2011.
17. Bendavid 2007, 82–87; Connelly and Pitney 1994, 121; Whalen 1990.
18. The other is providing resources. Cox and Katz 1996; interview with former Democratic leader, January 6, 2011; interview with NRCC aide, August 26, 2011.
19. Balz and Brownstein 1996, 145–46, quote 145; Draper 2011; Kolodny 1998, 117; interview with former Democratic leader, January 6, 2011; interview with former Republican campaign aide, September 20, 2011; see also Kolodny 1998, 199–205. Outside interest groups sometimes get in the recruitment game, too (Davidson, Oleszek, and Lee 2012, 59).
20. Drucker 2006; interview with former Republican campaign aide, September 20, 2011; interview with former DCCC aide, September 29, 2011. Incumbents who win with less than 60% are, statistically speaking, the most vulnerable (Jacobson 2009, 34). Emanuel followed a somewhat similar rubric for the 2005–6 cycle (Bendavid 2007, 76).
21. Herrnson (2012) notes that such candidates are also useful to "expand the farm team" and give the local party something to rally around (53).
22. Babington and Weisman 2006. The ultimate goal is to have roughly three times the number of seats needed to win back the House, a goal that usually seems so daunting at first that, as one DCCC aide said, "you usually say, 'holy crap, this isn't possible.'" Interview with former DCCC aide, September 29, 2011.

23. Dannheisser 2007; Herrnson 2012, 51–52; Maestas, Maisel, and Stone 2005; L. Sandy Maisel, Cherie Maestas, and Walter J. Stone, "The Party Role in Congressional Competition," from Maisel 2002; interview with former Republican campaign aide, September 20, 2011; interview with NRCC aide, August 26, 2011. Some factors will matter more than others, given the nature of the election cycle. In 2007–8, for example, minority Republicans gave considerable attention to rich candidates as a means of countering the NRCC's relative lack of money (Hernandez 2007).
24. Bendavid 2007, 99–100; Cantor and Herrnson 1997; Herrnson 2012, 52; Kane 2010; Kolodny 1998, 10, 102; Lawless 2012, ch. 7; interview with former DCCC aide, September 29, 2011. In 2010, for instance, Republicans stood behind losing primary candidates in Idaho and Pennsylvania, while in 2006 Democrats endorsed candidates in primaries in California, New Hampshire, and New York who subsequently lost. The winners of these primaries all went on to win the general election (Gonzales 2010).
25. Eilperin 1999; Herrnson 2012, 51–52; Toeplitz 2010. Special elections are given great weight by lawmakers as indicators of how the general election will go (see e.g. Balz and Brownstein 1996, 23–26 and Bendavid 2007, 137). So even though "they're squirrely," in the words of a onetime NRCC staffer, it is not surprising that congressional parties will give particular attention to winning these races. However, as one DCCC campaign staffer put it, "if a district is an absolute stinker for you, it's usually best to say 'uh uh, not going to go for it'" (interview with former Republican campaign aide, September 20, 2011; interview with former DCCC aide, September 29, 2011).
26. For instance, Bill Clinton helped recruit Rep. Mike Honda to run in 1999, and Barack Obama offered to assist with candidate recruitment in 2013. See below.
27. Interview with former DCCC aide, September 29, 2011; Herrnson 2012, 101; Maestas, Maisel, and Stone 2005; Rowley 2010.
28. Herrnson 2012, 101–2; Wallison 2002; interview with Steve Elmendorf, September 30, 2011; interview with former DCCC aide, September 29, 2011; interview with former NRCC aide, September 30, 2011. If an incumbent cannot be persuaded to stay, the party may try to time the person's retirement to help the party. Late retirements, for instance, allow the party to secretly groom replacements in advance, while a "drum beat of retirements" can create negative press (interview with former DCCC aide, September 29, 2011).

29. Baker 2009; Balz and Brownstein 1996, 146; Bendavid 2007, 21–23; Draper 2012, 78; McArdle and Toeplitz 2009; Weisman 2006; interview with former Democratic leader, September 15, 2011.
30. Nyhan 2010; see also Jacobson and Kernell 1983, 30.
31. Berkman and Eisenstein 1999; Fowler and McClure 1989, 224–30; Fox and Lawless 2005, quote 652; Geraghty 2009; Hernandez 2008; Jacobson 2009, 168–74; Jacobson and Kernell 1983, ch. 3; Krasno and Green 1988; Lawless 2012; Maisel, Maestas, and Stone, "The Party Role," from Maisel 2002; "Prelude to Our Race for Leader," Robert H. Michel Papers, Leadership Box 2, Folder 96th Leadership Contests, 1980(1); Stone and Maisel 2003; Wrighton and Squire 1997; and York 2010. For more on what leads individuals to run, see Kazee and Thornberry 1990.
32. Lawless 2012; Maestas, Fulton, Maisel, and Stone 2006; Maisel, Maestas, and Stone, "The Party Role," from Maisel 2002; see also Kazee and Thornberry 1990.
33. See e.g. Cox and Katz 1996 and Green and Krasno 1988.
34. Nor is it clear how one can best measure candidate quality. Personal traits may also matter. See e.g. Stone and Maisel 2003.
35. Jacobson and Kernell 1983.
36. The other important resource, according to Parker, is reputation. Parker 2008, 11.
37. Currinder 2009, 175–79; Heberlig and Larson 2012, 5, 54, 204–5; Jacobson 2009, 76. For more, see Herrnson 2012, 100 and Ornstein 1997, 10.
38. The final year's figures are provisional as of this writing.
39. Eilperin 2006, 23–24. Lamented one former DCCC staffer, after BCRA passed "we went from a $100 million budget to a $32 million budget overnight" (interview with former DCCC aide, September 29, 2011).
40. Balz and Brownstein 1996, 49; Bendavid 2007, 56, 109; Murray 2010; Toeplitz 2010. The name "Hammer" first appeared in a 1995 *Washington Post* article critical of DeLay's fund-raising operation (Pershing 2004). On GOPAC's critical financial help to the NRCC in the early 1990s, see Bruck 1995.
41. Carney 1999; Cillizza 2003; Eilperin 1999; Liptak 2013; Wilson and Rucker 2013; interview with former NRCC aide, September 30, 2011. See also Herrnson 2012, 96–97 and Kolodny 1998, 8–9.
42. Jacobson 2009, 79; Parker 2008, 21–23. Individual candidates get the largest percentage of their campaign funds (over half) from individuals (Jacobson 2009).

43. Herrnson 2012, 100, 105, 107; Jacobson 2009, 74–75; Ornstein 1997, 10. Other approaches include giving money to state party organizations, which then give the money to candidates, or asking other party committees and legislator PACs to give their funding to certain candidates (Herrnson 2012, 107, 109).
44. Herrnson 2012, 101–3; Maisel, Maestas, and Stone, "The Party Role," from Maisel 2002. The parties have even been known to "trade" people on watch lists if each party has an equal number of seats they would prefer not be challenged by the other. Tony Coelho, for instance, removed Carroll Campbell (R-SC) from the DCCC's list of targeted incumbents in exchange for the NRCC deprioritizing its campaign against Robin Talent (D-NC). Interview with former Democratic leader, December 4, 2002.
45. Heberlig and Larson 2012, 141; Herrnson 2012, 102–4, quote 107; Jacobson and Kernell 1983, 39–42; interview with former NRCC aide, September 30, 2011. Nor is there evidence that spending on a candidate noticeably affects that person's subsequent voting behavior (Cantor and Herrnson 1997; Damore and Hansford 1999).
46. Interview with former Republican campaign aide, September 20, 2011; interview with former DCCC aide, September 29, 2011; interview with former NRCC aide, September 30, 2011; see also Bendavid 2007, 25–26. Whether party pressures to retire actually work is unclear; Jacobson and Kernell (1983) suggest that retirements may be more the consequence of how incumbents perceive the likely partisan swing of the next election (ch. 5). For more on retirement from Congress, see Theriault 1998 and Stone, Fulton, Maestas, and Maisel 2010.
47. Herrnson 2012, 104–5, 119; interview with former DCCC aide, September 29, 2011. Candidates must meet fairly stringent requirements to be added to these list, including having strong campaign organizations and fund-raising operations, in order (as one erstwhile Republican campaign staffer put it) to "keep the integrity of the brand" (interview with former Republican campaign aide, September 20, 2011).
48. Data on fund-raising taken from FEC reports in 2004, 2006, and 2010. Data on election results and equivalent districts taken from FEC data, CQ's 2006 *Politics in America*, and the 2008 *Almanac of American Politics*. Equivalent districts are those in proximity to candidates on each list, with similar partisan index and occupational balance, and with a candidate showing a relatively competitive rate of fund-raising. Only the data from list members who have matched pairs are included (12 Democrats for 2004, 12 Democrats for 2006, and 9 Republicans for 2010).

49. Democrats believed they would have lost even more seats in 2010 had they not spent money on behalf of some vulnerable incumbents, but it is impossible to know that with certainty (Herrnson 2012, 105). In 2012, twenty-six of the fifty-five Democratic Red to Blue candidates won their elections.
50. Gerber, Gimpel, Green, and Shaw 2011; Jacobson 2009, 48–51; Levitt 1994; McGhee and Sides 2011; Parker 2008, ch. 6; Stratmann 2009.
51. Fiorina 1981; Miller 1977, 264 (emphasis his).
52. Grynaviski 2010, 181–87; see also Bader 1996, 181 and Hunter 2010. In mid-2006, for instance, Republicans issued an American Values Agenda of bills designed to appeal to right-leaning voters (Bendavid 2007, 145). On party "record building" more generally, see Cox and McCubbins 1993, 110. Sellers (2010, 46–47) notes that their breadth provides flexibility for lawmakers seeking issues that may best suit their districts or campaigns.
53. Interview with Republican House member, November 17, 2011; see also Balz and Brownstein 1996, 52. In the spring of 2009, Republicans tried to hold events that emphasized conservative policy proposals, as "prominent Republicans" grew "worried that the GOP is being portrayed only as the opposition party" (Bacon 2009). For more on obstruction and delay, see Chapter 4.
54. Albright 1968; "Congress Enacts President Reagan's Tax Plan," from *CQ Almanac* 1981, 91–104; Groeling 2010, 14–15; Herrnson 2012, 92–93; Kenneally 2003, 120–21; Sinclair 2006; Smith 2005, 217. The 1968 agenda was later published as a book called *The Futile System*. The 1980 agenda included a pledge to pass the Kemp-Roth tax-reduction proposal, which later became Reagan's signature budget bill in 1981.
55. Reprinted in Bader 1996, 175. One Gephardt aide's notes from a leadership meeting to develop the party's 1996 agenda observed: "Develop agenda to enact—rebuild confidence of American people in government. Contract-concept—good idea." Memo, Richard Gephardt Papers, Series 5 Subsection 8 Sub-subsection 9, Box 169, Folder 2.
56. Bader 1996, 186–88; Espo 2006; Koopman 1996, 144–45; notes from consultant meeting, June 12, 1997, "Research Plan" memo, and "Review of Polling on Proposed Issues" memo, July 1, 1997, Gephardt Papers, Box 827, Folder 2.
57. Bader 1996, 171–73; Koopman 1996, 146; Lott 2005, 127. In 1996, for instance, Democrats held teleconferences to announce their Families First agenda in four cities, quickly sent out an ad touting the

agenda, developed "monthly message themes" related to the agenda, and encouraged Democrats to use those themes in their campaigns (B. Bradley 1996; *CongressDaily* 1996; "Discussion Draft: Marketing of Democratic Agenda," Gephardt Papers, Series 5 Subsection 8 Sub-subsection 9, Box 169, Folder 2). During the August 2006 recess, Democrats were given pocket-size cards that summarized the New Direction agenda and were encouraged to hold events in their district to discuss it.

58. Fagan and Dinan 2002.
59. Republican whip Robert Michel also ran a whip count to maximize attendance at the September 1980 rally. Letter to John Anderson, September 8, 1980, Michel Papers, RHM Leadership, Box 3, Folder 96th Whip Rolls. For more on the Contract and how it was developed and marketed, see Bader 1996, ch. 7; Balz and Brownstein 1996; Gimpel 1996; and Koopman 1996, 142–47.
60. Draper 2012, 48; Kucinich 2010d.
61. Bader 1996, 184; Grynaviski 2010, 184. Agreement is sometimes tried across chambers and with the White House. The Democrats' 1998 agenda was, in fact, based on items from President Clinton's State of the Union address the previous month (Rankin and Pugh 1998, *White House Bulletin* 1998; see also Tackett and Gregory 1996).
62. Fights within the G.O.P. in 1994 emerged over whether to include school prayer, for instance, and Democrats in 2006 tried to come up with an agenda that "threatened to come apart, then it would come together, then it would threaten to come apart," recounted George Miller (CA). Balz and Brownstein 1996, 38–39; Bendavid 2007, 141. In 1996, Gephardt's staff advised that because the party's campaign agenda was unlikely to garner the full support of the party or its candidates, the "announcement event should avoid 'head count' of supporters." "Discussion Draft: Marketing of Democratic Agenda," Gephardt Papers, Series 5 Subsection 8 Sub-subsection 9, Box 169, Folder 2.
63. For a somewhat different view of the Contract, see Bader 1996. Minority parties might still tout these agendas after an election, as Democrats sometimes did with their Families First agenda.
64. The Democrats' 2006 agenda had six proposals because campaign consultants had recommended that number (Bendavid 2007, 141). Reportedly Gingrich wanted ten items in the Contract with America because he "believed in the 'mythic power' of the number ten" (Balz and Brownstein 1996, 38).

65. Bader 1996, 187–88; "Slogan Ideas" memo, Gephardt Papers, Box 835, Folder 20. Polling was used by 1994 Republicans and 2002 Democrats to figure out their agenda and how to present it (Bader 1996, 188; Espo 2002).
66. Balz and Brownstein 1996, 37; Groeling 2010, 31; Pelosi 2006.
67. Balz and Brownstein 1996, 36; Groeling 2010, 18; Koopman 1996, 147–48; Lippmann 1969 [1914], 186. Grynaviski (2010, 187) suggests the 1994 and 2006 campaign agendas made a difference, given how close the races in those years were. But of course we cannot know how those elections might have differed had there been no agenda.
68. Fiorina 1981. Opinion polls support this claim. For example, after the November 2006 election, one survey showed that only 13% believed the Democrats had won based on their agenda, while a whopping 79% believed it was a repudiation of President George W. Bush or opposition to Republican programs. Several major issues negatively associated with the Bush White House were salient in that election, including the war in Iraq and the government's failed response to Hurricane Katrina. CNN poll, November 2006 [USORC.200629.Q06].
69. Lippmann 1969 [1914], 186; Sellers 1998.
70. See e.g. Rhodes 1995, 134. A search in LexisNexis of stories mentioning the agendas (by name) of minority parties between 1994 and 2010 turned up a median of 29 newspaper articles published in the two months before an election. But 497 newspaper stories mentioned the Contract with America, while 629 referred to the Pledge to America.
71. CNN/*USA Today*/Gallup survey, November 28–29, 1994 [USA IPOCNUS1994-5001002]; ABC News/*Washington Post* survey, September 30–October 3, 2010 [USABCWP.100510.R09]; Wolfensberger 2000, 167–68; interview with Steve Elmendorf, September 30, 2011. A Princeton/*Newsweek* survey held in January 2007 found that about one-third of respondents did not know if Democrats were keeping the promises they made in 2006 [USPSRNEW.011907.R13], though some of those saying this may, in theory, have known of the Democrats' agenda but had not been following Congress since the 2006 elections.
72. Herrnson and Curry 2011; memo to Dick Gephardt from Laura Nichols, May 7, 1998, Gephardt Papers, Box 835, Folder 7.
73. See e.g. Billings 2005 and Herrnson 2012, 117–18. Challengers tend to focus their energy on criticizing incumbents, and parties tend to go negative, so that candidates can stay positive in their own messages (Jacobson 2009, 94–95).

74. Herrnson 2012, 112–13; "Language: A Key Mechanism of Control," GOPAC memo, Gephardt Papers, Box 917, Folder 3. For an account of how Rahm Emanuel pressed candidates to highlight certain issues in the 2005–6 cycle, see Bendavid 2007, 109, 117, 119, and 175.
75. Herrnson 2012, 114–17; Singer 2010. Some of these activities may bring about greater voting unity within the minority party, at least on critical votes (Cantor and Herrnson 1997).
76. Some former Democratic Party leaders interviewed for this book insisted that their campaign efforts were successful even if their party had failed to win control of the House, because their efforts had kept the margins between the two parties narrow. But as a onetime Democratic campaign aide put it, "If at the end of the day you haven't taken back the House, you've failed. Period." Interview, September 29, 2011.
77. See e.g. Campbell 1985; Jacobson 2009; Mayhew 1974, 30–31. For a contrary view, see Cox and McCubbins 1993, 110–20.
78. Bendavid 2007, 73; Connelly and Pitney 1994, ch. 6; Jacobson 2011; Lott 2005, 71–72; McKee 2010; Nyhan, McGhee, Sides, Masket, and Greene 2012; interview with former Republican leadership aide, September 15, 2011; interview with former NRCC aide, September 30, 2011; interview with former House Republican leader, December 7, 2011.
79. Bendavid 2007, 208; Cook 1998; Kolodny 1998, 13; Wallison 2001a; interview with Steve Elmendorf, September 30, 2011.

Chapter Three. Messaging

Epigraph 1. Quoted in Bradley 1997.

Epigraph 2. Quoted in Hulse 2009a.

1. Fenno 2000.
2. Boorstin 1961, Mayhew 1974. Credit-claiming and position-taking, unlike advertising, can also be achieved through legislative activity (e.g. with recorded votes or providing benefits to one's district).
3. Highton and Rocca (2005) argue that other activities are more subject to party discipline than floor statements—particularly voting, because it is a direct means of influencing policy. But since the minority rarely can expect to have much policy influence, it is just as rational for it to develop, and encourage maximum participation in, partisan messaging.
4. Cox and McCubbins 1993, 112–17. Congressional parties that develop strong party reputations may also benefit electorally; see Grynaviski 2010.

5. Quoted in Sinclair 1995, 289. In addition, because the media tends to write "process" stories—stories about party tactics and strategy—a party that fails to run a strong media campaign may tempt reporters to write negative stories about it. On messaging in the Senate, see Lee 2011.
6. Interview with David Bonior, July 3, 2012; interview with Republican leadership aide, August 29, 2011; interview with former Republican aide, August 31, 2011.
7. Arnold 1990, 58; Cox and McCubbins 1993; Lee 2009, 8–10; Sellers 2010.
8. Cook 1989; Ehrenhalt 1986; Graber 2006, 278; Kedrowski 1996; quote from Bach and Smith 1988, 91. In 1993, House Republicans tried to highlight complaints about closed rules with a "battle plan" that "included press kits, op-ed articles, and graphic depictions on the House floor" of restrictive rules. Democrats did provide an open rule on a bill shortly thereafter, but the overall use of restrictive rules did not diminish in the 103rd Congress (see Figure 5.1). Foerstel 1993e, Wolfensberger 2000, 156–57. Relatedly, the minority can use messaging to suggest institutional corruption and connect it with Democratic governance. In mid-1994, for example, the Republicans issued a twenty-eight-page report, *It's Long Enough*, making that very case.
9. Interview with John Feehery, August 31, 2011; interview with Republican leadership aide, October 18, 2011; interview with Democratic House member, October 27, 2011; interview with Republican House member, November 17, 2011. Similarly, presidents may use the public sphere to educate voters, "articulate the common good," or do other nationally minded duties not just to help win reelection (Mayhew 2011, 57).
10. See e.g. C. Lawrence Evans, "Committees, Leaders, and Message Politics," from Dodd and Oppenheimer 2001; Sinclair 2006, ch. 8.
11. Finocchiaro 2003; Jones 2010; Jones and McDermott 2009; interview with Democratic leadership aide, August 26, 2011.
12. See e.g. Evans, from Dodd and Oppenheimer 2001, 220. In 1997 one Gephardt aide urged that the party's agenda be introduced jointly with Clinton and Senate Democrats, for "we need something positive that pulls Democrats together" (memo from Laura Nichols to Steve Elmendorf, Richard Gephardt Papers, Series 7 Subsection 29, Box 832, Folder 17). Later, Nancy Pelosi would run coordinated weekly messages with Senate leader Tom Daschle in 2003, known as Operation Home Front (Epstein 2003).

13. Larry Evans describes an excellent example from the 106th Congress (1999–2000) in which minority Democrats opposed a G.O.P. prescription drug bill with discharge petitions, publicized trips for constituents to buy prescription drugs in other countries, and coordinated visits to congressional districts (Evans, from Dodd and Oppenheimer 2001, 218).
14. Thomas Curtis (R-MO), for example, complained that Johnson was ignoring "an implied constitutional restriction" against "reporting directly to the people over the heads" of Congress "on matters which are essentially legislative" (Thomas Curtis, "The Executive Dominates the News," from Blanchard 1974, 101).
15. Ben H. Bagdikian, "Congress and the Media: Partners in Propaganda," Mark J. Green, James M. Fallows, and David R. Zwick, ". . . And, Frankly, Getting Reelected," and Lewis W. Wolfson, "The Press and Washington's Own Suburban Five," from Blanchard 1974; Mayhew 2000, 230–31. John J. Rhodes, for instance, met weekly with the congressional press corps as minority leader, and Ford and Rhodes did so when Rhodes was chair of the Republican Policy Committee (Smith 2005, 214). Coverage of Congress, at least on television, continued to decline through the early 1990s (Stephen Hess, "The Decline and Fall of Congressional News," and S. Robert Lichter and Daniel R. Amundson, "Less News Is Worse News: Television News Coverage of Congress, 1972–1992, from Mann and Ornstein 1994). See also Cook 1989, ch. 2.
16. Galvin 2010, 62; Lott 2005, 93; interview with former House Republican leader, December 7, 2011.
17. Ehrenhalt 1986; Farrell 2001, 632–36; Granat 1984; Dear Republican Colleague letter from Robert Michel and Trent Lott, September 28, 1983, Robert Michel Papers, RHM Leadership, Box 6, Folder 98th, Dear C.; see also Connelly and Pitney 1994, 77–79.
18. Connelly and Pitney 1994, 42–43; Evans, from Dodd and Oppenheimer 2001, 220; Kedrowski 1996, 91–94; Sinclair 1995, 269–70; letter from Gillis Long to Dick Gephardt, March 20, 1981, from Gephardt Papers, Series 7 Subsection 5, Box 4, Folder 22.
19. Connelly and Pitney 1994, 43; Koopman 1996, 141–42; "Leadership Structure," Gephardt Papers, Box 837, Folder 3. Between March and July 1997, for instance, the DPC sent out nearly thirty messages of the day and another nine "outrage" or "reality check" memos (Gephardt Papers, Series 5 Subsection 11 Sub-subsection 3, Box 388, Folder 2).

20. Wallison 2001b; interview with Democratic House member, October 27, 2011.
21. Billings 2003b; Groeling 2010, 106, 108–10.
22. Graber 2006, 250–51, 272–77; Groeling 2010; Sinclair 1995, 268–69; interview with Republican House member, November 17, 2011. Studies have shown that minority party leaders in the House get less media coverage than majority leaders, and much less than the president (e.g. Cook 1989, 192–98). Between 2006 and 2011, the minority leader was mentioned in news programs 77 times per year, on average; the speaker of the House, over 131 times per year on average; and President Barack Obama, 2,900 times in 2009 alone (Vanderbilt Television News Archives).
23. Cook 1989, 8–9, 30; see also Stanton 2011b. The party does much the same for its campaign agendas; see Chapter 2.
24. Bendery 2011; Glassman, Straus, and Shogan 2009. The majority party, especially when facing an opposite-party president or fearing an imminent loss of power, can also be a source of innovation in communication and messaging. Speaker Tip O'Neill, for example, introduced a now-common "public speakership" style to combat the Republican White House after 1980 (Farrell 2001; Harris 1998). For more on "media entrepreneurs" and how and why individual members use media, see Kedrowski 1996.
25. Roth 2007; interview with former Democratic leader, January 6, 2011; interview with Republican leadership aide, August 29, 2011.
26. Sinclair 1995, 215; interview with NRCC aide, August 26, 2011; interview with former Democratic leader, July 1, 2003; interview with former Democratic leader, December 4, 2002; interview with Democratic House member, October 27, 2011. For more on the particular messaging topics chosen by legislative parties, albeit in the Senate, see Sellers 2010, ch. 3.
27. Evans, from Dodd and Oppenheimer 2001, 230–31; Graber 2006, 276; Kedrowski 1996, 91; Sinclair 1995, 265, 292–93; interview with Democratic leadership aide, August 26, 2011; interview with John Feehery, August 31, 2011; interview with former Republican aide, August 31, 2011.
28. See e.g. Keller 1997a. A message should be "repeated, and repeated, and repeated, and repeated," as one former Republican aide put it (interview, August 31, 2011).
29. Bellantoni 2010; interview with former Republican aide, August 29, 2011; interview with Republican leadership aide, August 31, 2011; Crabtree 2003; Eilperin 2003.

30. Interview with former Republican aide, August 31, 2011. One Democratic leadership staffer recalled how a conservative party member warned that the party's national message was hurting her in her district; she lost reelection in 2010 (interview with Democratic leadership aide, September 28, 2011).
31. Interview with Steve Elmendorf, September 30, 2011; interview with Democratic House member, October 27, 2011. In May 1997, for instance, an aide to Minority Leader Gephardt argued in a memo that the first messaging objective should be to "carve out a message and a position in the budget debate for Dick *that will stand up in* 2000" (memo from Laura Nichols to Steve Elmendorf, Gephardt Papers, Series 7 Subsection 29, Box 832, Folder 17, emphasis added). For more on how parties try to develop message unity, see Sellers 2010, 47.
32. This also limits the coverage of the majority party if the president is of the same party (Groeling 2010, 59–70, ch. 3, and 123–24).
33. See e.g. Brady and Shiner 2012. In November 2005, for instance, 81% of respondents in one survey correctly identified the Republican Party as controlling Congress, but in August 2008 only 56% knew that Democrats were in charge (GWU Battleground poll, August 2008; Democracy Corps poll, November 2005). For more on voter knowledge of the ideological predisposition of Congress, see Jones and McDermott 2009.
34. Groeling 2010, 124; Pianin 1987; Wasson and Lillis 2011; interview with John Feehery, August 31, 2011; interview with Steve Elmendorf, September 30, 2011; interview with Republican House member, October 14, 2011; memorandum from Daschle staff to Gephardt staff, December 22, 1997, from Gephardt Papers, Box 979, Folder 1.
35. Rothenberg 2009; Wallison 1999b, 2000a; interview with Democratic House member, October 27, 2011.
36. Sellers 2010, 42–44; interview with Democratic leadership aide, August 26, 2011. For more on the "inside" audience of lawmakers, see Kedrowski 1996, 16; Sinclair 1995, 266–69, 289.
37. Five-minute speeches are given less frequently than one-minute speeches, and hour-long "special order" speeches are popular with a smaller group of lawmakers, though they were central to the communication strategy of House Republicans in the 1970s and '80s.
38. Interview with Democratic House member, October 27, 2011; interview with Republican House member, November 17, 2011.
39. Members were allowed have extended versions of one-minute speeches printed in the *Congressional Record*, but they became so lengthy that

Speaker Sam Rayburn eventually required that they be reprinted in the appendix of the *Record* (Deschler 1977, v. 6, ch. 21, §6.1).

40. Garay 1984, 140–41. In a random sample of one-minute speeches from 1975, the most frequent partisan speech-givers were party leaders Tip O'Neill and John Rhodes, but in 1980 rank-and-file members delivered the bulk of speeches with partisan content or commentary about the president. The percentage of one-minutes given by minority Republicans also grew from 32% to 59%.
41. See e.g. *Congressional Record*, January 22, 1980, 220; March 5, 1980, 4779, 4780; March 20, 1980, 6017; and April 2, 1980, 7474–75. Republicans also used the same argument in special order speeches given that year; see e.g. February 11, 1980, 2597–2603.
42. *Congressional Record*, August 21, 1980, 22231. When Democrats announced that one-minutes would be moved to the end of the day for the rest of the 1980 session, Republicans cried foul, claiming it was an effort to prevent their speeches from getting television coverage. See *Congressional Record*, July 24, 1980, 19443.
43. *Congressional Record*, August 19, 1980, 21943, and August 26, 1980, 23100. Excessive partisanship in one-minutes remained a complaint among a number of members of both parties, and in the 1990s some legislators proposed limiting one-minutes or moving them to the end of the legislative day because of their sharp partisan content (J. Bradley 1996; Keller 1999).
44. Deschler 1977, v. 12, ch. 29, §10, §10.48; Harris 2005; Simpson 1990; Sinclair 1995, 270. The same August 1984 ruling instituted a similar policy for special order speeches as well, and it followed the famous incident in May of that year in which Speaker O'Neill was formally admonished by the House for criticizing Newt Gingrich's language in a special order on the floor of the House (*Congressional Record*, May 15, 1984, 12201). The DMB is not to be confused with the Democratic Message Group, led by the party's top leaders, which chooses year- or Congress-long themes, though those themes might guide the specific topics of one-minute speeches solicited by the DMB (Harris 2005, 129).
45. Koopman 1996, 141; interview with John Feehery, August 31, 2011; "A Blueprint for Leadership," Office of the Republican Leader, April 16, 1993, RHM Legislative, Special Subjects, Other, Box 6, Folder 103rd, Reform, Grandy-Gunderson.
46. Kucinich 2009b.

47. The House sometimes allows lawmakers to deliver longer, five-minute speeches (during what is known as "morning hour debate") before the time set aside for one-minute speeches.
48. The average number of one-minutes does not capture the total amount of floor time each party dedicates to speeches, since its members also use five-minute and hour-long "special order" speeches. For more on how the House treats one-minute speeches under its rules and customs, see Mulvihill 1999.
49. Garay 1984, 140. A smaller sampling of one-minute speeches taken in 1992, 1993, 2008, and 2009 suggests that the minority did dramatically increase its share of one-minute speeches in 1993 and 2009 compared to the previous year. However, a sample from 2004 suggests that it was the majority party—not the minority—that was responsible for the increase in one-minute speeches in 2005.
50. Maltzman and Sigelman 1996; interview with Republican House member, November 17, 2011.
51. Harris 2005, interview with Republican House member, November 17, 2011. Evans (from Dodd and Oppenheimer 2001) sees one-minute speeches as sufficiently party-oriented and party-coordinated that he uses them to measure the parties' overall message priorities. In 1996, one-minute speeches were among those tools proposed by Democratic leadership as a way of advertising the party's campaign agenda. "Discussion Draft: Marketing of Democratic Agenda," Gephardt Papers, Series 5 Subsection 8 Sub-subsection 9, Box 169, Folder 2.
52. Fenno 2000. Ironically, giving more one-minute speeches may hurt a lawmaker's chances of getting reelected (Box-Steffensmeier, Kimball, Meinke, and Tate 2003).
53. For an example of archival data used to determine party coordination of one-minutes, see Harris 2005. Maltzman and Sigelman (1996) use certain characteristics of speech-givers themselves to divine motivation. Shogan, Glassman, and McMillon (2013), analyzing their own sample of one-minute speeches, find many of the same patterns between parties as I do.
54. Such statements could also include references to collective concerns, but were primarily focused on a parochial matter. Statements that could not be clearly traced to a local district matter were not included in the total (e.g. praising an ethnic group without referring to their large population in one's district), nor were speeches that referred to constituents

in general when discussing national policy (e.g. "the health care bill will hurt my constituents").

55. The data consist of all one-minute speeches given in eight randomly selected weeks, stratified by quarter (i.e. two weeks chosen randomly from each of four quarters of the year). In 2010, 286 were given by majority party Democrats and 271 by minority party Republicans.
56. Larry Evans analyzes in more detail the policy content of one-minute speeches in 1999, demonstrating that variation by party does exist (Evans, from Dodd and Oppenheimer 2001).
57. Speeches discussing procedural rights included statements criticizing procedures used to consider a bill or structure debate on the floor (e.g. a floor rule), the partisan balance of committee seats, or failure to schedule or allow a vote on a bill. They do not include criticisms that a committee has not released a bill, since that may not necessarily be the fault of the majority party.
58. Two-tailed test, $p<.05$.
59. In 1975, 1985, and 1990, Democrats controlled the House but not the White House; in 1995 and 2000, Republicans were in the same boat; in 1980 and 2010, minority Republicans faced a Democratic president; and in 2005, the reverse was true.
60. One-minute speeches delivered by the majority tend to emphasize the work of Congress as a whole, bipartisanship, or unity.
61. Interview with Republican House member, October 14, 2011. Not that lawmakers fail to try getting such media attention for their floor speeches; see e.g. Sinclair 1995, 270. About 25% of Americans eligible to vote watch the U.S. House on C-SPAN, though estimates of the number of C-SPAN viewers range from 39 million to 54 million (C-SPAN 2010, Miller 2009).
62. A CBS/*New York Times* poll taken a few days after the event showed 57% believed the stimulus bill passed earlier that year had already, or soon would, create more jobs, though 62% of Republicans surveyed thought it would not. CBS/*New York Times* poll, July 24–28, 2009 [USCBSNYT.072909B.R26].
63. Graber 2006, 253.
64. Other ways that parties communicate with the media include press releases and background ("pen-and-pad") briefings (Graber 2006, 276–77).
65. Alexander 2010, 286–87, 291; Graber 2006, 249, 277–78. Sellers (2010, 13–15) describes what he calls the "cycle of spin" in which lawmakers

develop and promote messages, the press repeats it, and their reportage affects what lawmakers do.

66. Cook 1989, 35; Ehrenhalt 1986; Graber 2006, 276; Michael J. Robinson, "Three Faces of Congressional Media," from Mann and Ornstein 1981, 65, 82–84, quote 55. In November 2009, for example, House Republicans, led by the vocal and high-profile Michele Bachmann (MN), held a rally outside the Capitol against the Democratic health care reform bill before an audience of reporters and Tea Party activists. Other creative press events have included taking constituents to Canada to buy cheap prescription drugs and sleeping outside to dramatize homelessness (e.g. Sinclair 1995, 270).
67. Barbara Sinclair (1995) highlights several goals of majority leaders in going public, but emphasizes the electoral and policy goals of the party as motivating communication (266–71, 289).
68. Arnold 2004, 47; Graber 2006, 278; Groeling 2010, 53–55, 100; Sinclair 1995, 263. For more on how majority party leaders and their staff interact with the press, see Sinclair 1995, 263–65. Transcripts were selected using LexisNexis; press conferences at bill signings, at the White House, or with visiting dignitaries were excluded. Some press conference transcripts were unavailable, especially older ones, which could have introduced some bias into the data. It is also possible that the content of leadership conferences reflects the particular rhetorical style of leaders rather than systemic differences between the parties.
69. It should be noted that *people* is one of the most common nouns in spoken English (Davies and Gardner 2010). But in the context of congressional press conferences, I would argue, that word takes on particular weight.
70. Graber 2006, ch. 7; Kimball 2005; interview with Republican House member, November 17, 2011; see also Groeling 2010, 45–46, 122; Kedrowski 1996, 96.
71. For more on symbolism in politics, see Edelman 1967 and March and Olsen 1984.
72. Interview with David Bonior, July 3, 2012.
73. This account is taken from Gugliotta 1995 and the author's own observation of the event.
74. Coile 2008; interview with Rep. Tom Price, October 2011; interview with Republican House member, November 17, 2011. Gas price data provided by the Energy Information Administration, Department of

Energy (http://www.eia.doe.gov/oil_gas/petroleum/data_publications/wrgp/mogas_history.html, accessed March 20, 1999). Republicans also filed discharge petitions on oil-related bills; see Chapter 5.

75. Orndorff 2008; Reilly and Bresnahan 2008; interview with Republican House member, October 14, 2011; interview with Republican House member, November 17, 2011; interview with Republican leadership aide, October 18, 2011.
76. Past interpretations of the chamber's constitutional quorum requirement have given minority parties considerably more influence, most famously in the 1880s when lawmakers could deny a quorum by simply refusing to respond when the clerk called their name. In some state legislatures, minority parties have been able to block legislative action with walkouts by exploiting supermajority rules in their chambers, as happened in Texas in 2003 (to halt a redistricting bill) and in Wisconsin in 2011 (to stop a budget bill that curtailed union rights).
77. All cases were found via searches in the *CQ Almanac* from 1983 to 2008 with the search term *walkout*; and the LexisNexis Academic database, using the search terms *Republican walkout and Congress*, *Democrats walkout and house floor*, *protests and walkout and Congress*, *walkout protests and house floor*, and *house floor protest and Congress*. Walkouts can also happen at the committee level (see e.g. Edwards 2012, 139).
78. Barshay 2003; Connelly and Pitney 1994, 79–81; Plattner 1985. The conference voted on, and approved, the tactics in advance (memo from Mike Johnson, April 25, 1985, Michel Papers, RHM Staff Pitts, Box 8, Folder McIntyre Correspondence (2); Dear Republican Colleague letter, April 29, 1985, Michel Papers, RHM Leadership, Box 9, Folder 99th, Joint Letters).
79. Carey 2000, Starks 2008.
80. Carey 2000, *CQ Weekly* 1992, Plattner 1985.
81. Refusals to leave the floor, by contrast, have fewer negative connotations, and their biggest impediment is party members who would prefer to go to their districts during recess.
82. Richert 2007. Many minority party members avoided the 1995 and 2008 "mock" sessions as well. But because they are rare, and attendance at these sorts of events is not publicized, a lack of full participation is not necessarily a liability for the party. In 1995, well over 100 Democrats (including family members, in some cases) attended the November "sit-in," and 124 Republicans—over 60% of the party—gave at least one speech during the August 2008 mock session.

83. Connelly and Pitney 1994, 80, 156; Plattner 1985. Nor was this solely about the walkout. According to one reporter at the time, "an internal debate within the House GOP has been under way for months about whether the party's strategy should be one of confrontation or of compromise" (Plattner 1985).
84. Palmer 2008.
85. Interview with Republican House member, November 17, 2011.
86. Arnold 1990, 68–71; Edwards 2003; Lippmann 1946 [1922], 36.
87. Groeling 2010, ch. 5; House G.O.P. news conference, May 20, 2008; Kenski, Hardy, and Jamieson 2010, 110, 118; Sellers 2010, 177–80, 198.
88. Republican support also fell from 27% to 15% during that time period. The polls did not, however, drop immediately after the one-minute speeches. ABC/*Washington Post* survey question, "Do you approve or disapprove of the way Obama is handling the economy?" taken April 21–24, June 18–21, July 15–18, and August 13–17, 2009. Presidential rhetoric may follow a similar pattern (Canes-Wrone 2005).
89. Connelly and Pitney 1994, 63; Groeling 2010, 44.

Chapter Four: Obstructing

Epigraph. Interview with former Republican campaign aide, September 30, 2011.

1. Technically, McHenry's amendment was a second-degree amendment, revising Gingrey's earlier amendment.
2. *Congressional Record*, July 31, 2007, H9249–H9271. Democrats tried a similar method of delaying floor proceedings by discussing nongermane issues in early 1995 (Kahn 1995a).
3. Plutarch 1919, 8:31. There are countless examples of obstruction in other legislative institutions as well. In the British Parliament, for instance, the opposition party successfully used the chamber's procedures in unexpected ways to stop an excise tax in 1733, and Irish delegates conducted notable obstruction in 1877 (Foord 1964, 177–82; Jellinek 1904, 580). Dion (1997, 8) argues that obstruction is a minority right.
4. On the filibuster, see, for example, Bell 2010, Binder and Smith 1997, Koger 2010, and Wawro and Schickler 2006. Very few have written about delaying tactics in the House; notable exceptions are Binder 1997 and Koger 2010.
5. See e.g. Bell 2010; Koger 2002, 2010; Wawro and Schickler 2006. Many of these studies also seek explanations for the frequency of dilatory acts in each Congress.

6. Some scholars use the term *filibuster* to describe delaying techniques of many types (e.g. Beth and Heitshusen 2013; Koger 2010, 16—18). But to avoid confusion, since the filibuster is usually associated with just the Senate, I largely stick with the terms *obstruction*, *delay*, and *dilatory* to describe what happens in the House. Note that by obstruction I do not mean killing a bill, which I consider a kind of legislating, but rather delay. Obstruction could also be pursued by a minority of either or both parties.
7. Rawls 2009. Techniques not in Table 4.1 include offering non-germane motions to recommit, then demanding a vote to challenge a ruling that they are not germane; and objecting to a unanimous consent request to dispense with reading a bill, amendment, or motions to recommit with instructions. The latter was used by House Republicans in late 1978 to defeat the creation of the Department of Education ("Department of Education," from *CQ Almanac* 1978, 571–76). See also Evans 2000.
8. Wolfensberger 2005, 1.
9. Babson 1995; Balz and Brownstein 1996, 120; Cloud 1994; Oleszek 2007, 162; interview with Republican leadership aide, December 2007. In the early 1980s, Newt Gingrich and COS members were "outnumbered" but used dilatory schemes in part because, according to one reporter, they felt they could "publicize their viewpoint and perhaps win some converts" (Roberts 1983). Some survey data suggest that voters unhappy with Congress blame both parties, not solely the majority; if so, obstruction that makes the House look poorly may yield little electoral advantage for minority party candidates. See Adler and Wilkerson 2012.
10. Foerstel 1993d; Koger 2010; Oleszek 2007, 162; *Roll Call* 1993; Wawro and Schickler 2006; Wayne and Armstrong 2007.
11. Cox and McCubbins 1993. As former floor objector Robert Walker put it, "People can see it as delaying necessary work" (Crabtree 2002). But not all agree that this cost is significant. Opined political scientist Jack Pitney in 2008, minority Republicans were using dilatory methods at the time because "they've learned that being labeled as obstructionist isn't a very effective attack. Being obstructionist hasn't hurt in the past, so why not?" If the minority party is likely to lose seats in the next election regardless, obstruction may also be a "nothing-to-lose proposition" (Epstein and Jansen 2008).
12. *Congressional Record*, August 2, 2007, H9579–9580 and November 6, 2007, H13198; Crabtree 2002; Curran 1995; Dennis 2007; Dion 1997; Koger 2010, ch. 2 and 148; Wines 1995.

13. See e.g. Connelly and Pitney 1994, 162–63; Granat 1984; and Sinclair 1995, 243.
14. By contrast, Lincoln Diaz-Balart (R-FL) got his party in hot water for making a motion to adjourn in February 2008 that disrupted a memorial service for former congressman Tom Lantos (*Congressional Quarterly Today* 2008 and Werner 2008). Staff is an especially important resource. G.O.P. procedural maven Billy Pitts helped Republicans delay a Democratic budget in 1983 so that the party could find ways to respond to it and later blocked a tax bill long enough to force some desired changes to the bill (Shapiro 1986).
15. Foerstel 1993b; interview with Republican leadership aide, November 2007; interview with Robert Walker, May 2008; Ted Van Der Meid notes, March 25, 1993, Robert Michel Papers, RHM Legislative, Special Subjects, Other, Box 6, Folder 103rd, Reform, Grandy-Gunderson.
16. Hook 1986; Kucinich 2009b; interview with Republican leadership aide, December 2007; interview with David Bonior, July 3, 2012. A G.O.P. aide to the House Rules Committee suggested in an interview that the large number of dilatory procedures used in 2007 were because "I think we're riled up . . . I think a lot of Republicans are mad they lost the majority." The aide also acknowledged that more dilatory motions may appear near the time of a scheduled recess or adjournment, "when tensions are running high" (interview, November 2007).
17. Hulse 2009c, interview with Republican leadership aide, October 18, 2011; see also Wines 1995. Delay could also be used to bring the party together around a certain set of issues—in other words, to build *ideological* unity. One Rules Committee minority aide interviewed suggested that some Republicans in the 110th Congress offered dilatory motions as "an effort to try to rally the conservative base, [to] *bring the party back to its conservative roots*" (anonymous interview, November 2007, emphasis added).
18. Kosseff 2006; interview with Republican leadership aide, November 2007; interview with Republican leadership aide, December 2007; interview with David Bonior, July 3, 2012; interview with Steve Elmendorf, September 30, 2011. David Bonior noted that, if done late in the evening, obstruction can risk ticking off the press as well, since it requires reporters covering the House to stay in the Capitol.
19. Wawro and Schickler 2006, 34–35; interview with Republican leadership aide, October 18, 2011.
20. Hunter 1964. The Johnson poverty bill eventually passed, 226–184.

21. Two other changes along with the elimination of the demand for engrossment were also designed to limit dilatory tactics: the Speaker was given the power to permit bills held by the Rules Committee to go directly to the floor, and an individual member was denied the right to block a bill from being reconciled with the Senate (Bolling 1968, 230–31).
22. Most of the rules changes were designed to increase transparency, reduce organizational complexity, or improve the general efficiency of the House without regard to either party. Cox and McCubbins (1993) argue that the cartel model explains the House before 1977 as well, but Schickler and Rich (1997) show otherwise. See also Mayhew 2011, 173.
23. Averill 1974; Schwieder and Schwieder 2006; Smith 1989, 157; Smith 2005, 254. "Bauman was one of the brightest," one aide recalled. Interview with former Republican leadership aide, September 13, 2011.
24. Examples include restrictions on quorum calls and motions related to the *Journal*, adopted in 1979; more quorum call limits in 1981; limits to the right to demand a vote to order a second on motions to suspend, passed in 1979; an end to forced votes on motions to enter the Committee of the Whole, enacted in 1983; and the elimination of teller voting in 1986 (Binder 1997; Green 2011; Smith 1989, 39). In recent years, the majority party has shown a preference for clamping down on delaying devices by using restrictive rules for considering individual bills, rather than by changing the chamber's procedures outright.
25. Jerry Lewis (CA), a Republican appropriator, openly expressed worry that obstructionist efforts by lawmakers like Walker were the reason Democrats were passing more closed or restrictive rules on bills (Horowitz 1992). For more on restrictive floor rules, see Chapter 5.
26. Republicans made numerous delaying motions and objections on the floor between mid-April and May 2, 1985, including a series of delays on April 25 which Republicans nicknamed "sample Thursday" to give a taste of what might be in store for Democrats if they ultimately seated their candidate (Plattner 1985).
27. Connelly and Pitney 1994, 57; Foerstel 1993d; Idelson 1994; Wolfensberger 2000, 156; interview with John Feehery, August 31, 2011; see also Foerstel 1993a, 1993b, and 1993f; Jacoby 1993; and *Roll Call* 1993. For a brief summary of these and earlier initiatives, see Connelly and Pitney 1994, 27, 49–50 and Koopman 1996, 141–42.
28. Kahn 1995b, Keller 1997b, Oleszek 2007, 163; Vande Hei 1997b; Wines 1995; interview with former Democratic leader, January 6, 2011.

29. Price 2010; interview with Republican leadership aide, April 15, 2009; interview with Republican leadership aide, October 18, 2011. See also Horowitz 1992.
30. Broder 1968; "Maneuvers Late in the Session Kill TV Debate Bill," from *CQ Almanac* 1968, 9–651–9–656; McMahon 2011, 45; "Political Debates on TV," from *CQ Almanac* 1960, 9–290–9–291.
31. "Maneuvers," from *CQ Almanac* 1968. Only 4% of the 980 individuals polled thought a refusal to debate by Nixon would hurt Humphrey; 71% said it would make no difference. Nixon poll, October 7–10, 1968 [USORC.101068.R14]. Retrieved July 12, 2011, from the iPOLL Databank, Roper Center for Public Opinion Research, University of Connecticut (http://www.ropercenter.uconn.edu.proxycu.wrlc.org/data_access/ipoll/ipoll.html).
32. Rumsfeld 2011, 116. It is unlikely Rumsfeld thought the move would do enough to help his party win the House. The party also faced a steep uphill climb in the elections: it needed to win thirty seats to become a majority, and on October 6 a *Washington Post* news story reported that the G.O.P. was unlikely to gain more than a dozen (Broder 1968).
33. Kling 1968; Rumsfeld 2011, 116–17; *Congressional Record*, 30091; see also *Congressional Record*, October 14, 1968, 31774; July 13, 1970, 23908; July 23, 1970, 21044. This tactic was somewhat akin to the famous "disappearing quorum" technique used prior to the adoption of Reed's Rules in 1890, the difference being that under the disappearing quorum lawmakers could avoid being counted without having to leave the chamber.
34. *Congressional Record*, 30092, 30097; Rumsfeld 2011, 117; Warden 1968.
35. *Chicago Tribune* 1969; comments by Rep. William Steiger, *Congressional Record*, July 13, 1970, 23908; Rumsfeld 2011, 117, 121–23. The mini-filibuster was not enough to help Rumsfeld's House career—he lost a close race to chair the Republican Research and Planning Committee shortly thereafter—but he ended up taking a job in the Nixon White House and would later become a top Nixon aide and, a few decades later, secretary of defense under President George W. Bush.
36. *Congressional Record*, July 17, 1997, H5441–5448; Doherty 1997a, 1997b.
37. *Congressional Record*, May 7, 2008, H3149.
38. *Congressional Record*, May 7, 2008, H3147–H3148; Pierce and Dennis 2008; http://www.c-spanvideo.org/program/HouseSession3552, 7:59–8:14. Two Democrats also switched, Carolyn McCarthy and Michael Capuano, but it is exceedingly unlikely they switched for purposes of delay.

39. For instance, a Harris poll showed 20% of voters having an excellent or pretty good view of House Republicans in April 2008; in early June, that had risen only slightly, to 21%. Republicans' strategic voting on the Iraq measure is also discussed in Chapter 5.
40. Milbank 2008.
41. A methodological advantage of these motions is that they not only delay floor proceedings but are easily observable. Similarly, one measure used by Binder and Smith of Senate delay is the number of recorded votes to adjourn (Binder and Smith 1997, 47–49).
42. The House provides fifteen minutes to complete a vote on a motion to adjourn, and five minutes on a motion to rise. A motion to rise can also include a motion to strike the enacting clause of a bill, which if successful defeats the bill. It is possible for a minority motion to rise or adjourn to be considered—or even pass—by voice vote, with no subsequent request that the vote be recorded (e.g. Foerstel 1993b). But this is rare.
43. Wolfensberger 2007.
44. There are some noteworthy examples of individuals from both the minority and majority parties offering these motions for their own purposes. In October 1992, a departing and bitter William Dannemeyer (R-CA) twice offered motions to adjourn in one day because, he said, "I hate this process. The place is miserable. I only have an hour and a half left, and I'm going to cause as much damage as I can" (Winneker 1992). Other noteworthy examples involved Reps. Gene Taylor (D-MS), Neil Abercrombie (D-HI), John Ensign (R-NV), and Mike Forbes (R-NY) (Dennis 2007, Eilperin and Vande Hei 1997, Foerstel 1993c, Hume 1997).
45. "Party leadership" here includes the minority leader, whip, conference chair, or campaign committee chair. Only eleven motions since 1991 have been initiated by minority leaders without support from their own party. The largest percent of motions with majority support were those justified in terms of irregular order (63% of the total); the smallest were those targeting the legislative agenda (29%). A good number of motions with no accompanying explanation were likely employed to meet intraparty tactical needs. A minority staff aide on the House Rules Committee noted, for instance, that if Democrats call for fewer than three floor votes in a row, Republicans may call for a motion to adjourn (a "backstop" vote) to gain extra time for whipping on a future vote (anonymous interview, November 2007). Party leaders may offer motions to rise or adjourn to give their vulnerable members an opportunity to vote

"against" their party, or allow the rank and file to signal their degree of support for an underlying issue or the tactics being employed.

46. Interview with Republican leadership aide, April 15, 2009. For example, the May 2007 protest against limiting the motion to recommit was approved and coordinated by Republican Party leaders (Davis and Yachnin 2007a).
47. A legislator may openly state opposition to a bill, for instance, but privately hope that delay will yield compromise with bill supporters or slow consideration of another bill (Wawro and Schickler 2006, 117).
48. Some notable examples not in these categories: Congressman Obey used dilatory maneuvers in retaliation against House Republicans when they tried to keep the House in session late (*Congressional Record*, July 13, 1995); and two years later, Democratic caucus chairman Vic Fazio (CA) offered a motion to adjourn knowing that not enough Republicans were in town to vote against it (Javers 1997).
49. In one exception, from 2010, Republicans successfully demonized the Democrats' special "deemed to have passed" rule to consider health care reform, forcing the party to use a different rule.
50. The motions to adjourn used to protest the 1985 contested-election case fall into this category. That event earned House Democrats considerable outside criticism, and Republicans may have hoped that their procedural protests would deter the majority from getting involved in future contested elections.
51. This is also seen in the U.S. Senate (Koger 2010, 112).
52. Bradsher 1995; Cloud and Gruenwald 1995. Speaking at the time, Democratic caucus chairman Vic Fazio observed that "what unifies us as a party is that we can't deal with any of our concerns unless we stick up for our rights as a minority" (Kahn 1995b).
53. Interview with Republican House member, November 17, 2011.
54. This becomes more clear when contrasted with the success rate of motions to rise or adjourn that do not gain votes from a majority of the minority party: of the 197 in this category between 1993 and 2010, only 14% (28) were followed by some sort of change in political outcome.
55. "Department of Education," from *CQ Almanac* 1978, 571–76.

Chapter Five. Legislating

Epigraph 1. Quoted in Mayhew 1974, 90.
Epigraph 2. Smith 2005, 211.

1. "Congress Enacts President Reagan's Tax Plan," from *CQ Almanac* 1981, 91–104; Connelly and Pitney 1994, 116; Karol 2009, 169–70; Roberts 1980, 158–60; Stockman 1986. The bill was sponsored in the Senate by William Roth (DE) and thus became known as Roth-Kemp (or Kemp-Roth).
2. See e.g. Anderson, Box-Steffensmeier, and Sinclair-Chapman 2003.
3. I do not examine activity within committees because it is difficult to observe or associate that activity with the party's collective needs. Also, I do not discuss the development of policy proposals by the minority, even though it can be an important guide to legislative strategy for the party. For more on these subjects, see Evans 2000 and, on the development of the Republicans' Policy Committee specifically, Jones 1964.
4. See e.g. Lebo, McGlynn, and Koger 2007, 466. Waxman was referring to a policy battle *within* the majority party, but his observation applies equally well to fights between the majority and minority parties (Waxman 2009, 78).
5. Hook 1986; Jones 1970, 24. Sometimes this happens without the minority's consent; the Pelosi abortion amendment discussed below is an example.
6. See e.g. Canes-Wrone, Brady, and Cogan 2002. The majority party uses legislative techniques for symbolic purposes too, of course, but it faces a greater expectation that it will use those techniques to govern.
7. Koszczuk 1995; interview with former Democratic leader, January 2011; interview with former Republican aide, August 31, 2011.
8. Jones 2005; Lott 2005, 79–80; acceptance speech by Robert Michel, December 8, 1980, 5 and 7 (http://www.dirksencenter.org/images/RHMichel/rhmleader1980.PDF).
9. "Budget Adopted after Long Battle," from *CQ Almanac* 1990, 111–66; Javers 1995; Lott 2005, 89–91; Pianin and Harris 1995. The deep unhappiness of House Democrats with the final debt-limit deal made by Obama made it challenging for its leaders to garner support for the measure, though they ultimately did get exactly half the party to vote for it. Draper 2012, 257–59; Woodward 2012, 127–29, 170, 186, 283, 355, quote 285.
10. *Congressional Record*, February 23, 1993, 3277. Wolf's entreaties may have worked: the bill failed on the suspension calendar the day after his statement, falling 15 votes shy of the needed 290, despite near unanimous Democratic support. A modified version was amended by Republicans on the floor and passed a month later.

11. The Democrats' affirmative votes were finally cast when Rep. Gabrielle Giffords, who had been severely injured by a gunman earlier that year, arrived unexpectedly on the floor and voted for the measure (Draper 2012, 258–62; Lochhead 2011). Pelosi's warning may have also been intended to demonstrate to other congressional Democrats her independence from the White House (Woodward 2012, 148, quote 170).
12. For more on the origin of legislative proposals, see Kingdon 1984.
13. Kucinich 2009a; Rogin and Higa 2008; interview with Republican leadership aide, October 27, 2011.
14. Jones 1970, 24; Mayhew 1974, 104; interview with former Republican leadership aide, September 15, 2011; see also Connelly and Pitney 1994, 70–71. This was true of earlier decades as well; see e.g. Sundquist 1968.
15. Beckman 1971; Hess and Broder 1967, 28. Writing in 1965, Charles O. Jones had a more favorable view of the Policy Committee, arguing it was "perhaps the most active and effective policy committee on Capitol Hill" (103). The House Democratic Steering Committee, the Policy Committee's majority party counterpart, also lacked funding for staff. Steven Smith (2007, 199–200) notes that lawmakers from the minority were more likely to be on the winning side of votes in the early 1970s than afterward.
16. See Chapter 4.
17. Bach and Smith 1988; "Congressional Reforms Made in 1975," from *CQ Almanac* 1975, 26–40; Marshall 2005; Smith 1989; *CQ Weekly* 1987; see also *Congressional Record*, January 14, 1975, 23–31. The quorum call, for instance, was effectively eliminated in 1977 in large part because "old bulls" in the Democratic Party "were calling quorum calls every two minutes to prevent us from getting any business done," as it was later described by former Rep. Abner Mikva (D-IL) who had helped curtail the call (interview, March 2010).
18. Bach and Smith 1988, 28–33. Rhodes (1995, 233–34) claimed O'Neill's statement embodied an attitude that first emerged with the Democratic freshman class of 1974.
19. "House Rejects Labor-Backed Picketing Bill," from *CQ Almanac* 1977, 122–26; C. Lawrence Evans and Claire E. Grandy, "The Whip Systems of Congress," from Dodd and Oppenheimer 2009, 196–97; Lott 2005, 79; interview with former Republican leadership aide, September 13, 2011.
20. The data are averaged across the two years of each Congress. The year 1982 was the first in which the majority had a higher unity score than the minority.

21. "Rape," from U.S. House 1992, 115–18; Connelly and Pitney 1994, 76–77, 81–83; Lott 2005, 98; Martinez 2003. Republicans were angered again the next year when Democrats reneged on a deal to allow a vote on a G.O.P. proposal for funding the Nicaraguan Contras; see Connelly and Pitney 1994, 83–84.
22. The data include floor rules that were either closed, allowing no amendments; "modified" closed, allowing only a select few amendments, and "structured" such that the right to participate in the debate or offer amendments was significantly curtailed. The data may undercount the number of restrictive rules; see e.g. Owens and Wrighton 2008 and Wolfensberger 2003.
23. These party rules were adopted in response to the unpopular decision of Jack Kemp, as chairman of the Republican conference, to make a deal with President Reagan on tax reform in late 1985 despite many Republicans' opposition to the bill. Connelly and Pitney 1994, 49–50.
24. Connelly and Pitney 1994; Foerstel 1993e; "Management Model for Republican Leadership," Robert Michel Papers, RHM Legislative, Special Subjects, Other, Box 6, Folder 103rd, Reform; Wolfensberger 2003; "Setting Legislative Goals" letter, January 27, 1994, Robert Michel Papers, RHM Leadership, Box 17, Folder 103rd. Some Democrats also chafed at how restrictive rules hindered their opportunities to legislate on the floor (Cohen 1993).
25. Balz and Brownstein 1996, 249–53; Johnson and Broder 1997, 187, 234, 363–65, 428. More generally, each party has reduced its degree of support on the floor for opposite-party presidents; see e.g. Lee 2011.
26. Duff and Rohde 2012; Eilperin 2006, 63, 69; C. Lawrence Evans, "Committees, Leaders, and Message Politics," from Dodd and Oppenheimer 2001, 229–30; Kahn 1995a; Martinez 2003; Price 2010; Sinclair 2006; Vande Hei and Babington 2005; interview with Democratic leadership aide, August 1, 2003. Former whip Tom DeLay described the "Hastert Rule" not as a firm axiom but as a guideline that bills reflect the party's wishes, lest it be unable to govern due to its narrow margin of control. Otherwise, remarked DeLay, "you might as well turn the floor over to the Democrats and say, 'Have it' " (DeLay interview, July 19, 2006, John Brademas Center, Segment 3, 8:42–8:47, http://www.nyu.edu/brademas/resources/video.delay.3.html). Former congressman Sherwood Boehlert (R-NY) argued that it was the necessary consequence of minority Democrats uniformly opposing G.O.P. proposals (Boehlert interview, October 12, 2006, John Brademas Center,

segment 2, 0:54–1:23, http://www.nyu.edu/brademas/resources/video.boehlert.2.html).

27. By contrast, while Republicans introduced no more than 109 bills cosponsored by a majority of their party in that Congress, a far greater percentage of them (72%, or 78) passed the House. Data from Adler and Wilkerson 2005–6, corrected by the author. The views expressed are those of the authors and not the National Science Foundation.
28. These bills were H.R. 2072, H.R. 2429, H.R. 1696, and H.R. 5642.
29. These bills were H.R. 550, H.R. 3764, H.R. 1157, and H.R. 3003. None of the 81 were related to the procedures or rules of the House.
30. Interview with Republican leadership aide, October 27, 2011, emphasis added.
31. Bacon 2006; Bendavid 2007, 145; Brownstein 2007, 342; interview with Democratic aide, June 10, 2006. For more on cosponsorship and messaging, see Highton and Rocca 2005.
32. Duff and Rohde 2012; Finocchiaro and Jenkins 2008; Hunter and Palmer 2011; Newhauser 2012a; interview with Democratic aide, June 10, 2006. David Mayhew notes that the sponsors of individual-oriented amendments often did not even bother lobbying for votes (Mayhew 1974, 119). Lee (2011) argues that, at least in the Senate, symbolic amendments became more popular when Senate control became increasingly competitive after 1980; see also C. Lawrence Evans and Walter J. Oleszek, "Message Politics and Senate Procedure," from Campbell and Rae 2001.
33. Attributed to Frank Annunzio. Interview with former Democratic leadership aide, October 9, 2002.
34. Bai 2009; Baumann 2007; Eilperin 2006, 49; Evans and Grandy, from Dodd and Oppenheimer 2009, 195; Hess and Broder 1967, 29; Hulse 2005; Smith 2005, 219; Wallison 2000c; interview with former Republican aide, August 31, 2011. Matt Bai used the "jury box" phrase to describe the result of unanimous Republican opposition to the Obama stimulus bill in 2009.
35. See e.g. Maraniss 1982. Charles O. Jones calls these sorts of minorities potentially "unrestricted" (Jones 1970, ch. 6). Steven Smith (2007, 201) notes that party size also matters: larger majority parties tend to yield less voting success for the minority.
36. Cox and McCubbins 2005, 117–22; Lott 2005, 79–80, 83.
37. They tried this gambit in January and again in March of 2010. Drucker 2010, Kucinich 2010a.

38. Kaiser 2013, 206–7; interview with Republican leadership aide, April 7, 2010. See also Kady 2006.
39. Abramowitz 2010; Lee 2009; McCarty, Poole, and Rosenthal 2008; and Theriault 1998.
40. Baumann 2007; Blunt 2006 (emphasis added); Eilperin 2003; see also Allen 2007a; Barry 1989, 458–72, 551; and Sinclair 2006, 180.
41. Evans and Grandy, from Dodd and Oppenheimer 2009; Meinke 2008. The minority party has sometimes tried to get rid of powerful majority whips by launching ethics charges, as Republicans threatened to do against Tony Coelho in 1989 and Democrats successfully did against Tom DeLay in 2005 (Allen 2007a).
42. Baumann 2007; Connelly and Pitney 1994, 37; interview with David Bonior, July 3, 2012.
43. Generally speaking, minority whips tend to focus on motions to recommit, veto overrides, and amendments to bills, while majority whips pay the most attention to procedural votes and votes on the final passage of bills (Evans and Grandy, from Dodd and Oppenheimer 2009, 195).
44. Interview with Republican leadership aide, April 15, 2009. This phrase, spoken by former Speaker Newt Gingrich, referred to the House Republicans' position vis-à-vis President Obama (Bai 2009).
45. Gephardt did manage—perhaps thanks to his film screenings—to avoid a looming threat of forty Democrats voting for the bill; only five did. Wallison 2000c.
46. Eilperin 2006, 62–65; Epstein 2003; Sinclair 2006, 177–80; interview with Democratic leadership aide, August 1, 2003.
47. Bai 2009. Former representative Cal Dooley noted that Democrats who wanted to support the Medicare bill were asked to at least "hold their vote until the very end" to make Republicans sweat for the needed votes; interview with Cal Dooley, September 8, 2011. See also Sinclair 2006, 178–79.
48. Brady and Newhauser 2011; Draper 2012, 269–70; Palmer and Hunter 2011. Democrats flexed their muscle again in September 2011, with all but six voting against a short-term spending bill, defeating it and suggesting majority Republicans "still need Democratic votes to help them govern" (Sherman and Bresnahan 2011).
49. Foerstel and Foerstel 1996, quote 131; Lott 2005, 84; Margolies-Mezvinsky 1994; Rubin 1993; Rubin and Zuckman 1993; Shapiro 1986. The motion was to rise from the Committee of the Whole; if it was

rejected, the House allowed "disfavored" amendments (like Hyde's) to be offered.

50. Cox and McCubbins 2005, 41, 91–94. The minority may also be hindered by the likelihood that the majority party responds to floor losses by working to improve its own party unity (Lebo, McGlynn, and Koger 2007).
51. Binder 2013; Krehbiel and Woon 2005.
52. Gary Cox and Mathew McCubbins may have first used the term in an earlier, unpublished version of their book *Setting the Agenda*. Thanks to Chris Den Hartog for this observation. For more on disappointments, see Jenkins and Monroe 2013.
53. See also Duff and Rohde 2012; Ethridge 2012; and Smith 2005, 219–21. During their time in the minority between 1995 and 2006, for instance, Democrats sometimes deliberately called for votes on non-controversial measures requiring a two-thirds vote, then voted against them to protest the lack of Democratic bills coming to the floor. They were able to defeat several bills this way (Wolfensberger 2002). Nearly half (40) of the 82 veto override attempts made in the House between 1971 and 2000 failed.
54. Cox and McCubbins 2005, 107.
55. Draper 2012, 147–48. Other noteworthy examples of strategic voting since 1970 include a Nicaraguan Contra aid amendment in 1986 and a presidential impeachment-related vote in 2007 (Connelly and Pitney 1994, 61; Mattingly 1990; Yachnin 2007b).
56. Technically the petition discharges the committee from further consideration of the bill, and it does not necessarily guarantee the bill will come to the floor. For more, see Beth 2003.
57. Their numbers have ranged from five (in 1987–88) to twenty-five (in 1981–82).
58. Oleszek 2007, 144. The minimum threshold of signatures to discharge a measure from a committee has changed several times in the House's history and was actually less than a majority of the House during two brief periods (1924–25 and 1931–34) (Schickler 2001, 102–3, 109–14, 126–28).
59. Connelly and Pitney 1994, 89; Oleszek 2007, 143. Before 1993, interested lobbying groups and entrepreneurial reporters who put in the legwork could usually find out who had signed a petition, and enterprising minority members could get public attention for their petitions without advertising who signed them.

60. The minority may also designate the filing of a petition to an electorally vulnerable party member for credit-claiming purposes. In 2003, for instance, House Democrats intentionally gave Jim Marshall, who hailed from a marginally Democratic district in Georgia, the opportunity to file a petition on concurrent receipts for veterans (petition #2) (interview with Democratic leadership aide, August 1, 2003).
61. The table excludes another eleven petitions between 1971 and 2012 that were signed by the minority leader but not by a majority of the minority party.
62. Mayhew 2002, 149–50. These include corporate-regulation legislation in 2002, following the bankruptcy of Enron (see *Congressional Record, Extension of Remarks*, February 28, 2002, E238 and April 9, 2002, E463–64); campaign-finance reform in the 1990s; a measure requiring that bills be published three days before consideration; and a bill to ban insider trading by lawmakers.
63. Evans, from Dodd and Oppenheimer 2001, 229; Oleszek 2007, 144.
64. Petitions #8, 9, 10, 12, 13, 15, and 16. An eighth petition (#17) was filed on an energy bill in September 2008, but it received few signatures.
65. Petitions #11, 12, and 13.
66. Two that come closest to fitting this description are the 1993 petition that successfully brought to the floor the House rule change making petition signatures public and a 2009 petition (#6) targeting a proposed rule to require that legislation be available on the Internet three days before coming to the floor.
67. "Lawmakers Agree on Need for Changes in Managed Care—But Only in Principle," from *CQ Almanac* 1998, 14-3–14-15. Democrats followed up the petition with a motion to recommit that contained the bill's language and waged a major media campaign on behalf of HMO reform.
68. Discharge petitions #1 and #7.
69. Discharge petition #7.
70. "School Prayer Amendment: House Vote Defeats Move," from *CQ Almanac* 1971, 03-624–03-629; "House Rejects Anti-Busing Amendment," from *CQ Almanac* 1979, 482–84.
71. Beth 2003. Sometimes a petition leads to unilateral action by the White House, as arguably was the case when President George W. Bush imposed tariffs on steel imports in 2002 following a petition filed by a House Democrat to bring a tariff bill to the chamber floor. At least one minority party petition since 2002 has yielded legislative fruit: a

2003 petition related to retirement and disability benefits for veterans, which received over two hundred signatures before majority Republicans agreed to a version of the proposal ("Lawmakers Expand Vets' Benefits," from *CQ Almanac* 2003, 7-9–7-10).

72. As noted below, prior to 2009 the motion could include instructions phrased in a way that required the committee's time to act, thereby defeating it. I do not include here the rare but related *motion to commit*, which sends a bill to a committee different from the one that considered it (or to a committee if none had considered the bill at all).
73. Lynch 2008; Nickels 1989; Oleszek 2006; Wolfensberger 2003. Technically any opponent of a bill can offer the motion to recommit (Deschler v. 7, ch. 23, §31.2 and v. 16, ch. 33, §32.17; Nickels 1989). In the 1970s and '80s, the majority party sometimes found sympathetic lawmakers from the minority who would offer "friendly" motions to recommit, infuriating genuine bill opponents (Tiefer 1989, 458; testimony by Mr. Murray, U.S. House 1992, 39).
74. Oleszek 2006, 10; see also Tiefer 1989, 456. Nonetheless, recalled one leadership aide from the period, the motion "wasn't considered a tool of leadership because bills were considered under an open process, generally." Interview with former Republican leadership aide, September 13, 2011.
75. Tiefer 1989, 459; Wolfensberger statement, U.S. House 1992, 82. As minority leader, Nancy Pelosi had primary authority to determine what the party's motion to recommit would be. Interview with Democratic leadership aide, August 1, 2003. Republicans continued this practice as a minority party after 2006 (Pierce and Yachnin 2008).
76. Quote from Tiefer 1989, 454; see also statement by Eric Cantor, *Congressional Record*, March 9, 2007. The guaranteed opportunity for those opposed to a bill to offer the motion to recommit dates back to 1909 (Nickels 1989, 5; Schickler 2001, 76–77).
77. See e.g. motion by Mark Kirk, *Congressional Record*, July 9, 2009. Motions may be debated for up to an hour at the discretion of the majority party (Lynch 2008, 7).
78. Wolfensberger 2003; see also Donald R. Wolfensberger, "The Motion to Recommit in the House: The Rape of a Minority Right," reprinted in U.S. House 1992, 93–153. To try to block the passage of Reagan's budget in early 1981, for instance, Democrats proposed a floor rule that limited what could be included in a recommittal motion, but the rule was

defeated. Republicans pointedly revised the House's rules after taking control in 1994 to guarantee a motion to recommit with instructions for the minority (Oleszek 2007, 183).

79. In fact, sometimes the majority has used that guarantee as an excuse to offer bills under otherwise highly restrictive rules. Oleszek 2007, 181–82; Wolfensberger 2003.
80. Lynch 2008, 11; Oleszek 2007, 168. In 2009, the House allowed debate on motions without instructions, so in theory these, too, could be offered with the hope of electoral messaging (Weyl 2010).
81. Republicans did this not infrequently in the 2000s. The motion can also allow minority party members to go on the record on a particular provision of the bill, but still support the bill itself—a sort of "conditional" support (Nickels 1989, 7).
82. Lynch 2008, 12; O'Connor 2008.
83. Lynch 2008, 10; Oleszek 2007, 183; Tiefer 1989, 455. Before 2009, chamber rules prohibited certain language in a "forthwith" motion to recommit, compelling the minority to offer a motion to recommit without "forthwith" instructions (Lynch 2008, 4–5). Motions on conference reports are prohibited from including instructions.
84. Lynch 2008, 11; U.S. House 1992, 38, 80. In October 2007, Steny Hoyer denounced these motions for serving "political purposes, not substantive purposes. Substantive purposes would be trying to change policy," though he admitted that "to some degree, we did that as well" (Yachnin 2007a).
85. This includes motions not subject to recorded vote, and excludes motions ruled out of order or withdrawn but followed by a second motion. They constituted 13% (8 of 61) in the 109th Congress, 19% (25 of 132) in the 110th, 9% (7 of 79) in the 111th, and 5% (6 of 114) in the 112th.
86. Examples include a 1977 motion that instructed a committee to consider a potentially problematic statement made by President Carter; motions to limit the White House from generating partisan propaganda (May 4, 2005) and urge investigations into the abuses of terrorist detainees (June 21, 2005); and motions that made references to energy prices (in 2008) and the non-profit group ACORN, an organization under investigation that Republicans sought to connect with President Obama (March 18 and May 7, 2009).
87. In the 93rd Congress, for example, Republicans offered a recommittal motion guaranteeing the party a percentage of committee funding.
88. Lynch 2008, 13.

89. Data collected by the author from the *Congressional Record* and Lynch 2008. My data differ from that collected by others (e.g. Lynch 2008), most notably because they include all motions, not just those subject to recorded votes. I excluded the eight motions between 1971 and 2010 offered by a member of the majority party but not voted for by a majority of the minority.
90. The 101st Congress (1989–90) marked a particularly important period in this change. The percent of motions with instructions surpassed the 60% mark for the first time and did so despite an increase in the absolute number of motions over the previous Congress. This came just before a noticeable hike in the number of rules limiting the minority's amending opportunities; see Figure 5.1.
91. It was also not always guaranteed that an amendment would get a recorded vote, so the minority sometimes took an amendment that had lost by voice vote and put it in the instructions of a motion to recommit, demanding a roll call vote (Nickels 1989; Oleszek 1978, 121, 128; Tiefer 1989, 457n343).
92. The overall fluctuation in the number of motions offered since 1971 is probably due not to changes in how often the minority can offer motions but on the case-by-case decisions of the minority party of whether to offer one (Lynch 2008, 15).
93. Interview with Republican leadership aide, October 18, 2011. This decision, which some believed was made by Caucus Chairman Rahm Emanuel—perhaps to protect vulnerable freshmen—led to the passage of many motions to recommit and became a sore spot for senior and more liberal Democratic members (see e.g. Price 2010; Soraghan 2009; Waldman 2008; Whittington and Dennis 2008). Democrats learned the hard way, noted one former Gingrich aide, that "once you breach the wall, you create a new political dynamic" (interview with former Republican leadership aide, March 14, 2003).
94. This motion was itself in order because Democrats had adopted new House rules that unintentionally expanded the scope of issues allowable in a motion to recommit. See Ferrechio 2007.
95. Allen 2007b; O'Connor 2008; Roth 2009; see also Starks 2007.
96. Lynch (2008), from which data on motions to recommit were obtained for the 1991 to 2002 period, did not include data on whether motions to recommit were resolved by voice or recorded vote. Cox, Hartog, and McCubbins (from Brady and McCubbins 2006) argue that the motion to recommit is even less influential because it rarely leads to the

majority party being rolled on the bill's final passage. But this incorrectly assumes that the majority party will remain opposed to a bill because a recommittal motion has passed, when the party may have policy or electoral reasons to still vote for the bill.

97. Gary Cox, Chris Den Hartog, and Mathew McCubbins, "The Motion to Recommit in the U.S. House of Representatives," from Brady and McCubbins 2006; Oleszek 2007, 184; Roberts 2005; but see Krehbiel and Meirowitz 2002. For other examples, see Foerstel and Nitschke 2001 and Nather 2000.
98. Jones 1970.
99. For further analysis of the factors which may increase the degree of minority party influence in the legislature, collectively or among its individual members, see Clark 2007 and Hasecke and Mycoff 2008.
100. Unified G.O.P. opposition to several key measures in the 111th Congress (2009–11), including energy legislation and health care reform, may have helped make the votes for those bills toxic enough to cost some Democrats their seats in 2010. Nyhan, McGhee, Sides, Masket, and Greene 2012.

Chapter Six. The Minority Party and American Politics

Epigraph 1. Quoted in Paumgarten 2007.

Epigraph 2. Quoted in Eigen and Siegel 1993, 483.

1. Interview with Republican aide, November 17, 2011.
2. Cohen 1997; Stanton and Hunter 2010; interview with Republican leadership aide, October 18, 2011. This dynamic echoes the "thermostatic" model of politics, in which the public reacts to government policies it deems too extreme by swinging to the other side of the ideological spectrum. Erikson, MacKuen, and Stimson 2002.
3. Balz and Brownstein 1996, 29, 45–46, 54, 91–94, 120, 122, 195–96; Bendavid 2007, 52–57, 211; Kenworthy 1988; Koopman 1996, 147; interview with former Democratic House leader, December 4, 2002; interview with former Republican aide, August 31, 2011; interview with former Democratic House leader, September 15, 2011.
4. Ehrenhalt 1986; Mayhew 1974; Rohde 1991; Rhodes 1995, 233–34, 237.
5. Eilperin 2006, 50; Sinclair 2006, 368.
6. See e.g. Bendix 2012; Eilperin 2006, 49; Mann and Ornstein 2006, 145; Sinclair 2006, 352.
7. U.S. House 1992, 40–41; U.S. House 1997; Burke quote from *Reflections on the Revolution in France*, quoted in Eigen and Siegel 1993, 464. Arend

Lijphart argues that consensual forms of democratic government not only enact better policy but also treat minorities better than majoritarian systems (Lijphart 1999).

8. Baker 2008.
9. Evans 2004, 275; Jellinek 1904, 579; Lutz 1941; Rossiter 1960, 47; interview with Republican aide, November 17, 2011.
10. Boorstin 1961; Larry Evans, "Committees, Leaders, and Message Politics," from Dodd and Oppenheimer 2001, 219; Fahrenthold 2011; Jacobs and Shapiro 2000; Newhauser 2012b; Smith 1988, 104; see also Lee 2013.
11. Blumenthal 1982; Gutmann and Thompson 2012; Newhauser and Strong 2012. Exclusion of the minority may also encourage it to look to other institutions and groups—the White House, the Senate, special interest groups—to act as veto points to stop the House majority, exacerbating the fragmentation of power in the American political system (Ware 2011, 13).
12. See e.g. Abramowitz 2010; Bond and Fleisher 2000; McCarty, Poole, and Rosenthal 2008; Poole and Rosenthal 1997; Rohde 1991; and Stonecash, Brewer, and Mariani 2003. Some that look at party conflict in a broader fashion include Sinclair 2006 and Uslander 1994. Lee (2009) argues that political, not ideological, differences explain this growing chasm in voting. Lee, as well as Theriault (2008), is among the few who distinguish between roll call votes on policy versus procedural matters, noting (for instance) that votes on procedures have become more polarized over time than votes on substantive issues.
13. Some, including Fiorina, Abrams, and Pope (2011) and Roberts and Smith (2003), suggest that polarization in Congress may be the result of what lawmakers and party leaders do, rather than what voters want. See also Lee 2009.
14. Connelly 2010, 237, 240. Not all agree that these trends in Congress are inherently bad. Connelly, for instance, argues that obstruction and the "permanent campaign" reflect an important purpose of the Constitution: to prevent bad legislation from becoming law. Connelly 2010, 239.
15. Giroux 2013.
16. Dahl 1961; Mayhew 1974, 71. Some studies blame divided voters as the primary cause of polarization in Congress (e.g. Abramowitz 2010; Dahl, "Patterns of Opposition," from Dahl 1966, 376), but others disagree or suggest that other factors also matter (e.g. Bafumi and Herron 2010;

Fiorina, Abrams, and Pope 2011; Hetherington and Weiler 2009; Sinclair 2006).

17. Foord 1964, 3; Jellinek 1904, 584, 585.
18. See Chapter 3.
19. Remark by former Republican member of Congress, Wilson Center 2010.
20. Quote from Eilperin 2006, 127; "Leadership Structure" memo, Richard Gephardt Papers, Box 837, Folder 3.

BIBLIOGRAPHY

Abramowitz, Alan I. 2010. *The Disappearing Center: Engaged Citizens, Polarization, and American Democracy*. New Haven, CT: Yale University Press.

Adams, Rebecca. 2007. "Kids' Health Gets Political." *CQ Weekly*, July 23.

Adler, E. Scott and John D. Wilkerson. 2005–6. *Congressional Bills Project*. NSF 00880066 and 00880061.

Adler, E. Scott, and John D. Wilkerson. 2012. *Congress and the Politics of Problem Solving*. New York: Cambridge University Press.

Agar, Herbert. 1950. *The Price of Union*. Boston: Houghton Mifflin.

Albright, Robert C. 1968. "GOP Begins Drive to Win House." *Washington Post*, September 19.

Aldrich, John H. 1995. *Why Parties? The Origin and Transformation of Political Parties in America*. Chicago: University of Chicago Press.

Alexander, Jeffrey C. 2010. *The Performance of Politics: Obama's Victory and the Democratic Struggle for Power*. New York: Oxford University Press.

Allen, Jonathan. 2004. "Putting Party First Wins Pelosi Loyalty—And Hopes of Victory." *CQ Weekly*, July 31.

Allen, Jonathan. 2007a. "Cohesion the Key to Minority's Clout." *CQ Weekly*, January 1.

Allen, Jonathan. 2007b. "GOP Move Stalls D.C. Voting Rights Bill." *CQ Weekly*, March 26.

Allen, Jonathan, and John Bresnahan. 2010. "Nancy Pelosi Survives Democratic Revolt." *Politico*, November 17.

Anderson, William D., Janet M. Box-Steffensmeier, and Valeria Sinclair-Chapman. 2003. "The Keys to Legislative Success in the U.S. House of Representatives." *Legislative Studies Quarterly* 28 (3), 357–86.

Arnold, R. Douglas. 1990. *The Logic of Congressional Action*. New Haven, CT: Yale University Press.

Arnold, R. Douglas. 2004. *Congress, the Press, and Political Accountability*. New York: Russell Sage Foundation.

Averill, John H. 1974. "House's Great Nay-Sayer Decides to Quit." *Los Angeles Times*, June 16.

Babington, Charles and Jonathan Weisman. 2006. "Rep. Foley Quits In Page Scandal." *Washington Post*, September 30.

Babson, Jennifer. 1995. "Democrats Refine the Tactics of Minority Party Power." *CQ Weekly*, July 15.

Bach, Stanley, and Steven S. Smith. 1988. *Managing Uncertainty in the House of Representatives: Adaption and Innovation in Special Rules*. Washington, D.C.: Brookings Institution Press.

Bacon, Perry Jr. 2006. "Don't Mess with Nancy Pelosi." *Time*, August 27.

Bacon, Perry Jr. 2009. "GOP Leaders Try to Polish Party's Image." *Washington Post*, May 3.

Bacon, Perry Jr. 2010. "Rahm Emanuel, Mentor to Republicans?" *Washington Post*, April 13.

Bader, John B. 1996. *Taking the Initiative: Leadership Agendas in Congress and the "Contract with America."* Washington, D.C.: Georgetown University Press.

Bafumi, Joseph and Michael C. Herron. 2010. "Leapfrog Representation and Extremism: A Study of American Voters and Their Members in Congress." *American Political Science Review* 104 (3), 519–42.

Bai, Matt. 2009. "Newt. Again." *New York Times Magazine*, March 1.

Baker, Donald P. 1981. "Ex-Rep. Bauman Is Given Consulting Job on the Hill." *Washington Post*, January 8.

Baker, Peter. 2008. "Tom Davis Gives Up." *New York Times*, October 5.

Baker, Peter. 2009. "Film Celebrates Emanuel as Democrats' Dynamo." *New York Times*, October 22.

Balz, Dan, and Ronald Brownstein. 1996. *Storming the Gates: Protest Politics and the Republican Revival*. Boston: Little, Brown.

Barry, John M. 1989. *The Ambition and the Power*. Boston: Viking.

Barshay, Jill. 2003. "A Rough but Steady Hand at Helm of Ways and Means." *CQ Weekly*, July 5.

Baumann, David. 2007. "GOP Conservatives Push 'RINOs' to Become More Right-Minded." *Politico*, May 29.

Bawn, Kathleen, Martin Cohen, David Karol, Seth Masket, Hans Noel, and John Zaller. 2012. "A Theory of Political Parties: Groups, Policy Demands and Nominations in American Politics." *Perspectives on Politics* 10 (3), 571–97.

Beckman, Norman. 1971. "Congressional Information Processes for National Policy." *Annals of the American Academy of Political and Social Science* 394 (March), 84–99.

Bell, Lauren C. 2010. *Filibustering in the U.S. Senate*. Amherst, NY: Cambria Press.

Bellantoni, Christina. 2010. "Battle Lines Drawn over Jobs as Members Use Recess for Politicking." *Talking Points Memo*, July 6, http://tpmdc.talkingpointsmemo.com/2010/07/battle-lines-drawn-over-jobs-as-members-use-recess-for-election-agenda.php, accessed July 7, 2010.

Bendavid, Naftali. 2007. *The Thumpin': How Rahm Emanuel and the Democrats Learned to Be Ruthless and Ended the Republican Revolution*. New York: Doubleday.

Bendery, Jennifer. 2011. "Democrats Look to Twitter to Reverse Fortunes for 2012." *Roll Call*, March 14.

Bendix, William Claus. 2012. "One-Party Deliberations in the U.S. House of Representatives." Ph.D. dissertation, University of British Columbia.

Berkman, Michael, and James Eisenstein. 1999. "State Legislators as Congressional Candidates: The Effects of Prior Experience on Legislative Recruitment and Fundraising." *Political Research Quarterly* 52 (3), 481–98.

Berman, Russell, Molly K. Hooper, and Erik Wasson. 2013. "Farm Bill Setback Opens House GOP up to New Attacks about Ability to Lead." *Hill*, June 20, http://thehill.com/homenews/house/306981-farm-bill-setback-opens-gop-to-attacks-about-ability-to-lead, accessed June 26, 2013.

Berman, William C. 2001. *America's Right Turn: From Nixon to Clinton*. 2nd ed. Baltimore: Johns Hopkins University Press.

Beth, Richard, 2003. "The Discharge Rule in the House: Recent Use in Historical Context." *CRS Report* 97–856 GOV, April 17.

Beth, Richard, and Valerie Heitshusen. 2013. "Filibusters and Cloture in the Senate." *CRS Report* RL30360, May 31.

Bibby, John F., and Roger H. Davidson. 1972. *On Capitol Hill: Studies in the Legislative Process*. 2nd ed. Hinsdale, IL: Dryden Press.

Billings, Erin P. 2003a. "Caucus Resists 'Permanent Minority' Mind-Set." *Roll Call*, September 8.

Billings, Erin P. 2003b. "Democrats Clash on Communications." *Roll Call*, November 5.

Billings, Erin P. 2005. "Democrats Target GOP Members over Budget." *Roll Call*, November 15.

Binder, Sarah A. 1997. *Minority Rights, Majority Rule: Partisanship and the Development of Congress*. New York: Cambridge University Press.

Binder, Sarah A. 2013. "Oh 113th Congress Hastert Rule, We Hardly Knew Ye!" Blog post, *The Monkey Cage*, January 16, http://themonkeycage.org/2013/01/16/oh-113th-congress-hastert-rule-we-hardly-knew-ye/, accessed May 23, 2013.

Binder, Sarah A., and Steven S. Smith. 1997. *Politics or Principle? Filibustering in the United States Senate*. Washington, D.C.: Brookings Institution Press.

Black, Eric. 1998. "Democrats' Walkout Was a Symbolic Protest." *Minneapolis Star Tribune*, December 20.

Blanchard, Robert O., ed. 1974. *Congress and the News Media*. New York: Hastings House.

Blumenthal, Sidney. 1982. *The Permanent Campaign*. New York: Simon & Schuster.

Blunt, Roy. 2006. "24 Months to a New Republican Majority: A Plan for Victory." November 15.

Bolling, Richard. 1968. *Power in the House: A History of the Leadership of the House of Representatives*. New York: E. P. Dutton.

Bond, Jon R., and Richard Fleisher, eds. 2000. *Polarized Politics: Congress and the President in a Partisan Era*. Washington, D.C.: CQ Press.

Boorstin, Daniel J. 1961. *The Image: A Guide to Pseudo-Events in America*. New York: Harper & and Row.

Box-Steffensmeier, Janet M., David C. Kimball, Scott R. Meinke, and Katherine Tate. 2003. "The Effects of Political Representation on the Electoral Advantages of House Incumbents." *Political Research Quarterly* 56 (3), 259–70.

Bradley, Barbara. 1996. "House Democrats Unveil Families First Agenda." *All Things Considered*, National Public Radio, June 23.

Bradley, Jennifer. 1996. "'Soundbite Assaults' or Free Speech on the Floor?" *Roll Call*, July 29.

Bradley, Jennifer. 1997. "Dems Use Adjournment Debate to Hammer GOP." *Roll Call*, June 30.

Bradsher, Keith. 1995. "Democrats Vow to Slow the Budget Debate." *New York Times*, July 3.

Brady, David W., and Mathew D. McCubbins, eds. 2006. *Party, Process, and Political Change in Congress: Further New Perspectives on the History of Congress*. Stanford, CA: Stanford University Press.

Brady, Jessica, and Daniel Newhauser. 2011. "House Liberals Find Footing." *Roll Call*, October 5.

Brady, Jessica, and Meredith Shiner. 2012. "Democrats in Search of a Fiery Speech." *Roll Call*, January 23.

Broder, David S. 1968. "Nixon within 24 Votes—as of Today." *Washington Post*, October 6.

Brownstein, Ronald. 2007. *The Second Civil War: How Extreme Partisanship Has Paralyzed Washington and Polarized America*. New York: Penguin Press.

Bruck, Connie. 1995. "The Politics of Perception." *New Yorker*, October 9.

Burke, Edmund. 1770. *Thoughts On the Cause Of the Present Discontents*. London: J. Dodsley.

Burns, James MacGregor. 1963. *The Deadlock of Democracy: Four-Party Politics in America*. Englewood Cliffs, NJ: Prentice Hall.

Campbell, Colton C., and Nicol C. Rae, eds. 2001. *The Contentious Senate: Partisanship, Ideology, and the Myth of Cool Judgment*. Lanham, MD: Rowman & Littlefield.

Campbell, James E. 1985. "Explaining Presidential Losses in Midterm Congressional Elections." *Journal of Politics* 47 (4), 1140–57.

Canes-Wrone, Brandice. 2005. *Who Leads Whom? Presidents, Policy, and the Public*. Chicago: University of Chicago Press.

Canes-Wrone, Brandice, David W. Brady, and John F. Cogan. 2002. "Out of Step, Out of Office: Electoral Accountability and House Members' Voting." *American Political Science Review* 96 (1), 127–40.

Cantor, David M., and Paul S. Herrnson. 1997. "Party Campaign Activity and Party Unity in the U.S. House of Representatives." *Legislative Studies Quarterly* 22 (3), 393–415.

Carey, Mary Agnes. 2000. "GOP Drug Plan Prevails." *CQ Weekly*, July 1.

Carey, Mary Agnes. 2008. "House Votes to Issue Contempt Citations." *New York Times*, February 15.

Carney, Eliza Newlin. 1999. "Winner Take All." *National Journal*, March 20.

Chambers, William Nisbet. 1963. *Political Parties in a New Nation: The American Experience, 1776–1809*. New York: Oxford University Press.

Chicago Tribune. 1969. "Taft Elected to Head G.O.P. Research Unit." January 17.

Cillizza, Chris. 2003. "A Reluctant Warrior, Matsui Takes Helm at DCCC." *Roll Call*, January 6.

Clark, Jennifer Hayes. 2007. "Majority Party Dominance or Norm of Cooperation? Understanding the Causes and Consequences of Minority Party Influence in Legislative Decision-Making." Ph.D. dissertation, Indiana University.

Cloud, David S. 1994. "End of Session Marked By Partisan Stalemate." *CQ Weekly*, October 8.

Cloud, David S., and Juliana Gruenwald. 1995. "Democrats Find Their Footing in Minority Party Trenches." *CQ Weekly*, July 1.

CNN. 2002. "Gephardt Considers Future in Leadership." November 6, http://www.cnn.com/2002/ALLPOLITICS/11/06/elec02.main.wrap/index.html, accessed November 6, 2002.

Cohen, Marty, David Karol, Hans Noel, and John Zaller. 2008. *The Party Decides: Presidential Nominations before and after Reform*. Chicago: University of Chicago Press.

Cohen, Richard E. 1993. "Challenging the House's Traffic Cop." *National Journal*, April 24.

Cohen, Richard E. 1997. "Bumpy Road to a Democratic Agenda." *National Journal*, March 15.

Cohen, Richard E. 2002. "Congress: After Gephardt." *National Journal*, June 8.

Coile, Zachary. 2008. "Pelosi Using Power to Stymie GOP on Offshore Drilling Vote." *San Francisco Chronicle*, August 1.

Committee on Political Parties. 1950. "Toward a More Responsible Two Party System." *American Political Science Review Supplement* 44 (3), part 2.

CongressDaily. 1996. "Democrats Unveil New Ads on Their Agenda." *National Journal*, June 26.

Congressional Quarterly Almanac. Various Dates. Washington, DC: Congressional Quarterly Press.

Congressional Quarterly Today Midday Update. 2008. "Partisan Dustup Mars Lantos Memorial Service." February 14.

Connelly, William F. Jr. 2010. *James Madison Rules America: The Constitutional Origins of Congressional Partisanship*. Lanham, MD: Rowman & Littlefield.

Connelly, William F. Jr., and John J. Pitney, Jr. 1994. *Congress' Permanent Minority? Republicans in the U.S. House*. Lanham, MD: Rowman & Littlefield.

Cook, Charlie. 1998. "How the Campaign Committees Look Now." *National Journal*, November 14.

Cook, Timothy E. 1989. *Making Laws and Making News: Media Strategies in the U.S. House of Representatives*. Washington, D.C.: Brookings Institution.

Cox, Gary W., and Jonathan N. Katz. 1996. "Why Did the Incumbency Advantage in U.S. House Elections Grow?" *American Journal of Political Science* 40 (2), 478–97.

Cox, Gary W., and Mathew D. McCubbins. 1993. *Legislative Leviathan: Party Government in the House*. Berkeley: University of California Press.

Cox, Gary W., and Mathew D. McCubbins. 2005. *Setting the Agenda: Responsible Party Government in the U.S. House of Representatives*. New York: Cambridge University Press.

CQ Weekly. 1987. "Rep. Lott Protests Waivers of Points of Order." November 28.

CQ Weekly. 1992. "The House: Approval of Administrator Creates More Rancor." April 11.

Crabtree, Susan. 2002. "House GOP Plans Parliamentary Counterattack." *Roll Call*, June 13.

Crabtree, Susan. 2003. "GOP Unsure of Media Messenger." *Roll Call*, January 16.

Crossman, Richard, ed. 1965. *The God That Failed*. New York: Bantam Books.

C-SPAN. 2010. "American Voters Suggest How to Make Congress More Accessible." Press release, November 17, http://www.c-span.org/PDF/C-SPANHouseAccessibilityPollPressRelease.pdf, accessed August 7, 2011.

Curran, Tim. 1991. "Ed Rollins Looks Back on Two Tumultuous and Disappointing Years as Head of NRCC." *Roll Call*, February 7.

Curran, Tim. 1995. "Book Deal Sparks Nasty Floor Brawl." *Roll Call*, January 19.

Currinder, Marian. 2009. *Money in the House: Campaign Funds and Congressional Party Politics*. Boulder, CO: Westview Press.

Dahl, Robert A. 1961. *Who Governs? Democracy and Power in an American City*. New Haven, CT: Yale University Press.

Dahl, Robert A., ed. 1966. *Political Oppositions in Western Democracies*. New Haven, CT: Yale University Press.

Damore, David F. and Thomas G. Hansford. 1999. "The Allocation of Party Controlled Campaign Resources in the House of Representatives, 1989–1996." *Political Research Quarterly* 52 (2), 371–85.

Dannheisser, Ralph. 2007. "Major Parties Work to Recruit Winning Candidates for Congress." *USINFO*, U.S. Department of State, December 18.

Davidson, Roger H., Walter J. Oleszek, and Frances E. Lee. 2012. *Congress and Its Members*. 13th ed. Washington, D.C.: CQ Press.

Davies, Mark, and Dee Gardner. 2010. *A Frequency Dictionary of Contemporary American English: Word Sketches, Collocates and Thematic Lists*. New York: Routledge.

Davis, Susan. 2006. "GOP Keeps Team, Promises Changes." *Roll Call*, November 20.

Davis, Susan, and Jennifer Yachnin. 2007a. "GOP Halts Rules Change." *Roll Call*, May 17.

Davis, Susan, and Jennifer Yachnin. 2007b. "Democrats Feel Growing Pains; GOP Ties Up Majority on Floor." *Roll Call*, June 18.

Dennis, Steven T. 2007. "Health Bill OK'd after a Big Push." *Roll Call*, August 2.

Dennis, Steven T., and Kathleen Hunter. 2010. "Pelosi Inches Closer to Unifying Caucus." *Roll Call*, November 18.

Deschler, Lewis. 1977. *Deschler's Precedents of the United States House of Representatives*. Washington, D.C.: Government Printing Office.

de Waal, Frans B. M. 2011. "Prehuman Foundations of Morality." Chapter 7 in George Levine, ed., *The Joy of Secularism: 11 Essays for How We Live Now*. Princeton, NJ: Princeton University Press.

Dion, Douglas. 1997. *Turning the Legislative Thumbscrew: Minority Rights and Procedural Change in Legislative Politics*. Ann Arbor: University of Michigan Press.

Dodd, Lawrence C., and Bruce I. Oppenheimer, eds. 2001. *Congress Reconsidered*. 7th ed. Washington, D.C.: CQ Press.

Dodd, Lawrence C., and Bruce I. Oppenheimer, eds. 2009. *Congress Reconsidered*. 9th ed. Washington, D.C.: CQ Press.

Doherty, Carroll J. 1997a. "Democrats Stall to Protest Rules Slight." *CQ Weekly*, July 26.

Doherty, Carroll J. 1997b. "Abortion Controversy Stymies Two Foreign Policy Bills." *CQ Weekly*, July 26.

Downs, Anthony. 1957. *An Economic Theory of Democracy*. New York: Harper Press.

Draper, Robert. 2011. "How Kevin McCarthy Wrangles the Tea Party in Washington." *New York Times Sunday Magazine*, July 13.

Draper, Robert. 2012. *Do Not Ask What Good We Do: Inside the U.S. House of Representatives*. New York: Free Press.

Drew, Elizabeth. 2009. "The Thirty Days of Barack Obama." *New York Review of Books*, March 26.

Drucker, David M. 2006. "Emanuel, Lieutenants Resume Party Recruiting." *Roll Call*, December 11.

Drucker, David M. 2010. "GOP Team Targets Democrats." *Roll Call*, March 18.

Duff, Jeremy F., and David W. Rohde. 2012. "Rules to Live By: Agenda Control and the Partisan Use of Special Rules in the House." *Congress & the Presidency* 39, 28–50.

Durkheim, Emile. 2001 [1912], *The Elementary Forms of Religious Life*, part 1. New York: Oxford University Press.

Edelman, Murray. 1967 [1964]. *The Symbolic Uses of Politics*. Urbana: University of Illinois Press.

Edelman, Murray. 1971. *Politics as Symbolic Action: Mass Arousal and Quiescence*. Chicago: Markham.

Edwards, George C. III. 2003. *On Deaf Ears: The Limits of the Bully Pulpit*. New Haven, CT: Yale University Press.

Edwards, Mickey. 2012. *The Parties versus the People: How to Turn Republicans and Democrats into Americans*. New Haven, CT: Yale University Press.

Ehrenhalt, Alan. 1986. "Media, Power Shifts Dominate O'Neill's House." *CQ Weekly*, September 13.

Eigen, Lewis D., and Jonathan P. Siegel. 1993. *The Macmillan Dictionary of Political Quotations*. New York: Macmillan.

Eilperin, Juliet. 1999. "Democrats Elated over Recruitment Coups in California." *Washington Post*, December 12.

Eilperin, Juliet. 2003. "Democrats Laud Pelosi's Style." *Washington Post*, November 30.

Eilperin, Juliet. 2006. *Fight Club Politics: How Partisanship Is Poisoning the House of Representatives*. Lanham, MD: Rowman & Littlefield.

Eilperin, Juliet, and Jim Vande Hei. 1997. "Rep. Mike Forbes' Rebel Yell." *Roll Call*, June 23.

Elkins, Stanley M., and Eric L. McKitrick. 1993. *The Age of Federalism: The Early American Republic, 1788–1800*. New York: Oxford University Press.

Epstein, Edward. 2003. "Pelosi Makes Dems Toe The Line." *San Francisco Chronicle*, November 30.

Epstein, Edward, and Bart Jansen. 2008. "Role Reversal Yields Stalemate." *CQ Weekly*, January 7.

Erikson, Robert S., Michael B. MacKuen, and James A. Stimson. 2002. *The Macro Polity*. New York: Cambridge University Press.

Espo, David. 2002. "Democrats Ready to Start Highlighting Differences With GOP." Associated Press, April 22.

Espo, David. 2006. "Pelosi Says She Would Drain GOP 'Swamp' If She Becomes House Majority Leader." Associated Press, October 6.

Ethridge, Emily. 2012. "2011 Vote Studies: Party Unity." *CQ Weekly*, January 16.

Eulau, Heinz. 1984. "Legislative Committee Assignments." *Legislative Studies Quarterly* 9 (4), 587–633.

Evans, Richard J. 2004. *The Coming of the Third Reich*. New York: Penguin Press.

Evans, Sean Franklin. 2000. "Draw Your Pay and Make a Quorum: The Minority Party in Congress." Ph.D. dissertation, University of Colorado at Boulder.

Fagan, Amy, and Stephen Dinan. 2002. "Bush Appearance Captures Spotlight from Democrats." *Washington Times*, May 16.

Fahrenthold, David A. 2011. "Congress: So Many Taunts, So Few Deals." *Washington Post*, April 6.

Farrell, John A. 2001. *Tip O'Neill and the Democratic Century*. Boston: Little, Brown.

Fenno, Richard F. Jr. 1973. *Congressmen in Committees*. Boston: Little, Brown.

Fenno, Richard F. Jr. 2000. *Congress at the Grassroots: Representational Change in the South, 1970–1998*. Chapel Hill: University of North Carolina Press.

Ferrechio, Susan. 2007. "Pay-As-You-Go Change Planned to Limit GOP's Motions to Recommit." *CQ Weekly*, April 2.

Feulner, Edwin J. Jr. 1983. *Conservatives Stalk the House: The Republican Study Committee, 1970–1982*. Ottawa, IL: Green Hill Publishers.

Fiorina, Morris P. 1981. *Retrospective Voting in American National Elections*. New Haven, CT: Yale University Press.

Fiorina, Morris P., Samuel J. Abrams, and Jeremy C. Pope. 2011. *Culture War? The Myth of a Polarized America*. 3rd ed. Boston: Longman.

Finocchiaro, Charles J. 2003. "An Institutional View of Congressional Elections: The Impact of Congressional Images on Seat Change in the House." *Political Research Quarterly* 56 (1), 59–65.

Finocchiaro, Charles J., and Jeffrey Jenkins. 2008. "In Search of Killer Amendments in the Modern U.S. House." *Legislative Studies Quarterly* 33 (2), 263–94.

Foerstel, Karen. 1992. "In Surprise, Rep. Coughlin (R-PA) to Retire." *Roll Call*, February 24.

Foerstel, Karen. 1993a. "Guerilla Warfare Ahead as Republicans, Democrats Spar over Floor Proceedings." *Roll Call*, April 1.

Foerstel, Karen. 1993b. "Burton Bucks GOP Requests to Lay Off Stalling Tactics That Tie Up Floor Work." *Roll Call*, September 30.

Foerstel, Karen. 1993c. "Fight over Speeches Heats Up, Taylor Wins Adjournment Votes." *Roll Call*, March 29.

Foerstel, Karen. 1993d. "1st Open Rule Hits the Floor." *Roll Call*, May 6.

Foerstel, Karen. 1993e. "Republicans Unveil Strategy to Combat Restrictive Rules." *Roll Call*, April 22.

Foerstel, Karen. 1993f. "Closed Rules Irk Some Dems, Too." *Roll Call*, September 23.

Foerstel, Karen, and Herbert N. Foerstel. 1996. *Climbing the Hill: Gender Conflict in Congress*. Westport, CT: Praeger.

Foerstel, Karen, and Lori Nitschke. 2001. "Revolt of the Moderates Tests House Leadership." *CQ Weekly*, July 21.

Foord, Archibald S. 1964. *His Majesty's Opposition, 1714–1830*. London: Oxford University Press.

Ford, Gerald R. 1979. *A Time to Heal: The Autobiography of Gerald R. Ford*. New York: Harper & Row.

Fowler, Linda L., and Robert D. McClure. 1989. *Political Ambition: Who Decides to Run for Congress*. New Haven, CT: Yale University Press.

Fox, Richard L., and Jennifer L. Lawless. 2005. "To Run or Not to Run for Office: Explaining Nascent Political Ambition." *American Journal of Political Science* 49 (3), 642–59.

Frisch, Scott A., and Sean Q. Kelly. 2006. *Committee Assignment Politics in the U.S. House of Representatives*. Norman: University of Oklahoma Press.

Galvin, Daniel J. 2010. *Presidential Party Building: Dwight D. Eisenhower to George W. Bush*. Princeton, NJ: Princeton University Press.

Gamm, Gerald, and Steven Smith. 2003. "Steering the Senate: The Consolidation of Senate Party Leadership, 1879–1913." Prepared for presentation to the Congress and History Conference, Massachusetts Institute of Technology, Cambridge, MA, May 30–31, http://web.mit.edu/polisci/congress/gamm_smith.pdf.

Garay, Ronald. 1984. *Congressional Television: A Legislative History*. Westport, CT: Greenwood Press.

Geraghty, Jim. 2009. "The NRCC Gets Their Man . . . and Their Woman . . . and Their Man . . . and Their Woman . . ." *National Review*, July 9, http://www.nationalreview.com/campaign-spot/6837/nrcc-gets-their-man-and-their-woman-and-their-man-and-their-woman, accessed June 20, 2012.

Gerber, Alan S., James G. Gimpel, Donald P. Green, and Daron R. Shaw. 2011. "How Large and Long-Lasting Are the Persuasive Effects of Televised Campaign Ads? Results from a Randomized Field Experiment." *American Political Science Review* 105 (1), 135–50.

Gimpel, James G. 1996. *Fulfilling the Contract: The First 100 Days*. Boston: Allyn and Bacon.

Giroux, Greg. 2013. "State Super-Minorities Lead to 'Lone Ranger' Movie Trip." Bloomberg News, June 4.

Glasgow, Garrett. 2002. "The Efficiency of Congressional Campaign Committee Contributions in House Elections." *Party Politics* 8 (6), 657–72.

Glassman, Matthew Eric, Jacob R. Straus, and Colleen J. Shogan. 2009. "Social Networking and Constituent Communication: Member Use of Twitter during a Two-Week Period in the 111th Congress." *CRS Report* R40823, September 21.

Gonzales, Nathan L. 2010. "A Primary Loss Does Not Equate a Lost Cause." *Roll Call*, June 1.

Graber, Doris A. 2006. *Mass Media & American Politics*. 7th ed. Washington, D.C.: CQ Press.

Granat, Diane. 1984. "Televised Partisan Skirmishes Erupt in House." *CQ Weekly*, February 11.

Green, Donald P., and Jonathan S. Krasno. 1988. "Salvation for the Spendthrift Incumbent: Reestimating the Effects of Campaign Spending in House Elections." *American Journal of Political Science* 32 (4), 884–907.

Green, Matthew N. 2010. *The Speaker of the House: A Study of Leadership*. New Haven, CT: Yale University Press.

Green, Matthew N. 2011. "Explaining Changes to Resilient Rules: The U.S. House and the Struggle to Tame Quorum Calls." Working Paper.

Green, Matthew N., and Kristen Hudak. 2009. "Congress and the Bailout: Explaining the Bailout Votes and Their Electoral Effect." *Legislative Studies Section Newsletter* 32 (1).

Groeling, Tim. 2010. *When Politicians Attack! Party Cohesion in the Media*. New York: Cambridge University Press.

Grynaviski, Jeffrey D. 2010. *Partisan Bonds: Political Reputations and Legislative Accountability*. New York: Cambridge University Press.

Gugliotta, Guy. 1995. "The Inner Democrat: When the TV Lights Went Out, Liberal Hearts Started to Beat Again." *Washington Post*, November 26.

Gutmann, Amy, and Dennis Thompson. 2012. *The Spirit of Compromise: Why Governing Demands It and Campaigning Undermines It*. Princeton, NJ: Princeton University Press.

Harris, Douglas B. 1998. "The Rise of the Public Speakership." *Political Science Quarterly* 113 (2), 193–212.

Harris, Douglas B. 2005. "Orchestrating Party Talk: A Party-Based View of One-Minute Speeches in the House of Representatives." *Legislative Studies Quarterly* 30 (1), 127–41.

Hasecke, Edward, and Jason D. Mycoff. 2008. "Minority Party Success in the House of Representatives." Paper presented at the annual meeting of the Midwest Political Science Association, Chicago, IL.

Heberlig, Eric S. 2003. "Congressional Parties, Fundraising, and Committee Ambition." *Political Research Quarterly* 56 (2), 151–61.

Heberlig, Eric S. 2007. "Party Fundraising, Descriptive Representation, and the Battle for Majority Control: Shifting Leadership Appointment Strategies in the U.S. House of Representatives, 1990–2002." *Social Science Quarterly* 88 (2), 404–21.

Heberlig, Eric S., and Bruce A. Larson. 2012. *Congressional Parties, Institutional Ambition, and the Financing of Majority Control*. Ann Arbor: University of Michigan Press.

Heinberg, John Gilbert. 1926. "History of the Majority Principle." *American Political Science Review* 20 (1), 52–68.

Henry, Ed, and Timothy J. Burger. 1996. "Gephardt Hits Up His Democrats for Cash to Take Back the House." *Roll Call*, July 29.

Hernandez, Raymond. 2007. "Short of Money, G.O.P. Is Enlisting Rich Candidates." *New York Times*, November 26.

Hernandez, Raymond. 2008. "G.O.P. Struggles to Find Candidates for Congress." *New York Times*, April 8.

Herrnson, Paul S. 2012. *Congressional Elections: Campaigning at Home and in Washington*. 6th ed. Washington, D.C.: CQ Press.

Herrnson, Paul S. and James M. Curry. 2011. "Issue Voting and Partisan Defections in Congressional Elections." *Legislative Studies Quarterly* 36 (2), 281–307.

Hershey, Marjorie. 1984. *Running for Office: The Political Education of Campaigners*. Chatham, NY: Chatham House.

Hess, Stephen, and David S. Broder. 1967. *The Republican Establishment: The Present and Future of the G.O.P.* New York: Harper & Row.

Hetherington, Marc J., and Jonathan D. Weiler. 2009. *Authoritarianism and Polarization in American Politics*. New York: Cambridge University Press.

Highton, Benjamin, and Michael S. Rocca. 2005. "Beyond the Roll-Call Arena: The Determinants of Position Taking in Congress." *Political Research Quarterly* 58 (2), 303–16.

Hinckley, Barbara. 1971. *Stability and Change in Congress*. New York: Harper & Row.

Hofstadter, Richard. 1969. *The Idea of a Party System: The Rise of Legitimate Opposition in the United States, 1780–1840*. Berkeley: University of California Press.

Hook, Janet. 1986. "House GOP: Plight of a Permanent Minority." *CQ Weekly*, June 21.

Horowitz, Paul. 1992. "Anger Marks Budget Vote." *Roll Call*, June 25.

"House Turns Back GOP Bid to Require Pledge." 1988. *CQ Weekly*, September 10.

Hulse, Carl. 2005. "In Raucous House Vote, G.O.P. Oil Refinery Bill Squeaks By." *New York Times*, October 8.

Hulse, Carl. 2009a. "Republicans Split on Need to Offer Rival for Budget." *New York Times*, March 14.

Hulse, Carl. 2009b. "Gaps Appear in G.O.P. Solidarity." *New York Times*, May 10.

Hulse, Carl. 2009c. "A Rabble-Rouser, Then and Now." *New York Times*, July 5.

Hume, David. 1888 [1739]. *A Treatise of Human Nature*. New York: Macmillan.

Hume, Sandy. 1997. "Energy Ads Anger GOP Leaders." *Hill*, October 29.

Hunter, Kathleen. 2010. "Democrats Begin War with GOP on Agenda." *Roll Call*, September 21.

Hunter, Kathleen. 2011. "Democrats Force Votes with Eye on Campaigns." *Roll Call*, January 31.

Hunter, Kathleen, and Anna Palmer. 2011. "Democrats Searching for Unity." *Roll Call*, March 7.

Hunter, Marjorie. 1964. "Johnson Antipoverty Bill Approved in House, 228–190, but Foes Balk Final Vote." *New York Times*, August 8.

Idelson, Holly. 1994. "Partisan Fault Lines Spark Delay on Anti-Crime Bill." *CQ Weekly*, March 26.

Jackson, Brooks. 1988. *Honest Graft: Big Money and the American Political Process*. New York: Alfred A. Knopf.

Jacobs, Lawrence R., and Robert Y. Shapiro. 2000. *Politicians Don't Pander: Political Manipulation and the Loss of Democratic Responsiveness*. Chicago: University of Chicago Press.

Jacobson, Gary C. 2009. *The Politics of Congressional Elections*. 7th ed. New York: Pearson Longman.

Jacobson, Gary C. 2011. "The Republican Resurgence in 2010." *Political Science Quarterly* 126 (1), 27–52.

Jacobson, Gary C., and Samuel Kernell. 1983. *Strategy and Choice in Congressional Elections*. 2nd ed. New Haven, CT: Yale University Press.

Jacoby, Mary. 1993. "House Passes A $1.77 Billion Spending Bill." *Roll Call*, June 14.

Javers, Eamon. 1995. "Red Hot Rhetoric." *Hill*, June 21.

Javers, Eamon. 1997. "Members Just Don't Want to Go Away." *Hill*, May 28.

Jefferson, Thomas. 1997 [1812]. *Manual of Parliamentary Practice*. House Doc. 104–272, http://www.gpo.gov/fdsys/pkg/HMAN-105/pdf/HMAN-105.pdf.

Jellinek, Georg. 1904. "Parliamentary Obstruction." *Political Science Quarterly* 19 (4), 579–88.

Jenkins, Jeffrey A., and Nathan W. Monroe. 2013. "On Measuring Legislative Agenda Setting Power." Paper presented at the annual meeting of the American Political Science Association, Chicago IL.

Johnson, Haynes, and David S. Broder. 1997. *The System: The American Way of Politics at the Breaking Point*. Boston: Little, Brown.

Johnson, Nevil. 1997. "Opposition in the British Political System." *Government and Opposition* 32 (4), 487–510.

Jones, Charles O. 1964. *Party and Policy-Making: The House Republican Policy Committee*. New Brunswick, NJ: Rutgers University Press.

Jones, Charles O. 1965. *The Republican Party in American Politics*. New York: Macmillan.

Jones, Charles O. 1968. "Joseph G. Cannon and Howard W. Smith: An Essay on the Limits of Leadership in the House of Representatives." *Journal of Politics* 30 (3), 617–46.

Jones, Charles O. 1970. *The Minority Party in Congress*. Boston: Little, Brown.

Jones, Charles O. 2005. *The Presidency in a Separated System*. 2nd ed. Washington, D.C.: Brookings Institution Press.

Jones, David R. 2010. "Partisan Polarization and Congressional Accountability in House Elections." *American Journal of Political Science* 54 (2), 323–37.

Jones, David R., and Monika L. McDermott. 2009. *Americans, Congress, and Democratic Responsiveness: Public Evaluations of Congress and Electoral Consequences*. Ann Arbor: University of Michigan Press.

Kabaservice, Geoffrey. 2012. *Rule and Ruin: The Downfall of Moderation and the Destruction of the Republican Party from Eisenhower to the Tea Party*. New York: Oxford University Press.

Kady II, Martin. 2006. "Party Unity: Learning to Stick Together." *CQ Weekly*, January 9.

Kahn, Gabriel. 1995a. "A First: Democratic Floor Outcry Brings GOP Concession on New Rule for Committee Scheduling." *Roll Call*, February 2.

Kahn, Gabriel. 1995b. "Dems Vow More Floor Fireworks." *Roll Call*, July 3.

Kaiser, Robert G. 2013. *Act of Congress: How America's Essential Institution Works, and How It Doesn't*. New York: Alfred A. Knopf.

Kane, Paul. 2007. "Freshmen Padding Their Independence; Procedural Votes Become Safe Nays." *Washington Post*, December 26.

Kane, Paul. 2010. "Former U.S. Attorneys Argue the G.O.P.'s Case in House Races." *Washington Post*, June 6.

Karol, David. 2009. *Party Position Change in American Politics: Coalition Management*. New York: Cambridge University Press.

Katz, Jeffrey L., and Andrew Taylor. 1998. "House Accuses Clinton of Perjury, Obstruction." *CQ Weekly*, December 19.

Kazee, Thomas A., and Mary C. Thornberry. 1990. "Where's the Party? Congressional Candidate Recruitment and American Party Organizations." *Western Political Quarterly* 43 (1), 61–80.

Keller, Amy. 1997a. "House Democrats Embrace Obstruction Plan by Rep. Miller to Force Reform Vote." *Roll Call*, September 11.

Keller, Amy. 1997b. "Without House, Senate Reform Deal Doesn't Matter." *Roll Call*, September 25.

Keller, Amy. 1999. "Archer, Hall Push Change of Schedule." *Roll Call*, June 3.

Kedrowski, Karen M. 1996. *Media Entrepreneurs and the Media Enterprise in the U.S. Congress*. Cresskill, NJ: Hampton Press.

Kenneally, James J. 2003. *A Compassionate Conservative: A Political Biography of Joseph W. Martin Jr., Speaker of the U.S. House of Representatives*. Lanham, MD: Lexington Books.

Kenski, Kate, Bruce W. Hardy, and Kathleen Hall Jamieson. 2010. *The Obama Victory: How Media, Money, and Message Shaped the 2008 Election*. New York: Oxford University Press.

Kenworthy, Tom. 1988. "House GOP Signals It's in a Fighting Mood." *Washington Post*, December 26.

Kimball, David C. 2005. "Priming Partisan Evaluations of Congress." *Legislative Studies Quarterly* 30 (1), 63–84.

Kingdon, John W. 1984. *Agendas, Alternatives, and Public Policies*. Boston: Little, Brown.

Kling, William. 1968. "TV Election Debates OK'd." *Chicago Tribune*, October 10.

Klinker, Philip A. 1994. *The Losing Parties: Out-Party National Committees, 1956–1993*. New Haven, CT: Yale University Press.

Koger, Greg. 2002. "Obstructionism in the U.S. House and Senate: A Bicameral Analysis of Institutional Choice." Ph.D. dissertation, University of California Los Angeles.

Koger, Greg. 2010. *Filibustering: A Political History of Obstruction in the House and Senate*. Chicago: University of Chicago Press.

Kolodny, Robin. 1998. *Pursuing Majorities: Congressional Campaign Committees in American Politics*. Norman: University of Oklahoma Press.

Koopman, Douglas L. 1996. *Hostile Takeover: The House Republican Party, 1980–1995*. Lanham, MD: Rowman & Littlefield.

Kosseff, Jeff. 2006. "Leaders Annoy House to Aid Fishermen." *Oregonian*, 29 June.

Koszczuk, Jackie. 1995. "Democrats Find Strength, Unity in Anger over Medicare Plans." *CQ Weekly*, September 23.

Krasno, Jonathan S., and Donald Philip Green. 1988. "Preempting Quality Challengers in House Elections." *Journal of Politics* 50 (4), 920–36.

Krehbiel, Keith, and Adam Meirowitz. 2002. "Minority Rights and Majority Power: Theoretical Consequences of the Motion to Recommit." *Legislative Studies Quarterly* 27 (2), 191–217.

Krehbiel, Keith, and Alan E. Wiseman. 2005. "Joe Cannon and the Minority Party: Tyranny or Bipartisanship?" *Legislative Studies Quarterly* 30, 479–505.

Krehbiel, Keith, and Jonathan Woon. 2005. "Selection Criteria for Roll Call Votes." Research Paper No. 1943, Stanford Graduate School of Business.

Kucinich, Jackie. 2009a. "House Conservative Group Asserts Relevance." *Roll Call*, March 16.

Kucinich, Jackie. 2009b. "Republicans Wage Floor Games." *Roll Call*, July 27.

Kucinich, Jackie. 2010a. "GOP Campaign to Sway Democrats Moves Slowly." *Roll Call*, January 19.

Kucinich, Jackie. 2010b. "NRCC Sends Crew to Collect Dues." *Roll Call*, April 21.

Kucinich, Jackie. 2010c. "GOP Hopefuls Get Member Mentors." *Roll Call*, July 13.

Kucinich, Jackie. 2010d. "GOP Web Project Contributed Little to Pledge." *Roll Call*, September 27.

Larson, Bruce A. 2004. "Incumbent Contributions to the Congressional Campaign Committees, 1990–2000." *Political Research Quarterly* 57 (1), 155–61.

Lawless, Jennifer L. 2012. *Becoming a Candidate: Political Ambition and the Decision to Run for Office*. New York: Cambridge University Press.

Lebo, Matthew J., Adam J. McGlynn, and Gregory Koger. 2007. "Strategic Party Government: Party Influence in Congress, 1789–2000." *American Journal of Political Science* 51 (3), 464–81.

Lee, Frances E. 2009. *Beyond Ideology: Politics, Principles, and Partisanship in the U.S. Senate*. Chicago: University of Chicago Press.

Lee, Frances E. 2011. "Two-Party Competition and Senate Politics: The Permanent Campaign on the Floor of the U.S. Senate." Working Paper.

Lee, Frances E. 2013. "Legislative Parties in an Era of Alternating Majorities." Paper presented at Representation & Governance: A Conference in Honor of David Mayhew, Yale University.

Leonard, Gerald. 2002. *The Invention of Party Politics: Federalism, Popular Sovereignty, and Constitutional Development in Jacksonian Illinois*. Chapel Hill: University of North Carolina Press.

Levitt, Steven D. 1994. "Using Repeat Challengers to Estimate the Effect of Campaign Spending on Election Outcomes in the U.S. House." *Journal of Political Economy* 102 (4), 777–98.

Lijphart, Arend. 1999. *Patterns of Democracy: Government Forms and Performance in Thirty-Six Countries.* New Haven, CT: Yale University Press.

Lippmann, Walter. 1969 [1914]. *A Preface to Politics.* Ann Arbor: University of Michigan Press.

Lippmann, Walter. 1946 [1922]. *Public Opinion.* New York: Penguin Books.

Liptak, Kevin. 2013. "Electing House Dems 'Not a Focus' of Obama's For Now." *CNN Wire*, March 4, http://politicalticker.blogs.cnn.com/2013/03/04/electing-house-dems-not-a-focus-of-obamas-for-now/, accessed July 14, 2013.

Lochhead, Carolyn. 2011. "Nancy Pelosi to Members: Vote Your Conscience." Blog post, *Below the Beltway*, *San Francisco Chronicle*, August 1, http://blog.sfgate.com/nov05election/2011/08/01/nancy-pelosi-to-members-vote-your-conscience/, accessed November 4, 2011.

Lott, Trent. 2005. *Herding Cats: A Life in Politics.* New York: HarperCollins.

Lowi, Theodore. 1963. "Toward Functionalism in Political Science: The Case of Innovation in Party Systems." *American Political Science Review* 57 (3), 570–83.

Luce, Robert. 1972 [1922]. *Legislative Procedure.* New York: Da Capo.

Lutz, Ralph Haswell. 1941. "The Collapse of German Democracy under the Brüning Government." *Pacific Historical Review* 10 (1), 1–14.

Lynch, Megan S. 2008. "The Motion to Recommit in the House of Representatives: Effects, Recent Trends, and Options for Change." *CRS Report* RL34757, November 20.

Madison, James. 1910. *The Writings of James Madison: 1819–1836*, v. 9. New York: G. P. Putnam's Sons.

Maestas, Cherie D., Sarah Fulton, L. Sandy Maisel, and Walter J. Stone. 2006. "When to Risk It? Institutions, Ambitions, and the Decision to Run for the U.S. House." *American Journal of Political Science* 100 (2), 195–208.

Maestas, Cherie D., L. Sandy Maisel, and Walter J. Stone. 2005. "National Party Efforts to Recruit State Legislators to Run for the U.S. House." *Legislative Studies Quarterly* 30 (2), 277–300.

Maisel, L. Sandy, ed. 2002. *The Parties Respond: Changes in American Parties and Campaigns.* 4th ed. Boulder, CO: Westview Press.

Maltzman, Forrest, and Lee Sigelman. 1996. "The Politics of Talk: Unconstrained Floor Time in the U.S. House of Representatives." *Journal of Politics* 58 (3), 819–30.

Mann, Thomas E., and Norman J. Ornstein, eds. 1981. *The New Congress*. Washington, D.C.: American Enterprise Institute

Mann, Thomas E., and Norman J. Ornstein, eds. 1994. *Congress, the Press, and the Public*. Washington, D.C.: AEI and Brookings.

Mann, Thomas E., and Norman J. Ornstein. 2006. *The Broken Branch: How Congress Is Failing America and How to Get It Back on Track*. New York: Oxford University Press.

Mann, Thomas E., and Norman J. Ornstein. 2012. *It's Even Worse Than It Looks: How the American Constitutional System Collided with the New Politics of Extremism*. New York: Basic Books.

Manning, Jason. 2005. "Why BRAC Exists." PBS NewsHour, August 12, http://www.pbs.org/newshour/bb/military/brac/history.html, accessed August 3, 2012.

Maraniss, David. 1982. " 'Boll Weevil' Winners Feel Lost." *Washington Post*, November 21.

March, James G., and Johan P. Olsen. 1984. "The New Institutionalism: Organizational Factors in Political Life." *American Political Science Review* 78 (3), 734–49.

Margolies-Mezvinsky, Marjorie with Barbara Feinman. 1994. *A Woman's Place . . . The Freshmen Women Who Changed the Face of Congress*. New York: Crown Publishers.

Marshall, Bryan W. 2005. *Rules For War: Procedural Choice in the U.S. House of Representatives*. Burlington, VT: Ashgate.

Martinez, Gebe. 2003. "Long Back-and-Forth House Vote Ran Afoul of Democrats, not Rules." *CQ Weekly*, November 29.

Masket, Seth E. 2009. *No Middle Ground: How Informal Party Organizations Control Nominations and Polarize Legislatures*. Ann Arbor: University of Michigan Press.

Matson, Floyd W. 1958. "Party and Faction: The Principles of Politics vs. The Politics of Principle." *Antioch Review* 18 (3), 331–42.

Mattingly, Kim. 1990. "Campaign Reform Debate Now Heads to Conference." *Roll Call*, August 9.

Mayhew, David R. 1974. *Congress: The Electoral Connection*. New Haven, CT: Yale University Press.

Mayhew, David R. 2000. *America's Congress: Actions in the Public Sphere, James Madison through Newt Gingrich*. New Haven, CT: Yale University Press.

Mayhew, David R. 2002. *Electoral Realignments: A Critique of an American Genre*. New Haven, CT: Yale University Press.

Mayhew, David R. 2005. *Divided We Govern: Party Control, Lawmaking, and Investigations, 1946–2002*. 2nd ed. New Haven, CT: Yale University Press.

Mayhew, David. 2011. *Partisan Balance: Why Political Parties Don't Kill the U.S. Constitutional System*. Princeton, NJ: Princeton University Press.

McArdle, John. 2010. "GOP Sets $20 Million Goal to Fund TV Effort." *Roll Call*, June 16.

McArdle, John, and Shira Toeplitz. 2009. "NRCC Has Mixed Results on Recruiting Front." *Roll Call*, September 14.

McCarty, Nolan, Keith T. Poole, and Howard Rosenthal. 2008. *Polarized America: The Dance of Ideology and Unequal Riches*. Cambridge, MA: MIT Press.

McCormick, Richard P. 1966. *The Second American Party System: Party Formation in the Jacksonian Era*. Chapel Hill: University of North Carolina Press.

McCutcheon, Chuck, and Pat Towell with Walt Barron. 2000. "House Passes Defense Budget That Includes Kosovo Conditions, Military Retiree Benefits." *CQ Weekly*, May 20.

McGhee, Eric and John Sides. 2011. "Do Campaigns Drive Partisan Turnout?" *Political Behavior* 33 (2), 313–33.

McKee, Seth C. 2010. *Republican Ascendancy in Southern U.S. House Elections*. Boulder, CO: Westview Press.

McMahon, Kevin J. 2011. *Nixon's Court: His Challenge to Judicial Liberalism and Its Political Consequences*. Chicago: University of Chicago Press.

Meinke, Scott R. 2008. "Who Whips? Party Government and the House Extended Whip Networks." *American Politics Research* 36 (5), 639–68.

Mercurio, John, and Ethan Wallison. 1998. "Gephardt's Moves May Tip 2000 Plans." *Roll Call*, December 7.

Milbank, Dana. 2008. "Republicans Vote against Moms; No Word Yet on Puppies, Kittens." *Washington Post*, May 9.

Mill, John Stuart. 1991 [1861] *Considerations on Representative Government*. Buffalo, NY: Prometheus Books.

Miller, Tricia. 2009. "C-SPAN Marks 30 Years of Riveting Television." *Roll Call*, March 18.

Miller, William "Fishbait" (as told to Frances Spatz Leighton). 1977. *Doorkeeper: The Memoirs of the Congressional Doorkeeper*. Englewood Cliffs, NJ: Prentice-Hall.

Montaigne, Michel de. 1958 [1580]. *Essays*. Translated by J. M. Cohen. Baltimore: Penguin Books.

Müller, Wolfgang C., and Kaare Strøm, eds. 1999. *Policy, Office, or Votes? How Political Parties in Western Europe Make Hard Decisions*. New York: Cambridge University Press.

Mulvihill, Mary. 1999. "One-Minute Speeches: Current House Practices." *CRS Report* RL 30135, April 12.

Murray, Matthew. 2010. "NRCC Chides PACs." *Roll Call*, April 20.

Nather, David. 2000. "Education Savings Account Bill Stalls When GOP Moderates Push School Construction Plan." *CQ Weekly*, April 1.

Nather, David. 2006. "Emanuel Is the Embodiment of a Jolt for Democrats." *CQ Weekly*, March 27.

Newhauser, Daniel. 2012a. "Appropriators Seeking Order." *Roll Call*, January 30.

Newhauser, Daniel. 2012b. "House GOP Uses Once-Reviled Tactic for Budget Measure." *Roll Call*, April 18.

Newhauser, Daniel and Jonathan Strong. 2012. "Stop Us If You've Heard This One Before." *Roll Call*, July 12.

Newmyer, Tory, and John McArdle. 2010. "Pelosi Presses Her Caucus to Pay Dues." *Roll Call*, April 5.

Nichols, Roy F. 1967. *The Invention of the American Political Parties*. New York: Free Press.

Nicholson, Stephen P., and Gary M. Segura. 1999. "Midterm Elections and Divided Government: An Information-Driven Theory of Electoral Volatility." *Political Research Quarterly* 52 (3), 609–29.

Nickels, Ilona. 1989. "The Motion to Recommit in The House: The Minority's Motion." *CRS Report* 89–641 GOV, November 28.

Noel, Hans. 2014. *Political Ideologies and Political Parties in America*. New York: Cambridge University Press.

Nyhan, Brendan. 2010. "How Much Are Tea Party Candidates Hurting the GOP?" Blog post, *Brendan Nyhan*, October 21, http://www.brendan-nyhan.com/blog/2010/10/did-the-tea-party-weaken-gop-candidate-quality.html, accessed March 31, 2014.

Nyhan, Brendan, Eric McGhee, John Sides, Seth Masket, and Steven Greene. 2012. "One Vote out of Step? The Effects of Salient Roll Call Votes in the 2010 Election." *American Politics Research* 40 (5), 844–79.

O'Connor, Patrick. 2008. "Dapper Duo Commits to Recommit Strategy—And to Peace within the Republican Ranks." *Politico*, April 23.

Oakeshott, Michael. 1981 [1962]. *Rationalism in Politics and Other Essays*. New York: Methuen.

Oleszek, Walter J. 1978. *Congressional Procedures and the Policy Process*. Washington, D.C.: CQ Press.

Oleszek, Walter J. 2006. "The Role of the House Minority Leader: An Overview." *CRS Report* RL30666, December 12.

Oleszek, Walter J. 2007. *Congressional Procedures and the Policy Process*. 7th ed. Washington, D.C.: CQ Press.

Olson, Mancur. 1966. *The Logic of Collective Action*. Cambridge, MA: Harvard University Press.

Orndorff, Mary. 2008. "Republicans Keep Talking after Cameras Leave." *Birmingham News*, August 7.

Ornstein, Norman. 2010. "The Motion to Recommit, Hijacked by Politics." *Roll Call*, May 19.

Ornstein, Norman J. with Jeremy C. Pope. 1997. *Campaign Finance: An Illustrated Guide*. Washington, D.C.: AEI Press.

Owens, John E., and J. Mark Wrighton. 2008. "Partisan Polarization, Procedural Control, and Partisan Emulation in the U.S. House: An Explanation of Rules Restrictiveness over Time." Paper presented at the History of Congress Conference, George Washington University, Washington, D.C.

Palmer, Ann, and Kathleen Hunter. 2011. "GOP Hopes Unity Lies Ahead." *Roll Call*, April 18.

Palmer, Avery. 2008. "Democrats' Drilling Bill Passes." *CQ Weekly*, September 22.

Parker, David C. W. 2008. *The Power of Money in Congressional Campaigns, 1880–2006*. Norman: University of Oklahoma Press.

Paumgarten, Nick. 2007. "The Humbling of Eliot Spitzer." *New Yorker*, December 10.

Peabody, Robert L. 1976. *Leadership in Congress: Stability, Succession, and Change*. Boston: Little, Brown.

Pear, Robert, and Jennifer Steinhauer. 2011. "House Rebukes G.O.P. Leaders over Spending." *New York Times*, September 21.

Pelosi, Nancy. 2006. *A New Direction for America*. http://www.democraticleader.gov/pdf/thebook.pdf, accessed June 20, 2012.

Pershing, Ben. 2004. "Time to Put a Nail in DeLay Monker?" *Roll Call*, March 3.

Pianin, Eric. 1987. "House GOP's Frustrations Intensify." *Washington Post*, December 21.

Pianin, Eric, and John F. Harris. 1995. "Clinton Budget Plan Stirs GOP Warmth, Democratic Wrath." *Washington Post*, June 15.

Pierce, Emily, and Steven T. Dennis. 2008. "Supplemental Roils Congress." *Roll Call*, May 8.

Pierce, Emily, and Jennifer Yachnin. 2008. "Rules of Debate; Tactical Skirmishes Intensified in 110th Congress." *Roll Call*, January 22.

Plattner, Andy. 1985. "Partisan Ill-Will Remains High." *CQ Weekly*, May 4.

Plutarch. 1919. *Lives*, v. 8. Trans. Bernadotte Perrin. Loeb Classical Library. Cambridge, MA: Harvard University Press.

Poole, Keith T., and Howard Rosenthal. 1997. *Congress: A Political-Economic History of Roll Call Voting*. New York: Oxford University Press.

Price, David E. 2010. "After the 'Housequake': Leadership and Partisanship in the Post-2006 House." *Forum* 8 (1).

Rae, Nicol. 1989. *The Decline and Fall of the Liberal Republicans from 1952 to the Present*. New York: Oxford University Press.

Rankin, Robert A., and Tony Pugh. 1998. "Clinton Lists Democrats' Priorities." *Philadelphia Inquirer*, February 13.

Rawls, W. Lee. 2009. *In Praise of Deadlock: How Partisan Struggle Makes Better Laws*. Washington, D.C.: Woodrow Wilson Center Press.

Reilly, Daniel W., and John Bresnahan. 2008. "House GOP Returns with No Plans to Stop." *Politico*, August 4.

Rhodes, John J. with Dean Smith. 1995. *I Was There*. Salt Lake City, UT: Northwest.

Richard A. Gephardt Papers, Missouri History Museum, St. Louis, MO.

Richert, Catharine. 2007. "GOP Walks Out as Agriculture Bill Passes." *CQ Weekly*, August 6.

Robert H. Michel Papers, Dirksen Congressional Center, Pekin, IL.

Roberts, James C. 1980. *The Conservative Decade: Emerging Leaders of the 1980s*. Westport, CT: Arlington House.

Roberts, Jason M. 2005. "Minority Rights and Majority Power: Conditional Party Government and the Motion to Recommit in the House." *Legislative Studies Quarterly* 30 (2), 219–34.

Roberts, Jason M., and Steven S. Smith. 2003. "Procedural Contexts, Party Strategy, and Conditional Party Voting in the U.S. House of Representatives, 1971–2000." *American Journal of Political Science* 47 (2), 305–17.

Roberts, Steven V. 1979. "House G.O.P. Freshmen Are Speaking Up on Party Issues." *New York Times*, October 29.

Roberts, Steven V. 1983. "One Conservative Faults Two Parties." *New York Times*, August 11.

Roberts, Steven V. 1985. "House Democrats Seat Indianian, and the Republicans Walk Out." *New York Times*, May 2.

Rogin, Josh, and Liriel Higa. 2008. "War Supplemental Vote Is Split." *CQ Weekly*, May 19.

Rohde, David W. 1991. *Parties and Leaders in the Postreform House*. Chicago: University of Chicago Press.

Rohde, David W. 2004. *Roll Call Voting Data for the United States House of Representatives, 1953–2004*. Compiled by the Political Institutions and Public Choice Program, Michigan State University, East Lansing, MI.

Roll Call. 1993. "Play By the Rules." Editorial, September 23.

Rosenblum, Nancy L. 2008. *On The Side of Angels: An Appreciation of Parties and Partisanship*. Princeton, NJ: Princeton University Press.

Rossiter, Clinton. 1960. *Parties and Politics in America*. Ithaca, NY: Cornell University Press.

Roth, Bennett. 2009. "House Adopts Package of Rule Changes." *CQ Weekly*, January 12.

Roth, Zachary. 2007. "The Upstart." *Washington Monthly*, May.

Rothenberg, Stuart. 2009. "House GOP Finds the Right Economic Stimulus Strategy." *Roll Call*, February 2.

Rowley, James. 2010. "Republican Recruiter Targets Obama Democrats with House Majority 'in Play.'" *Bloomberg News*, August 31.

Rubin, Alissa J. 1993. "By the Book and for the Books." *CQ Weekly*, July 3.

Rubin, Alissa J., and Jill Zuckman. 1993. "Abortion Funding Rebuff Shows House Divided." *CQ Weekly*, July 3.

Rumsfeld, Donald. 2011. *Known and Unknown: A Memoir*. New York: Sentinel.

Schickler, Eric. 2001. *Disjointed Pluralism: Institutional Innovation and the Development of the U.S. Congress*. Princeton, NJ: Princeton University Press.

Schickler, Eric and Andrew Rich. 1997. "Controlling the Floor: Parties as Procedural Coalitions in the House." *American Journal of Political Science* 41 (4), 1340–75.

Schwieder, David W., and Dorothy Schwieder. 2006. "The Power of Prickliness: Iowa's H. R. Gross in the U.S. House of Representatives." *Annals of Iowa* 65 (4), 329–68.

Selinger, Jeffrey S. 2012. "Rethinking the Development of Legitimate Party Opposition in the United States, 1793–1828." *Political Science Quarterly* 127 (2), 263–87.

Sellers, Patrick J. 1998. "Strategy and Background in Congressional Campaigns." *American Political Science Review* 92 (1), 159–71.

Sellers, Patrick J. 2010. *Cycles of Spin: Strategic Communication in the U.S. Congress*. New York: Cambridge University Press.

Shapiro, Margaret. 1986. "William R. Pitts Jr.: The Republican Minority's House Know-It-All." *Washington Post*, August 11.
Sherman, Jake, and John Bresnahan. 2011. "Vote Shows Boehner's Lack of Control." *Politico*, September 21.
Shogan, Colleen J., Matthew Glassman, and Barry J. McMillon. 2013. "Longitudinal Analysis of One-Minute Speeches in the House of Representatives." Paper presented at the annual meeting of the American Political Science Association, Chicago IL.
Simpson, Glenn R. 1990. "As One-Minutes Grow More Coordinated, a Great Tradition May Be Self-Destructing." *Roll Call*, May 7.
Sinclair, Barbara. 1995. *Legislators, Leaders, and Lawmaking: The U.S. House of Representative in the Postreform Era*. Baltimore: Johns Hopkins University Press.
Sinclair, Barbara. 2006. *Party Wars: Polarization and the Politics of National Policy Making*. Norman: University of Oklahoma Press.
Sindler, Allan P. 1966. *Political Parties in the United States*. New York: St. Martin's Press.
Singer, Paul. 2010. "Finding Dirt Steps Out of the Shadows." *Roll Call*, October 18.
Sjöblom, Gunnar. 1968. *Party Strategies in a Multiparty System*. Lund, Sweden: Studentlitteratur.
Skowronek, Stephen, and Matthew Glassman, eds. 2007. *Formative Acts: American Politics in the Making*. Philadelphia: University of Pennsylvania Press.
Smith, Hedrick. 1988. *The Power Game: How Washington Works*. New York: Random House.
Smith, J. Brian. 2005. *John J. Rhodes: Man of the House*. Phoenix, AZ: Primer.
Smith, Steven S. 1989. *Call To Order*. Washington, D.C.: Brookings Institution.
Smith, Steven S. 2007. *Party Influence in Congress*. New York: Cambridge University Press.
Soraghan, Mike. 2009. "Dem Campaign Anxiety." *Hill*, September 24.
Sorauf, Frank J. 1992. *Inside Campaign Finance: Myths and Realities*. New Haven, CT: Yale University Press.
Stanton, John. 2011a. "Democrats Feel the Short End of the Stick." *Roll Call*, August 2.
Stanton, John. 2011b. "GOP Jobs Message Has Had Competition." *Roll Call*, October 13.

Stanton, John, and Kathleen Hunter. 2010. "Democrats' Hope for Unity Rests in Health Care Fight." *Roll Call*, January 10.

Starks, Tim. 2007. "Spy Bill Future Still up in Air." *CQ Weekly*, October 22.

Starks, Tim. 2008. "House Allows FISA Law to Expire." *CQ Weekly*, February 18.

Stockman, David A. 1986. *The Triumph of Politics: The Inside Story of the Reagan Revolution*. New York: Avon Books.

Stone, Walter J., Sarah A. Fulton, Cherie D. Maestas, and L. Sandy Maisel. 2010. "Incumbency Reconsidered: Prospects, Strategic Retirement, and Incumbent Quality in U.S. House Elections." *Journal of Politics* 72 (1), 178–90.

Stone, Walter J., and L. Sandy Maisel. 2003. "The Not-So-Simple Calculus of Winning: Potential U.S. House Candidates' Nomination and General Election Prospects." *Journal of Politics* 65 (4), 951–77.

Stonecash, Jeffrey M., Mark D. Brewer, and Mack D. Mariani. 2003. *Diverging Parties: Social Change, Realignment, and Party Polarization*. Boulder, CO: Westview Press.

Stratmann, Thomas. 2009. "How Prices Matter in Politics: The Returns to Campaign Advertising." *Public Choice* 140, 357–77.

Strong, Jonathan. 2011. "Dingell Deplores House Climate." *Roll Call*, December 15.

Sundquist, James L. 1968. *Politics and Policy: The Eisenhower, Kennedy, and Johnson Years*. Washington, D.C.: Brookings Institution.

Tackett, Michael, and Ted Gregory. 1996. "Democratic Agenda Gets Personal." *Chicago Tribune*, August 20.

Theriault, Sean M. 1998. "Moving Up or Moving Out: Career Ceilings and Congressional Retirement." *Legislative Studies Quarterly* 23 (3), 419–33.

Theriault, Sean M. 2008. *Party Polarization in Congress*. New York: Cambridge University Press.

Tiefer, Charles. 1989. *Congressional Practice and Procedure: A Reference, Research, and Legislative Guide*. New York: Greenwood Press.

Tocqueville, Alexis de. 1969 [1848]. *Democracy in America*. New York: Harper & Row.

Toeplitz, Shira. 2010. "GOP Works to Channel Euphoria." *Roll Call*, January 21.

Toner, Robin. 2000. "Willing Contenders at a Premium in Fierce Fight to Rule Congress." *New York Times*, January 3.

Towell, Pat. 1987. "Controversy Shoots Down Gorbachev Speech." *CQ Weekly*, November 21.

Towell, Pat. 2000. "Coalition of Interests, Budget Surplus Won New Benefits for Military Retirees." *CQ Weekly*, October 28.

Trollope, Anthony. 1969 [1869]. *Phineas Finn*. London: Oxford University Press.

U.S. House of Representatives. 1983. *Hearing on the Regulatory Reform Act*. Committee on the Judiciary, Subcommittee on Administrative Law and Governmental Relations, June 15, 98–1.

U.S. House of Representatives. 1992. *Roundtable Discussion on the Motion to Recommit*. Committee on Rules, Subcommittee on the Rules of the House, May 6.

U.S. House of Representatives. 1997. *Civility in the House of Representatives*. Committee on Rules, Subcommittee on Rules and Organization of the House, April 17.

Uslander, Eric M. 1994. *The Decline of Comity in Congress*. Ann Arbor: University of Michigan Press.

Vande Hei, Jim. 1997a. "White House Sidesteps Gephardt's Leadership." *Roll Call*, July 7.

Vande Hei, Jim. 1997b. "Hopes for Early Adjournment Begin to Fade." *Roll Call*, September 11.

Vande Hei, Jim. 1997c. "The Message Wars: During Long Recess Dems Struggle to Find Common Theme." *Roll Call*, November 24.

Vande Hei, Jim. 1997d. "Gephardt's Speech Riles His Colleagues, Who Fear Party Division Will Hurt Chances in 1998." *Roll Call*, December 8.

Vande Hei, Jim, and Charles Babington. 2005. "Newly Emboldened Congress Has Dogged Bush This Year." *Washington Post*, December 23.

Vanderbilt Television News Archives, Vanderbilt University, Nashville, Tennessee.

Waldman, David. 2008. "Our Old friend, the Motion to Recommit . . ." Blog post, *Daily Kos*, May 14, http://www.dailykos.com/story/2008/05/14/511596/-Our-old-friend-the-motion-to-recommit-, accessed April 19, 2012.

Wallison, Ethan. 1999a. "Liberal House Democrats Learn to Work with Moderates." *Roll Call*, January 18.

Wallison, Ethan. 1999b. "Bush-Bashing Strategy Rejected." *Roll Call*, July 29.

Wallison, Ethan. 2000a. "Gore, Hill Democrats Plan to Sing off Same Page." *Roll Call*, March 27.

Wallison, Ethan. 2000b. "Debate Turns into Day at the Circus." *Roll Call*, June 29.

Wallison, Ethan. 2000c. "Gephardt Uses Theatrics to Keep His Troops in Line." *Roll Call*, July 6.

Wallison, Ethan. 2001a. "Frost Eyes Next Move." *Roll Call*, March 1.

Wallison, Ethan. 2001b. "Democrats Start 'Rapid-Response' Teams to Check Bush." *Roll Call*, March 12.

Wallison, Ethan. 2002. "Cramer Wins Spot on Intel Panel." *Roll Call*, April 15.

Walsh, Edward. 1985. "To Every Campaign, There Is a Recruiting Season." *Washington Post*, November 12.

Warden, Philip. 1968. "Dems Battle House Filibuster by G.O.P." *Chicago Tribune*, October 9.

Ware, Alan. 2011. *Political Conflict in America*. New York: Palgrave Macmillan.

Wasson, Erik and Mike Lillis. 2011. "Democrats Try to Pivot to Jobs Agenda." *Hill*, August 2.

Wawro, Gregory J., and Eric Schickler. 2006. *Filibuster: Obstruction and Lawmaking in the U.S. Senate*. Princeton, NJ: Princeton University Press.

Waxman, Henry, with Joshua Green. 2009. *The Waxman Report: How Congress Really Works*. New York: Twelve.

Wayne, Drew, and Alex Armstrong. 2007. "Divided House Stalls Action on SCHIP." *CQ Weekly*, July 30.

Wegner, Mark. 2001. "Frustrated Dems Caucusing More Often." *National Journal's CongressDailyAM*, September 25.

Weisman, Jonathan. 2006. "Democrats Face Uphill Battle to Retake House." *Washington Post*, April 13.

Weisman, Jonathan. 2007. "Allowed to Break Ranks This Year, Some in GOP Vote like Democrats." *Washington Post*, April 20.

Weiss, Carol H. 1980. "Knowledge Creep and Decision Accretion." *Science Communication* 1 (3), 381–404.

Werner, Erica. 2008. "Bono, Condoleeza Rice among Those Honoring Rep. Lantos." Associated Press, February 15.

Weyl, Ben. 2010. "Political Class: The Malleable Motion to Recommit." *CQ Weekly*, May 24.

Whalen, Bill. 1990. "Party Animal." *Campaigns and Elections*, October/November 1990.

White House Bulletin. 1998. "Democrats Prepare to Unveil Four-Item National Agenda." February 11.

Whittington, Lauren W., and Steven T. Dennis. 2008. "Waters Issues Warning to House Leadership." *Roll Call*, May 8.

Wilson Center. 2010. "The Role of Minority Parties in Congress." Roundtable, November 15, http://www.wilsoncenter.org/event/the-role-minority-parties-congress.

Wilson, Scott, and Philip Rucker. 2013. "Obama Sees 2014 as Key to Legacy." *Washington Post*, March 3.

Wines, Michael. 1995. "Irate Democrats Tie Up the House till Daylight." *New York Times*, June 30.

Winneker, Craig. 1992. "Heard on the Hill." *Roll Call*, October 8.

Wolfensberger, Donald R. 2000. *Congress and the People: Deliberative Democracy on Trial*. Washington, D.C.: Woodrow Wilson Center Press.

Wolfensberger, Donald R. 2002. "Suspended Partisanship in the House: How Most Laws Are Really Made." Paper presented at annual meeting of American Political Science Association, Boston, MA.

Wolfensberger, Donald R. 2003. "The Motion to Recommit in the House: The Creation, Evisceration, and Restoration of a Minority Right." Paper presented at the History of Congress Conference, San Diego, CA.

Wolfensberger, Donald R. 2005. "Question of Privilege in the House: Minority Party Tools for Unity, Accountability, and Reform." Paper presented at the annual meeting of the American Political Science Association, Washington, D.C.

Wolfensberger, Donald R. 2007. "'Vote Pummeling' Can Soften Majority's Hard Line in House." *Roll Call*, June 4.

Woodward, Bob. 2011. "Debut of a Power Player." *Washington Post*, December 25.

Woodward, Bob. 2012. *The Price of Politics*. New York: Simon & Schuster.

Wrighton, J. Mark, and Peverill Squire. 1997. "Uncontested Seats and Electoral Competition for the U.S. House of Representatives Over Time." *Journal of Politics* 59 (2), 452–68.

Yachnin, Jennifer. 2007a. "Democrats Again Look to Change GOP Motions." *Roll Call*, October 31.

Yachnin, Jennifer. 2007b. "Kucinich, GOP Trigger Debate." *Roll Call*, November 7.

York, Byron. 2010. "As Dems Struggle, GOP Candidates Line Up to Run." *Examiner*, March 19.

INDEX